S0-BRS-617

CARL A. RUDISILL LIBRARY
LENOIR-RHYNE COLLEGE

speechreading

speechreading
principles and methods

KENNETH W. BERGER

TEACHER TRAINING LIBRARY
NORTH CAROLINA SCHOOL FOR THE DEAF

 NATIONAL EDUCATIONAL PRESS

CARL A. RUDISILL LIBRARY
LENOIR RHYNE COLLEGE

362.42
B45s
101580
July 1977

Copyright © 1972 by National Educational Press, Inc. All rights reserved. No portion of this book may be reprinted or otherwise reproduced or used in any manner whatsoever without prior written permission from the publisher except in the case of short extracts embodied in critical articles and reviews.

First Edition

International Standard Book Number: 0-87971-005-5
Library of Congress Catalog Card Number: 72-76597

National Educational Press, Inc.
711 St. Paul Street
Baltimore, Maryland 21202

Printed in the United States of America

table of contents

introduction

The lengthy bibliography of this book attests to the abundance of articles and books on the subject of speechreading. Nonetheless, considering the large number of hearing-impaired individuals in the world and the fact that knowledge of deafness dates from antiquity, it is surprising that there is not a much greater wealth of writings. Not only is the quantity of scholarly writings disappointing, but the quality, for the most part, is poor. Nor has deaf education or auditory rehabilitation been well supported financially by private or public funds, and of the allocated support only a small amount has gone toward the improvement of techniques and methods.

Perhaps the lack of quality and quantity of scholarly work on speechreading is partially because members of the two professions most closely related to the subject, teachers of the deaf and audiologists, seem to have been busy with other pursuits and have had neither the interest nor the time to develop scientific studies in this area. Teachers of the deaf have tended to treat speechreading solely as an art and have been concerned mainly with teaching academic subject matter to their students. Audiologists, on the other hand, have been deeply involved in diagnostic hearing testing and have been criticized—in large measure, rightfully so—for apparent disinterest in the long-range habilitation and rehabilitation of the individual with a hearing loss. Psychologists have shown interest in visual perception, both verbal and nonverbal, but their experimental work has been conducted largely on static visual stimuli that, unfortunately, do not appear to relate closely to speechreading.

One small illustration of the lack of scientific interest in speechreading is the fact that the thirty-ninth meeting of the Convention of the American Instructors of the Deaf included only one paper on speechreading, and the fortieth and forty-second meetings contained none. The several journals published by the American Speech and Hearing Association have included relatively few reports on speechreading, and the small number of such publications internationally is reflected by their infrequent appearance in *dsh Abstracts*. The attention paid to speechreading at the various professional conventions and in scholarly journals leads one to suspect that speechreading receives but scant lip service from those who should be most interested in it.

This book was designed to bring together pertinent procedures, theories, and research on speechreading, both from the standpoint of the practices of the teacher of the deaf and from assorted studies that have endeavored to isolate and examine various aspects of the speechreading process. So that comparisons from one writing to another may be made, all hearing-level quotations herein have been converted to the I.S.O. (1964) standard; and the International Phonetic Association (I.P.A.) symbols, broad transcription, have been employed to spell out the sounds of speech. In quoting correlations, we commit the statistical sin of using the symbol r, regardless of the type of correlation. References dealing with the phenomena of receptive communication by concentrating visual attention on the articulators of the speaker use the terms speechreading or lipreading, write the terms each as two words, or hyphenate them. We have used the term speechreading throughout, except where narrower meanings of the term lipreading are occasionally discussed.

In some ways the reader may be disappointed at how little we really "know" about speechreading, or he may become frustrated to the point of disillusionment. It is hoped that the reader will be challenged to make scholarly, pedagogical, and research efforts to define, examine, explain, and improve further the many facets of speechreading.

The reader is asked to be indulgent of the sometimes detailed procedural quotations. The reason for the repetition of details is because at this juncture there is not a good understanding of many potential and critical variables involved in speechreading. To omit the details which differentiate one approach from another might confuse further inquiry or hide possible important procedural or population differences in some of the areas where the greatest need of research exists.

This book is intended primarily for use in classes preparing university students to teach speechreading to deaf and hard-of-hearing children or adults. It is trusted that many others interested in or involved with the hearing impaired will also find the information basic to the speechreading processes beneficial. For class use it is suggested that it will be profitable for the group to discuss many of the findings as well as the figures contained herein in greater detail than that given in the text. In many instances having students investigate and report on more complete data from the studies mentioned will be helpful.

The author wishes to express thanks to his students in speechreading classes at Kent State University. They provided the challenge to develop this book and were instrumental in clarifying and criticizing many of the issues as they appeared in the manuscript draft. Grateful acknowledgement is also given to Dan L. Bode, William W. Green, Joseph P. Millin, Katherine D. Miner, R. David Nelson, and Henry D. Schmitz for critically reading one or more chapters of the manuscript. Thanks are also given to the editor of *Hearing* for permission to reproduce Figures 2-1 and 3-3.

Kenneth W. Berger, Ph.D.
Director of Audiology
School of Speech
Kent State University

I
a brief history of
communication by the deaf

In the Talmud the deaf and dumb were classed with fools and children, not responsible for their actions and exempt from the ordinances of the law. Before Christ, Aristotle judged the deaf as incapable of thought, and the Roman law classified the deaf and dumb with the mentally incompetent. In some of the older references to the deaf, justifiable indignation is expressed because "the Spartan law consigned them to the great pit in Taygetus, into which the deformed were cast as useless to the state," and "in Athens they were without pity put to death without a single voice being raised against the monstrous deed" (83, p.4). The Justinian Code, of the sixth century A.D., denied the deaf and dumb the rights and duties of citizenship but should be credited as the first classification of the legal rights of the deaf. Before the sixteenth century many of the misconceptions regarding the deaf developed from the notion that "dumbness" was the fate of the untaught deaf.

Because so little was known of deafness, the anatomy of the ear, or medical treatment of hearing defects, little was done for the deaf. Their state was considered predestined, to be alleviated only by a miracle. The prevailing attitude is well described in the book of Leviticus: "Thou shalt not curse the deaf nor put a stumbling-block before the blind." These statements reveal that the deaf were not only uneducated but that they were considered incapable of learning. Consequently, it is apparent that the deaf were not educated up to this time. Such ideas prevailed until the sixteenth century.

A NEW ERA FOR THE DEAF

The time of Girolamo Cardano (or Jerome Cardan, 1501-1576), who was a distinguished Italian physician, astronomer, and mathematician, marks the boundary between the dark ages for the deaf and the first glimmer of hope for them. In his book *Paralipomenon* he stated that the deaf could be taught to comprehend written symbols or combinations of symbols by associating them with the object or a picture of the object they are intended to represent. In another work he urged the importance of teaching the deaf to read and write and explained that many abstract ideas could be taught to them by signs. Despite Cardano's philosophical references to teaching the deaf, there is no evidence that he actually taught any deaf persons.

Spain has the honor of having produced the first known teacher of the prelingually deaf. Pedro Ponce de Leon (1520-1584), a monk of the Benedictine order, was successful in educating several deaf individuals. He left a legal document, dated August 24, 1578, dealing with the foundation of a chapel, that gives a short account of his work with the deaf: "With the industry which God has been pleased to give me, I have had pupils who were deaf and dumb from birth, children of great nobles and men of distinction, whom I have taught to speak, to read, to write, and to keep accounts; to repeat prayers, to serve Mass, to know the doctrine of the Christian religion, and to confess themselves with the living voice"[1] (14, p.40). Apparently Ponce emphasized the language of signs more than

---

[1]Excellent historical reviews of early and subsequent efforts by persons within the church to teach the deaf are given by Stone and Youngs (*357*) and Manson (*224*).

speechreading or the manual alphabet in his teaching.

Toward the end of the sixteenth century and the beginning of the seventeenth, a number of books about deafness were published, and teachers in various parts of Europe began to evolve methods of instruction for the deaf. Again, Spain was a pioneering area. *Simplification of the Letters of the Alphabet and the Method of Teaching Deaf-Mutes to Speak* by the Soldier-scholar Juan Martin Pablo Bonet, was published in Madrid in 1620. This is the earliest textbook on articulation teaching skill in existence.[2] Bonet was a pioneer in using the concept of "sense training" as it is used in the education of the deaf today. He also anticipated modern methods by insisting that, through giving letters their phonetic values, hearing children could be taught to read more rapidly than by using the alphabet only. Bonet was less modern on the subject of speechreading, feeling that it could be taught to only a few. He advocated the use of the manual alphabet in connection with speech teaching and thought that speechreading should not be a special object of instruction (83, p.33).

John Bulwer, also surnamed "The Chirosopher" or "lover of the wisdom of the hand," was influenced by the writings of Bonet. He authored *Chirologia* (or *The Natural Language of the Hand*) in 1644, in which an international language of gesture was proposed. He described the movement of the hand as being "the only speech that is natural to man" and said that "it may be called the tongue and general language of human nature, which, without teaching, men of all regions of the habitable world do at first sight most easily understand." Quotations or paraphrases of these philosophical statements are still too often unquestioningly accepted today.

Another book by Bulwer that was to have a profound effect on deaf education, *Philocophus*, or *The Deafe and Dumbe Mans Friend*, appeared in 1648. Bulwer, an English physician, believed in the possibility that a deaf person could learn to

---

[2]The first known book on deafness was *Oratio de Surdite et Mutitae* by Salmon Alberti (1540-1600), published in Nuremberg in 1591. He reported that some deaf individuals could lipread, but he seemed puzzled as to how.

reproduce sound through his use of the sense of touch, and he felt that "lip-grammar" (that is, speechreading) afforded the deaf a tool for learning speech. It should be recognized that up until the present century speechreading was typically regarded as a tool for teaching speech production rather than as a method for improvinig speech reception. Bulwer's second book is cited as the first English work treating lipreading and deafness extensively, along with the language problems of deafness. He published still another book on manual communication, *The Art of Manual Rhetoric*, and is also remembered for his statement that "men naturally (that is, born) deaf never learn speech without a teacher" (14, p.55). Bulwer's work with lipreading was motivated by two deaf gentlemen who were knowledgeable in communication by signs but who wished to develop speech. Even today this same desire to communicate orally has been observed in countless adults who were manually trained and constitutes a shortcoming of manualism which is difficult for its proponents to ignore.

Another English teacher of the deaf, Dr. William Holder (1616-1690), was a musician, clergyman, a Fellow of the Royal Society, and a brother-in-law of the famous English architect Sir Christopher Wren. In 1669 Holder wrote a summary of the method he used for teaching the deaf. The main portion of his book was a classification of the elements of speech and "an inquiry into the natural production of the letters, directing to a steady and effectual way of instructing Deaf and Dumb persons to obtain a reasonable perfection of utterance of speech, and to discern, in some measure, with their eyes, by observing the motions of their mouths what others speak" (83, p.52).

A Scotsman, George Dalgarno (1616-1687)[3] was a successful master of a private grammar school at Oxford. While engaged in formulating a "universal language," Dalgarno became interested in teaching language to the deaf. However, he was skeptical about the usefulness of speechreading. Somehow he felt that rather than understanding

---

[3]A birthdate of 1626 is sometimes quoted but is most unlikely, since Dalgarno was admitted to Marischal College in 1631.

speech by watching lip movements, the deaf probably understood merely because of a "concurrence of circumstance."
Dalgarno recommended the use of dactylology (the manual
alphabet) and typology (writing) as a means of communication.
Using a finger-spelling method similar to that of Holder, he
located the letters on the fingertips and palm of one hand.
These, in turn, were touched by the thumb or finger of the
other hand. Alexander Graham Bell used this method with his
pupil, George Sanders, and in a small notebook in the library
of the Volta Bureau is inscribed in Bell's handwriting, "Notes
on the Works of George Dalgarno, by A.G.B." (83, p.56). Bell's
notes are a resume of *Didascalocophus, Or The Deaf and
Dumb Mans Tutor,* published at Oxford in 1680 by Dalgarno,
and contain a sketch of Dalgarno's diagram of the hand with
the letters of the alphabet indicated on the fingers.

John Wallis (1616-1703) was an Oxford professor and a
mathematician of considerable repute. His work with the deaf
is noteworthy because of his scientific eminence rather than
his method of teaching. He accepted speechreading in the
teaching of others but did not use it in his own work with the
deaf. Meric Casaubon, a contemporary of Wallis and Dalgarno,
published a book entitled *A Treatise Concerning Enthusiasm* in
1665. In it are sections on the history of speechreading and the
mechanism of speech, "by the perfect knowledge whereof the
deaf and dumb may be taught not only to understand whatever
is spoken by others, but also to speak and to discourse."
Casaubon recommended speechreading instruction for normal-
hearing persons also, who "would be glad sometimes per-
chance, upon some special occasions, to know how they might
speak and be spoken unto at a convenient distance, without a
tongue or noise or sign discernible unto others" (83, p.60).

Johann Konrad Amman (1669-1724) was born in Switzer-
land and moved to The Netherlands in 1689. He was a
physician. In his *Dissertatio de Loquela* (Dissertation on
Speech)[4] published in 1700, he came to the conclusion that

---

[4]The title of Amman's first book on deafness was *De Doove Sprekende* (*The
Speaking Deaf*), published in Amsterdam by Pieter Rotterdam in 1692. The English
edition was published in 1694, and it was reprinted in facsimile by North-Holland
Publishing Company in 1965.

deaf-mutes were mute because of their deafness. This is the first publication to recognize this principle. He worked out his own method of teaching speech, based on the theory that the deaf could be taught to imitate sounds by means of speech-reading and watching their own movements in a mirror. Amman made use of the fact that his students could feel the vibrations of the voice by placing their hands on his throat as he taught them speech. If a pupil, upon being asked to give a certain sound, gave another by mistake, he was not corrected but shown instead the written symbol for the sound he had made and drilled in its repetition. Amman did not establish a school but he laid the foundation for oralism and had a great influence on his contemporaries (14, p.67).

In France the first notable teacher of the deaf was Jacob Rodriguez Pereira (1715-1780), a Portuguese Jew. He made primary use of the one-hand manual alphabet in his teaching, and his ideas of language instruction for the deaf were quite advanced. Some references claim that Pereira's first student was his wife, and others say it was his sister. He taught in Bordeaux, and from 1750, in Paris. After his students had progressed in their studies, Pereira gradually began using speech and speechreading with them.

Charles Michel de l'Epee,[5] a priest and lawyer, is sometimes called "The Apostle of the Deaf" because he was the first to make the education of the deaf a matter of public concern. His work with the deaf began in 1755. Although others had brought their pupils to a higher level of speech, speechreading, and general knowledge, no one had previously done as much for the deaf as a group. At first l'Epee used speech and speechreading in his teaching. After becoming acquainted with the works of Bonet and Amman on teaching the deaf, he incorporated their ideas into his teaching.

Historical notes on l'Epee often neglect to mention that he originally included oralism in his training program; the less time-consuming manual method became the sole mode of instruction in his school later because of a large increase in

[5]He was born 1712 in Versailles, the son of the king's architect, and died in 1789.

the number of students. In 1776 l'Epee wrote: "The only serious means of giving them (the deaf) back to society is to teach them to hear with their eyes and speak with their tongues" (176). In 1775 Louis XVI took l'Epee's school under his patronage and supported it with a small subsidy. At l'Epee's death Abbe Roch-Ambroise Cucurron Sicard (1742-1822) continued to operate the school. L'Epee's language of signs spread through most of Europe and to America. He employed the so-called natural signs, and he also developed "methodological signs" or grammatical signs, since he realized that natural signs would not permit adequate teaching of the French language.

Germany's foremost early name in the education of the deaf, and a man who could be called the father of the German oral method, was Samuel Heinicke (1727-1790), a schoolmaster, organist, and Lutheran pastor. He originally used the manual alphabet and writing to develop speech in his pupils. His school, founded in Leipzig in 1778, became the first public school for the deaf to be established in Germany. Rather than first teaching the letters as meaningless sounds, Heinicke advocated starting with words with functional meaning. Then the words were taken apart into syllables and finally into letters. However, the oral method fell into disuse in Germany at Heinicke's death and did not become widely used on the continent until F.M. Hill re-introduced it a half-century later.

Friedrich Moritz Hill (1805-1874), a native of Breslau and a student of Pestalozzi, in some ways can be considered the most influential of all the early educators of the deaf. He brought speech and language teaching to such a high degree of perfection that his teaching revolutionized the education of the deaf in Germany and finally in America. His method differed from that of even the most ardent oralists, who still used the grammatical method of teaching language. These were the principles of Hill's teaching: "Deaf children should be taught language in the same way that hearing children learn it, by constant use, associated with the proper objects and actions; speech must be the basis of all language; and speech must be used from the beginning as a basis for teaching and communication" (14, p.133). But Hill did not forbid the use of signing in the classroom. He made great use of picture sets in the development of language in deaf children. Hill was also highly successful in his training program for teachers.

An outstanding name in the education of the deaf in England was that of Thomas Braidwood (1715-1806), a Scotsman who was a teacher of mathematics. He began a private school for the deaf which was continued by three generations of his family. An authority on the Braidwood School was Francis Green, an American. Green sent his deaf son to the Braidwood School in 1780, and he visited the school himself the following year. Attempting to promulgate a free school for poor deaf children, Green published an exposition of Braidwood's method.[6] This book was the first publication by any American on the education of the deaf, but it was published without consulting the Braidwoods and consequently angered them. Although he left his son in the Braidwood School, Green stopped his efforts on behalf of a public school for the deaf. The significance of the Braidwoods' contribution to the education of the deaf has often been overemphasized. Primarily they should be credited with keeping the oral method alive in England at a time when the manual alphabet and signs were the chief methods used elsewhere in Europe, but they were secretive about their methods and did not share them with others. Henry Baker (1698-1774) of England and Jacob Pereira, who was mentioned previously, had already set examples of keeping their methods of teaching the deaf secret. As we shall see, oralism came to America from Germany rather than England.

Meanwhile, Francis Green transferred his interest to Abbe de l'Epee and to Sicard of France, and he translated l'Epee's book into English. His son died in 1787 by drowning, but later Green again initiated efforts to found a school for the deaf in America. He was also responsible for the first census of the deaf in America inasmuch as he solicited from the ministers of every denomination of Massachusetts the names of all the deaf and dumb in their parishes.

---

[6]Francis Green (1742-1809) published the monograph *Vox Oculis Subjecta* anonymously in 1783 in London. Green left America in 1776 because of his Tory leanings; he moved back to Boston in 1797.

Major Thomas Bolling of Virginia also had three deaf children in the Braidwood School, John, Thomas Jr., and Mary. Another child, William, had normal hearing, but he had two deaf children. At Colonel William Bolling's request John Braidwood, a grandson of Thomas Braidwood, opened a small, semipublic oral school for the deaf in Cobbs, Virginia, in 1813. Unfortunately, young Braidwood seems to have been quite irresponsible, and this first effort to introduce oralism in America soon faltered. The New York Institution for the Deaf, formed in 1817, grew out of the work of the earliest school for the deaf in America, which had been started in a poorhouse by the Reverend John Stanford in 1807.

The first permanent institution for the deaf in America, the Connecticut Asylum for the Deaf, was established through the efforts of Mason Fitch Cogswell, M.D., of Hartford. His daughter, Alice, acquired deafness caused by "spotted fever" at two years of age. Thomas Hopkins Gallaudet (1787-1851), a divinity student and a neighbor of the Cogswells, became Alice's first teacher. He began teaching her by associating an object with a written word, following this up with other words, and her vocabulary grew rapidly. Dr. Cogswell, following the initiative of Francis Green, obtained an approximate census of the deaf in the state of Connecticut. It was because of the census findings that a movement was begun to raise funds to send someone to Europe to "acquire the art of instructing the deaf and dumb" (83, p.100). Thomas Gallaudet was selected. He went to the Braidwood school, arriving in London in July, 1815, but soon broke off negotiations with them. He angered the Braidwoods because he proposed to remain a few months at their school to select what he wanted from their method and then to combine it with the sign method of Sicard. The war of the methods, begun by l'Epee and Heinicke, had intensified all over Europe at this time. It is interesting to speculate what the history of deaf education in America might have been had Gallaudet and the Braidwoods been able to work out a mutually agreeable arrangement. Although it is easy to fault the Braidwoods on the secrecy with which they guarded their method, it should be noted that Gallaudet had a reputation for being quite outspoken and difficult to get along with.

At this point Gallaudet went to France where he studied in Abbe Sicard's school. After two months one of the teachers from that school, Laurent Clerc, who was himself deaf, offered to help Gallaudet begin the Hartford institution. After fourteen weeks of training Gallaudet returned to America with Clerc in August, 1816, to open a school for the deaf. With the aid of funds from prominent men throughout the country and from the legislature of Connecticut, Gallaudet raised $17,000 to open the school. By 1818 so many pupils had been enrolled that it was thought best to solicit the aid of Congress. Laurent Clerc visited Washington for this purpose and made a favorable impression. His cause was sponsored by many members of Congress, among whom was Henry Clay, then Speaker of the House. An act was passed appropriating land for sale, and the Hartford Institution was endowed with the proceeds, amounting to $300,000. In 1821, the school was permanently established. The name of the school was changed to The American Asylum for the Deaf (now the American School for the Deaf), as it was thought that all the deaf in the nation could be educated in this building.

In 1819 Massachusetts provided for the education of her deaf children in the Hartford School. New Hampshire, Maine, South Carolina, Georegia, and Rhode Island also followed. Thus manualism spread and became the sole method of communication in deaf education in most of the states. In 1818 New York had opened its own school, the Fanwood School. Articulation was taught in the beginning, but Sicard's ideas as used by the Hartford School were soon adopted. The Pennsylvania Institution at Mt. Airy began as a private philanthropy in 1820, and a year later the school was incorporated and financed by the state legislature. At this time Laurent Clerc went to Pennsylvania to help reorganize the school and train the teachers. Gallaudet and Clerc traveled all over the country exhibiting their classes of deaf pupils. The appeal of the sign method, Clerc's intelligence, and his own unusual achievements made a strong public impression. As can be seen, education of the deaf in the United States was profoundly influenced by l'Epee through Clerc. Schools for the deaf opened in 1823 in Kentucky, in 1829 in Ohio, and in 1839 in Virginia. The first denominational school for the deaf, St. Joseph's Institute for the Deaf, Was established in St. Louis in 1830.

THE BEGINNING OF THE ORAL METHOD IN AMERICA

In 1842 Horace Mann, then secretary of the Massachusetts Board of Education, and Dr. Samuel Gridley Howe, the director of a school for the blind, went to Europe to study methods of education. On visiting schools in Germany, they were amazed to find deaf children speaking and reading lips. Upon returning, Horace Mann published a report strongly encouraging the introduction of this method in America. The report impressed a few parents who began to seek this training for their deaf children. As we saw above, a feeble effort was made to introduce the oral method into the Hartford School, but the impetus for speech and speechreading soon died out. By 1860 there were no teachers of the oral method in America. However, in 1867 through the efforts of Mrs. Lippit, Mrs. Hubbard, and Miss Rogers, the Clarke School for the Deaf was opened in Northhampton, Massachusetts, using the oral method.[7] Miss Rogers was its first principal (238). John Clarke, a Northhampton merchant and himself hard of hearing, donated the money to the State of Massachusetts to start the school. This was followed by the opening of an oral day school in Boston in 1869, the Boston School for Deaf Mutes, that became known as the Horace Mann School for the Deaf after 1873. It is still one of the more prominent day schools for the deaf in the United States.

Miss Sarah Fuller, who was previously at the Bowdich School and had received brief training from Miss Rogers, and Miss Mary True were associated with the Boston School and did all that they could to secure information on the teaching of speech and speechreading. They obtained much help from the works of Alexander Melville Bell, a Scottish master of phonetics and father of A.G. Bell, who had moved to Canada in 1870. Bell had perfected a system of symbols where any sound made by the human vocal organs could be expressed in

---

[7]Mrs. Lippit, wife of the Governor of Rhode Island, had a deaf daughter. Mrs. Hubbard was the wife of Gardiner Green Hubbard, a prominent attorney in Boston and founder of the National Geographic Society. Their daughter, Mabel, was deaf and received some oral education in Europe. Miss Harriet B. Rogers (1838-1919), with limited training in deaf education, opened a school for deaf children in 1866 in Chelmsford, Massachusetts. She retired as principal of the Clarke School in 1886 because of ill health.

writing. These symbols were pictorial as well as phonetic and therefore of considerable value to a deaf child in that they illustrated how he should manipulate his speech mechanism in forming the various sounds. The symbols were also useful to the teacher in writing the sounds that the pupil actually made. This provided a logical step from the sounds the pupil knew to the ones the teacher wanted him to form. Bell did not originally intend the system, called visible speech, for deaf students but had devised it as a method of universal language instruction.

in 1871 Sarah Fuller invited A.M. Bell to give lectures on visible speech at the Boston School; Bell sent his son Alex instead. Soon thereafter Alexander Graham Bell (1847-1922) opened a training class for teachers of the deaf in Boston. This "very little, experimental school," as he afterwards referred to it, was the beginning of an important epoch in deaf education in America, and it was here that Bell was converted to oralism (83, p.117). Bell opened a School of Vocal Physiology in Boston in 1872, advertised as "for the correction of stammering and other defects of utterance and for practical instruction in Visible Speech, conducted by Alexander Graham Bell, member of the Philological Society of London." Later he added Lip Reading to the subjects taught.

Bell was not originally convinced of the value of lip-reading, realizing that many of the sounds of speech are not readily visible. The teachers Bell trained became still stronger advocates of the oral method. The method war, oral-aural versus manual, was to continue, however. Bell was active in the method battle, and many articles, as well as reports of meetings of teachers of the deaf from that era, testify to the fury of the battle. Bell should also be credited with popularizing the term *deaf-mute* or simply *deaf*, as opposed to the older term *deaf and dumb*. The word *dumb*, correctly, refers to a lack of speech. But meanwhile a huge migration of Germans to the United States brought with it the word *dumm*, so that gradually dumb came to be used as meaning stupid or without intelligence.

Mabel Hubbard, the little deaf girl whose family had helped to start oralism in the United States, became the wife of

Alexander Graham Bell in 1877. Bell met Mabel when she was sixteen years old. She was not a pupil of his, despite some published statements to that effect. She had studied speechreading under Mary True. One of the prizes Bell received for his work with electricity, the invention of the telephone, was the Allessandro Volta Prize, named in memory of that pioneer of electricity. With half of the $220,000 resulting from an investment of his prize money, Bell founded the Volta Bureau in 1887 "for the increase and diffusion of knowledge relating to the deaf" (14, p.159). Because of Bell's efforts the American Association for Teaching Speech to the Deaf was organized in 1890. This developed into an influential national organization of teachers and educators interested in oral instruction for the deaf. Bell's personal beliefs on deaf education were that deaf children should be educated orally, and preferably in day schools where they would have normal social contacts. It was by Bell's efforts that the United States census forms were modified in 1890 so that the deaf could be more accurately counted in the total population.

During the latter part of the nineteenth century, methods of teaching the deaf were becoming better organized and were taking various forms around the world. A number of schools adopted what they called the simultaneous (or combined) method that consisted, ideally, of using the best from both the oral and manual approaches. The simultaneous method received the support of the Gallaudet family. In 1864 Gallaudet College (originally named the National Deaf-Mute College) in Washington, D.C., became the first institution of higher learning exclusively for the deaf in the world. In 1891, a teacher's college was added.

The increease in deaf education world-wide, as well as a desire to meet and exchange ideas, culminated in an international congress of educators of the deaf, which assembled in Milan in 1880. In a resolution the oral method was adopted as the preferred method in all countries by a vote of 116 to 16. The United States was part of the minority vote, still using predominantly the manual method. It was also noted at this time that in the education of the deaf in all countries, there was a shift from emphasis on subject matter to a stress on working with the child as an individual. Despite this congress, manualism continued in popularity in many educational institutions in the world, including the majority in the United States.

The first kindergarten for deaf children in the United States was opened in 1883 by Mary McCowen. Miss McCowen did much to influence the use of speechreading and speech. Her school, begun as a private enterprise, was later incorporated into the public school system of Chicago. Children as young as five years of age were enrolled, and adults were also enrolled there from time to time on a private basis. In 1888 Sarah Fuller, who was the principal of the Horace Mann School from 1869 to 1910, opened a school for very young deaf children in West Medford, Massachusetts. Ten children were enrolled in the first class. Although the value of early training in communication with the deaf has long been known, these early efforts at educating the young deaf were but isolated instances. Preschool deaf education has actually been a fairly recent phenomenon, with public school classes for the deaf which accepted children at about the age of four years becoming popular in some areas in America in the 1930's. The age was lowered to three years in a few areas in the 1960's. Despite early scattered efforts at educating young deaf children, a British visitor to the United States in 1923 observed that nursery schools for deaf infants did not exist, and although some state schools permitted enrollment at the age of five or six years, they usually did not encourage attendance until two or three years later (156).

This brief history of communication teaching with the deaf, in Europe and in America, may make it appear as though educational methodology had a gradual and smooth development. However, until the nineteenth century the education of the deaf was, at best, haphazard and isolated when viewed broadly. In particular, oralism was used sporadically. Further, until well into the twentieth century formal teacher-training standards, as well as the use of amplification by deaf students, was almost unknown, and unfortunately some schools today are still lacking in appropriate hearing aids.

PIONEER ORGANIZATIONS AND PUBLICATIONS IN THE UNITED STATES

The Convention of American Instructors of the Deaf and Dumb (now Convention of American Instructors of the Deaf) met for the first time in New York in 1850. Its official organ was *The American Annals of the Deaf and Dumb*, the first issue of which was published at the Hartford School in 1847. Except for several Civil War years this journal has had continuous publication. The *Annals* have been issued quarterly and have been open to proponents of the oral as well as the manual method (*83*, p.121). In recent years the journal appears to have become more manually oriented in emphasis, and at the same time the austere format has been brightened somewhat. The Convention of American Instructors of the Deaf has been subsidized by some public funds; the convention proceedings, by federal funds; and the *Annals* directly and indirectly has been financed in part by state schools for the deaf and in part by Gallaudet College.

Another important and early professional group, The Convention of Articulation Teachers, attracted large numbers as interest in speech and speechreading for the deaf became more widespread. There were more than two hundred persons present at a meeting in New York in 1884. In 1890 this group incorporated as the American Association to Promote the Teaching of Speech to the Deaf. Membership was open to anyone interested in the oral method of instruction, as contrasted with the Convention of American instructors of the Deaf, which has restricted its membership to teachers of the deaf. Part of the income from the Association's funds was used to pay the expenses of a training class for teachers at the Clarke School. Teachers from England, Japan, India, Greece, South Africa, and many other countries came to the United States for this training.

In 1890 the American Association to Promote the Teaching of Speech to the Deaf began to publish a magazine, *The Association Review*. In 1908 the Volta Fund, which Alexander Graham Bell had created in behalf of the deaf as we saw above, was placed under the direction of the Association. In 1910 the offices of the Association were moved to the Volta

Bureau in Washington, and their magazine became the monthly, *The Volta Review*. This publication has taken a strong pro-oral stance and has attempted the task of providing information to the deaf and their parents as well as to teachers of the deaf and others interested in hearing impairment.

The New York League for the Hard of Hearing, begun in 1910, became a powerful organization for social service. Edward B. Nitchie was instrumental in the establishment of this group and, in fact, the early membership was typically composed of "alumni" of the Nitchie School and other speechreading teachers. A similar group, the Speech Readers' Guild of Boston, was established in 1916, and soon thereafter the Chicago League was organized. Similar groups in Los Angeles and San Francisco, and one in Newark, New Jersey, were formed the following winter. In 1919 the directors of five eastern leagues met in New York City under the guidance of Dr. Wendell C. Phillips. At this time the groups united to form the American Association for the Hard of Hearing, which became the American Federation of Organizations for the Hard of Hearing in June, 1922. In 1946 this organization was renamed the American Hearing Society, more recently renamed the National Association of Hearing and Speech Agencies. These have been some of the aims of this Association: to establish organizations for the Hard of hearing, to establish speechreading classes in the public schools for children and for adults, to encourage audiometric tests of schools children, to educate employers to realize the potential efficiency of hearing-impaired employees, to investigate hearing aids, to reach the isolated deafened, to cooperate in research into causes of deafness, to encourage preventative measures against deafness, and to investigate discrimination against deafened persons by insurance companies. In more recent years there has been a de-emphasis on the social nature of the various leagues in cities around the country and an emphasis on professional diagnostic and rehabilitative services.

II
oral and manual communication

In almost every human society, primitive or complex, the primary mode of communication is by speaking-hearing. In the case of hearing impairment the hearing half of the typical communication system operates imperfectly, often with a resultant deficiency in speech production which is ordinarily dependent upon hearing.

The first efforts on the part of the deaf to supplement or substitute another communication method for speaking-hearing are lost in history. As we saw in the first chapter, at first sporadic and then more widespread written evidence of communication by manualism gradually appeared. Next we saw growing use of oralism. With time formal methods of educating the deaf began, and by published discourses the knowledge of communication methods spread from one nation to another. By the latter part of the nineteenth century, the perennial war of communication methods had begun.

Some schools for the deaf have attempted to be purely oral in their method, but manualism has gradually crept into the classroom. Some schools have changed from manualism to a combined method or to oralism. In other instances schools have gone from oralism to a combined method. For example, the St. Michielsgestel School for the Deaf in The Netherlands was originally manually oriented, began using some speech and speechreading along with manualism in 1852, and then changed to pure oralism in 1906 (377). In England the schools for the deaf, which were employing the manual method exclusively, introduced oralism both because of dissatisfaction with the product of manualism and also because of a desire to improve the opportunities of the deaf in social and vocational situations. In 1876 the Doncaster School was the first in England to adopt the oral method. The first school for the deaf in Russia was established in 1806 in Pavlovsk. In 1820 the St. Petersburg Institution included the teaching of Russian and French signs; oralism was introduced into Russian schools late in the nineteenth century (141). In 1880 the Institution Nationale des Sourds-Muets in Paris, the successor to l'Epee's school, became oral in instruction.

More recently, in 1946 the oral-aural method replaced the manual method at St. Mary's School for the Deaf in Dublin. Schools for the deaf were first organized in China in 1916, supported by parents' donations and using the manual method. In 1955 the oral method was introduced because it was considered to be advantageous to both pupils and instruction (142). This fact is remarkable, since the Chinese language, containing many guttural sounds and phonemic differences based upon pitch, might be expected to be one of the most difficult languages to speechread.

Looking broadly at the history of deaf education, one can see schools changing from the manual to the oral method. Or, schools have moved from manualism or oralism to a combined system. The combined approach is attaining some resurgence in the United States of late, and in England the social workers and ministers involved with the deaf have also made moves in that direction. Whether some combination of oralism and manualism will achieve greater popularity in the future cannot yet be determined from trends around the world. Inasmuch as speechreading is a vital part of one of the two methods involved in the oralism-manualism argument, it is appropriate to review briefly some of the propositions which constitute each of these methods and to discuss their relative strengths and weaknesses.

ORALISM

Oral education consists of two basic components: speech *by* the child and speech *to* the child. From its first inception to the present, oralism has placed its main stress on assisting the individual to use speech as the primary avenue for verbal communication. Although Kohl (196) states that there are four oral methods, for practical purposes there are only two, oral and aural; and typically these two blend into a single method today in most oral schools. With the advent of electronic hearing aids in the 1930's, the oral method should more accurately be called the oral-aural method. One difference of opinion within oralism involves the question of whether audition or speechreading should be used as the primary avenue for the reception of speech. A stress on the auditory avenue for speech reception is typified in the Acoustic Method (137), also referred to as the auricular or the unisensory method. Although a unisensory method could employ vision only, the term usually infers an emphasis on the use of audition when it appears in writings about rehabilitation of the hearing-impaired individual. Whether speechreading or audition should be used as the primary avenue for speech reception depends in large measure on the degree of hearing loss, as we shall see in the next chapter.

Other differences within the oral method are primarily methodological: utilizing one phase or part of the method more than another or introducing the teaching of certain skills, such as reading and writing, in varying orders. Other minor differences are that some oralists use one phonetic spelling system, while others prefer another; some insist that the deaf child wear a hearing aid, but other teachers are lax about the child's wearing amplification. Some teachers and schools supplement speechreading with phonetic or alphabet signs, and some do not. These signs will be briefly discussed below. Differences also involve the use of various schemes to develop grammatical structure and several ideas on the employment of "natural language."

The oral-aural method represents an attempt to assist the deaf child to become a member of society by helping him to communicate in the manner most commonly used in that society. Where oralism does not succeed perfectly, the goal is to permit the child to achieve as much integration into normal life as possible. The difficulty of attaining proficiency in oralism by those with a profound hearing loss should not obscure the desirability of reaching that goal. Not to attempt oralism with the deaf child will often separate him, communicatively, from his family and neighbors, since only about 10 percent of deaf children are born to deaf parents and not all deaf parents use manualism (*103*). Recent data show that 4.6 percent of hearing-impaired students in the United States have one parent with a hearing loss dating from before the age of six years; and for an additional 4.0 percent of the students, both parents have a hearing loss (*365*).

Sometimes the child who has been in an oral classroom, presumably with good teachers, may not progress satisfactorily. This child has often been referred to as the "oral failure." At present we have little good evidence as to the cause of oral failure, just as we often have no ready explanation for the reading or writing failure or for the occasional manual failure.[1] Oral failure includes those students who progressed adequately through the early stages of training but experienced a halt or even a regression in learning before their full potential was achieved. In other instances the child progressed well, but later his oral skills deteriorated. Evidently the most common oral failure is the child who achieves minimal or no success with speech and speechreading. Presumably oralism requires a higher intellect than does manual communication, and below-average intelligence may be a cause for oral failure. Another possibility is that the deaf child often has concomitant problems, such as a language dysfunction, which preclude complete success in oralism and language sophistication above a very concrete level. Approximately 32 percent of

---

[1]The inability to comprehend gestures or manual signs is an infrequently found aphasia called *amimia* (*257*, p.337).

the hearing-impaired children in school programs in the United States have one or more handicapping conditions in addition to hearing loss (365, p.5). Inadequate exploitation of amplification can also contribute to oral failure. Stronger evidence in reference to oral failure suggests that the majority are actually education failures, in that the child has not been appropriately guided through the numeroud and complex steplike processes required to learn speech and language in the absence of the important auditory avenue.

Without intent to detract from the work of countless excellent teachers of the deaf, Uden (377) blames oral failure less on the child than on the teacher. He also feels that another contributing factor is the too frequent substitution of reading-writing for speechreading. The adult deaf who use oralism have suggested that those adult deaf who have not been successful in oralism did not receive the training and confidence required when in school (46). That teachers of the deaf need special motivation and dedication is suggested from the results of one survey (253). Elementary classroom teachers, educational specialists, elementary school principlas, freshman teachers-to-be, and speech clinicians were asked to rank eight classes of exceptional children in terms of those they would "least prefer to teach" and "most prefer to teach." Classes of hearing-impaired children were ranked lowest or next-to-lowest in preference by all groups except ehs speech clinicians.

Formal teacher training for the deaf, except in isolated instances, is a relatively recent development. The first university training department for teachers of the deaf in England, for instance, was begun at Manchester University in 1918. In the United States such departments in universities have been slower to emerge and do not exist today in a large majority of the general teacher training colleges in universities. As a consequence, the teacher of the deaf often has minimal formal education qualifications for her specialty. Approximately 60 percent of the teachers in deaf classrooms in the United States have not had appropriate professional preparation for teaching hearing-impaired children.[2]

[2]*American Annals of the Deaf,* 1970 Directory issue.

Another factor contributing to oral failure might be teacher turnover, which could affect the smooth progress of children in classes for the deaf. At the University of Manchester in England, for example, from the school years 1956-57 through 1960-61 almost three hundred persons successfully completed the course of preparation for teaching the deaf; by 1967, 37.9 percent of these persons were no longer teaching the deaf. Also, 11.5 percent of those teaching the deaf had changed school assignment one or more times since graduating. From this it may be seen that many classes for the deaf do have a frequent change in teachers, which is not conducive to good continuity in education.[3] The various factors listed as possible contributors to oral failure are intended as explanations rather than excuses. It is easy to overlook the fact that formal teacher training in oralism is a fairly recent phenomenon or that well-trained and highly motivated teachers of the deaf constitute a minority. Repairing some of these deficiencies would seem to be an obvious and pressing need.

In training the deaf child, we should be mainly concerned with which method is most effective in developing receptive and expressive language. Having said this much, however, we should also recognize the possibility that the best method for training and teaching communication may not employ the best communication media for living and working in a hearing world. For example, use of sign language to the exclusion of oralism compels the deaf to form a society within a society; an isolated society of deaf people is inclined to be limited in opportunities for development (377). Unless the deaf child is to grow up and continue to live only in a world of other deaf persons who sign, at some point training and practice in oralism is mandatory. Obviously success with oralism opens the options of integration into a hearing classroom and integration into the social activities and the broader vocational opportunities of the hearing world. Certainly it is foolhardy for the deaf to expect the hearing world to adjust to their communication difficulties. Rather, there is an obligation to attempt to prepare the deaf the best we can to learn, live, work, and play in a hearing world. Should they later choose to segregate

[3]*Teacher of the Deaf* 65 (1967): 110-117.

themselves from the hearing world, that is their prerogative. Some adult deaf do choose the less competitive social world of the deaf. But for the teacher or school to make a judgement not to attempt oralism with the young deaf child seems manifestly unfair. Nor should discussions of any method of communication be made without considering the important advances in amplification or the teacher's attitude and her training in the method under use. One finds, for instance, too many "oral" classes where only the teacher is oral and no such demand is made or expected of the students.

Speechreading is a skill requiring much study and practice, proficiency coming perhaps only after some years of determined application.[4] In contrast, a working knowledge of finger spelling can be achieved in a matter of days, cued speech in weeks, and the language of signs in months, although proficiency with any of these manual modes requires a longer period of time. Regardless, the time required for attaining precision in speech-speechreading is surely greater than that of manualism. An important question, therefore, relates to whether the longer period of time necessary to become proficient in oralism is worth the time and effort.

One measure of the value of any communication method is the number of persons who have been successful with it. In the 1940's and 1950's, *The Volta Review* regularly published a list of deaf students who had successfully completed high school diplomas and university degrees in regular schools. The value of speechreading to these students is clearly shown. That same journal has frequently printed brief letters from individuals or descriptions by parents or of the deaf themselves relating to oral success; any one of the letters or descriptions alone could be considered an exception, but the large number of such reports is impressive. Similar reports are to be found in *The Teacher of the Deaf.* Speechreading can be considered

---

[4]Few authors have been willing to hazard an estimation of required training time. Nitchie (*274*) felt that three lessons a week for three months would give most pupils a satisfactory and practical skill. Pauls (*297*) found that twenty to thirty lessons on the average provided a basic achievement in speechreading. These estimates were for deafened adults, and prelingually deaf children would of course require a substantially longer period of time to acquire requisite skill.

a prime necessity for every person with any degree of hearing loss (239). Even ardent manualists acknowledge that speech and speechreading are valuable to the deaf (384, p.94). As for the deafened, about 94 percent of the rehabilitated military servicemen from one large program still need and use speechreading in addition to their hearing aids (297).

In one large city the hard-of-hearing students who had speechreading instruction repeated grades half as often as did those students without such instruction (412). More than half of the graduates from the same school system rated themselves as speechreading "very well" (152, p.212). In a survey of deaf adults, about three-fourths of whom had attended state-supported residential schools, it was found that 23 percent communicated within their homes primarily by oral means, and 65.7 percent combined speech, signs, and finger spelling (275). Among these same adults 23 percent use oralism with strangers, while almost 60 percent preferred writing; 12 percent said that strangers could understand "most" of what they said, 57 percent "some" of what was said, and 3.5 percent "all" of what was said. Interestingly, 26 percent said they could understand "most of what was said" by speechreading, 57 percent "some of what was said," and 12 percent nothing through speechreading. But 62 percent wished they had practiced speech more during their school years. Also note the absence of the use of manualism outside a close circle of family and friends.

In another survey of alumni from an oral school, 60 percent indicated complete dependence upon speech, 22 percent reported occasional recourse to gestures or notes, and 18 percent generally used gestures and notes; the same 18 percent reported they were inadequate in speechreading. Of these graduates approximately 60 percent were working in positions that they considered would have been closed to them or reduced in salary had they not been able to use speech and speechreading as the primary form of communication (46). An early survey showed that the median weekly wage for deaf males and females was higher for those who used spoken language than for those who used the manual method or writing (255); there is no reason to believe this situation has changed. From these and countless other similar statements and surveys, we see strong evidence of the importance of oralism, for both the deaf and the hard of hearing of all ages.

One criticism of oralism is that many orally trained persons are poorly understood by normal-hearing individuals. Although this may be a valid criticism, it hardly suggests that manualism would be a better alternative inasmuch as manualism discourages, if not prevents, communication with most other people. Rather, a careful look should be taken at what type of child or what kind of classroom is involved with oral failure, and with that knowledge steps can be taken to reduce the problem by improving oral instruction or by supplementing it with another method. It might be added that the argument that some deaf individuals find communication *among themselves* with manualism as being more facile is not evidence of oral failure.

Some criticize oralism, specifically speechreading, claiming that it has been overrated by many. In particular, fiction writers may have led the public to believe that any spy worth his salt can speechread the secrets of the enemy agent through binoculars, even if spoken in a foreign language! If there has been a too rosy picture presented of the perfection with which speech can be received by speechreading, it has not usually been made by the professional worker. In fact, comments by teachers of the deaf have typically been quite conservative in their estimation of overall accuracy by speechreading alone. Unrealistic statements on behalf of manualism can also be found. For example, one writer claimed that for the deaf child sign language is not only his original and natural language but also a God-given instinct.[5]

A quick scanning of the speechreading literature reveals many cautionary statements regarding inherent weaknesses and difficulties of speechreading. The following are but a sample of such published statements:

It should be understood from the beginning that

[5]*American Annals of the Deaf* 92 (1947): 305.

speechreading is not infallible, that mistakes will sometimes occur, and that often these mistakes are the result of circumstances which neither speaker nor watcher can control (53, p.6).

General conversation is hard for us to understand even though we be skillful readers of the lips (274, p.21). How imperfectly spoken language is fitted to the requirements of successful speechreading (p.26). I can sometimes understand a lecture or sermon, depending upon conditions of light, etc.; less often can I understand a play. I am called a good speechreader (p.29).

The speechreader must be ready to face the limitations inherent in the art—these the most skillful speechreader would be the first to acknowledge (168, p.9).

Neither audition or speechreading by themselves are entirely adequate in cases of hearing impairment, but the combination of both is exceedingly effective (102, p.5-6). Speechreading can never fully take the place of hearing, but for hundreds of deaf persons it leads to a quicker comprehension of speech and a more normal life than would be possible without its help (p.12).

Do not expect too much of speechreading, especially when nothing can be heard. Don't believe those extravagant tales of detectives sitting in dim downtown restaurants, reading the lips of plotting thieves. Speechreading has many limitations (169).

There are numbers of deaf—and hard-of-hearing —people who cannot master the art of speechreading despite extraordinary language skills, mental endowment, and life achievement (207, p.37).

Speechreading is a rather difficult skill to master (256, p.81).

MANUALISM

In addition to, or instead of, speechreading, the use of other visual communication systems can be employed for receptive language.[6] These other methods of receiving language are often referred to as "manual" communication, but it will be helpful to differentiate several levels of manual communication (64):

1. Language of Signs: These are ideographic signs that follow simple grammatical rules, but rules not necessarily related to the spoken language. Signs constitute a unique language and are not a translation from another language. The language of signs is one of generalities, much more concrete and with a smaller vocabulary than most other languages.

2. Finger Spelling: These represent alphabet signs used to "write in the air." In the United States the one-hand alphabet signs are popular; in England, a two-hand system.

3. Manual English: These are one- and two-hand signs that represent words that may be combined with alphabet signs. These signs are usually used within the grammatical context of the spoken language.

4. Phonetic Signs: These are supplementary hand or finger signs to augment identification of speech sounds through reduction of choices.

The language of signs has had wide use and acceptance as a formal teaching method with the deaf for more than two centuries,[7] and finger spelling has been utilized even longer

---

[6]Omitted from discussion here are such visual systems as the Morse Code by telegraph or by blinking lights, semaphore and other flag codes, smoke signals, or military land and underwater hand signals.

[7]The first historical reference to manual signs is much older than that of finger spelling, but common use with the deaf seems to be much more recent. Four hundred years B.C., Socrates (in *Cratylus*) stated: "If we had no voice or tongue and wished to make things clear to one another, should we not try, as dumb people actually do, to make signs with our hands, and head and person generally?"

(161).[8] Except for isolated uses, oralism has been slower to emerge, finding acceptance in England and in Germany a little over a century ago and in the United States not until even more recently. In the United States the percentage of deaf children receiving "articulation training" is said to have gone from zero in 1860 to 31 percent in 1887 and to 75 percent in 1917 (178). It should be added that these percentages refer to some use of oralism, but not necessarily to pure oralism.

One of the problems connected with the language of signs is that the signs lack standardization, a problem which is presently receiving considerable attention. The myth that manualism enables the deaf to be understood across languages or that manualism consists of "natural signs" should also be exploded. Since most proper nouns and numerous other words or concepts have no sign, using the language of signs also requires a knowledge of finger spelling.

It might be argued that the oralism-manualism disagreements could be settled by research. Perhaps this settlement will come about within the forseeable future. As a matter of fact, oralism has produced a large body of research; but, by comparison, research in manualism is negligible. Thus manualism seems more hampered than oralism from the standpoint of research. Rather, in expounding his method, the pro-manualist is, typically, restricted in his writings to the stating of opinions or the quoting of the opinions of other pro-manualists. For instance, Vernon and Mindel (384, p.93) claim that there is strong evidence to suggest that the early use of manual communication followed by oral and manual instruction can compensate for the deaf child's language deficit. Not only is such evidence meager and far from strong, the eight authors Vernon and Mindel use to support their position for the most part state personal opinion. One reference (362) did not inves-

---

[8]A book by the Franciscan monk, Melchor de Yebra (1524-1586), was published posthumously in 1593. It contains one-hand alphabet signs to be used in confession and in religious teaching; Yebra attributes the signs to St. Buenaventura. These signs, in almost identical form, appear in Bonet's work of 1620, and the one-hand alphabet signs used today in the United States are but a slight modification. The Venerable Bede mentions in the year 691 a manual alphabet that was possibly used by the deaf. The oldest known English reference to a two-hand alphabet system is contained in *Digiti-Lingua* of 1698.

tigate the conclusion attributed to them. Another supporting reference is that of Kohl (196), who merely reviewed language and education of the deaf from his viewpoint as an outside observer and in turn, uses for support the article by Hester (161), among others. Hester, in turn, supports his position by quoting the opinions of still others and presenting *post facto* research data obtained from two substantially variant groups of students.

Vernon and Mindel (p.94) also states that psychiatrists and clinically oriented psychologists experienced in deafness are almost unanimous in their support of the use of combined manual and oral methods in contrast to exclusively oral techniques. To support this rather broad statement, they give five sources, including an unpublished paper, a reputable but inaccessible Scandinavian reference, a report which gives a general description of a single case, and a report which makes only an offhand statement that can hardly be considered as evidence (i.e., "Another disturbing factor is that parents are rarely encouraged to learn the manual language ").

Kohl (196, p.13) concludes "from a thorough investigation of the literature on the education of the deaf" that oralism has failed; but his bibliography lists only forty-two items, many of which do not relate to communication of the deaf and eighteen of which are from a single convention report. He also echoes the occasionally found charge (p.4) that hearing teachers of the deaf as a rule prohibit signing, but he seems to contradict this statement by noting (p.13) that only two schools for the deaf in the United States have succeeded in remaining purely oral. Contemporary data are scarce, but in residential schools in the United States, the combination of oralism and finger spelling was found to be the most common teaching method in 1915 (82). Signs were typically discouraged but not prohibited, and in some activities (such as chapel exercises and dramatic productions) they were used rather commonly. In day schools the method was predominantly oral, aural, or both. Finger spelling and signing were discouraged if not prohibited. Day school students averaged smaller losses of hearing sensitivity. Indirect refutation of the charge that signing is prohibited at schools for the deaf is that between 1936 and

1940 forty graduates of Gallaudet College (where the simultaneous method is used) were given teaching positions in schools for the deaf, and from 1915 to 1940 the proportion of deaf teachers in residential schools for the deaf varied between 18.3 percent and 19.8 percent.[9] In addition, the *American Annals of the Deaf* in January, 1959, reported that in seventy-two residential schools for the deaf, approximately 15 percent of the students were being taught by the simultaneous method and another 15 percent by the combined method. We strongly suspect that these percentages are lower than the actual number of students taught by one of these methods and further that teachers using either the simultaneous or combined methods actually give minimal attention to the oral portion of them.

Evidence that manualism remains a strong force in deaf education in the United States is that in a survey of adult deaf individuals, 46 percent reported that in elementary school they had been taught primarily through oral methods, 16.5 percent primarily through manual methods, and 36.7 percent through some combination of methods (*275*). Of these same individuals 27.8 percent reported that they had been taught primarily through oral methods in high school; 20.6 percent, primarily through manual methods; and 50.8 percent, through some combination, showing a drop in oral instruction. The attitudes of professionals in England, often considered the bastion or oralism, are also revealing, as noted in the Lewis Report of 1968, based upon a survey in depth of the practices of education of the deaf. In one paragraph of that report it is stated that "...no organization or individual witness whom we approached suggested that oral methods and no other methods were entirely appropriate for all deaf pupils at all stages of their education."

Finger spelling, along with speechreading, has been employed for some years in classes for the deaf in the Soviet Union, and in the United States this method is sometimes referred to as the combined method or the Rochester Method (*338*). The combined method was popularized in the United States by Zenas Freeman Westervelt at the Rochester School for the Deaf beginning in 1878. Previously that school used the

[9]*American Annals of the Deaf* 85 (1940): 1951; and 86 (1941): 420.

language of signs. Some teachers find finger spelling particularly valuable as a supplement to speechreading in the early stages of the child's language training.

In 1953-54 N.G. Morozova and B.D. Korsunskaia, under the Moscow Institute of Defectology, introduced experiments combining oralism and finger spelling with kindergarten children. The goals were to enlarge the deaf child's communicative vocabulary and to accelerate the development of conversational speech and speechreading. Results showed a substantial increase in words spoken and perceived by speechreading and from flash cards (247). It should be recognized, however, that since Russian is a more phonetic language than English (that is, the alphabet and the speech sounds correspond to a high degree), the combination of finger spelling with speechreading might be expected better to facilitate learning with that language than would be true for English.

In 1934 it was suggested to Richard Paget that if a grammatical sign language could be devised, its use with speechreading and speech would be more efficient than that of manualism based on ideational signs. It may be recalled that l'Epee devised grammatical signs for his work with the deaf, but these rapidly deteriorated to the point where they were no longer functional. Paget worked on such a system and called it the New Sign Language. In this system each word had a sign, and the signs proceeded according to the grammatical structure of English. In the United States the term Manual English has been used for a somewhat different system of grammatical signs. After the death of Paget in 1955, his work was continued and modified by Pierre Gorman, who renamed the system Systematic Sign Language (SSL). SSL has been little used in deaf classes to date and seems to have been ignored, if not disliked, by the adult deaf who are more apt to use the language of signs (295). Furth (123) is sometimes quoted, correctly, as being strongly pro-manual, but he clearly champions manual English rather than other manual systems.

A more recent system of grammatical signs developed in the United States is called Seeing Essential English (SEE). SEE consists of a limited number of signs to be produced according to English syntax. The signs include forms for contractions, verb inflections, prefixes, and suffixes. The limited use of SEE does not permit an evaluation of its effectiveness at this time.

Another form of manualism used by some teachers of the deaf during classroom drill periods is occasionally to supplement their speech with a limited number of phonetic signs in an effort to clarify consonant categories: fingers along the bridge of the nose to indicate a nasal sound, fingers alongside the laryngeal area to indicate a voiced sound, hand in front of the chin for a plosive sound, and hand parallel to the ground and against the laryngeal area to indicate a velar sound. These arbitrary phonetic gestures or signs do not constitute an independent language but are merely used to clarify visual redundancies in the spoken language. Cued Speech is a more formal arrangement of phonetic signs, using four cues for vowel and eight for consonant distinctions (68, 69, 244). Cued Speech is intended as a supplement to, rather than a replacement for, speechreading. A similar system of fifteen consonant cues given by the hand near the mouth was devised about 1895 by G. Forchhammer of Denmark.[10] This system was introduced into Germany in the 1930's, but it is no longer used there (4).

SOME ARGUMENTS ON METHODS

The debate, pro and con, continues today over oralism and manualism. It might easily be argued that manualism is possible under poorer lighting conditions and at greater distances than is oralism. On the other hand, oralism allows the hands to remain free for other tasks and is not affected for the aged by arthritis. These and similar arguments are petty and relatively unimportant to the broader issues that need to be investigated and discussed. Meaningful comparisons of the several manual approaches and oralism, separately or in combination, have suffered from the emotional involvement of the professionals working with the deaf and of the various schools

---

[10]Dr. Forchhammer called this the mouth-hand system, or *manuemo*. He published several books and pamphlets on deafness. Dr. Forchhammer died in 1938.

themselves. Nor have the strong feelings of the parents of the deaf usually allowed meaningful experimentation. We suspect that the closer his family kinship to a deaf person, the more biased the proponent for one method or the other is likely to be.

FIGURE 2-1. "Next time you sign, put down your Martini first"

Parents of adventitiously deaf children tend to be strongly pro-oral and violently opposed to any form of manualism, while parents of genetically deaf children are often just as vehemently pro-manual. It is possible that some socio-economic differences confound this matter. If the columns of past issues of the *Deaf American* (formerly *The Silent Worker*) are typical of the thoughts and beliefs of the adult deaf on communication methods, the following conclusions can be reached: (1) adults who have been severely deaf since child-hood pay lip service to combined oralism-manualism but in fact are critical of oralism and stress manualism in most instances, (2) day classes for the deaf are considered an anathema, (3) using a hearing aid, if not discouraged, is looked down upon as

a crutch, and (4) if a person is not deaf, he can neither understand the communication problems involved nor speak with
authority on the subject. That hearing aids are not popular
with the deaf adult is brought out by a survey in which it was
found that almost 80 percent did not use amplification (275).
Even more pointed was the fact that only 62 percent had ever
tried a hearing aid. Previous inquiries have found a lower percentage of hearing-aid users in similar adult deaf populations,
but recent data on students with impaired hearing suggest that
the use of amplification is becoming more widespread in deaf
education (365, p.8).

As might be supposed, studies relating the several forms
of manualism to speech, speechreading, and other important
linguistic skills have been few. Too often those studies that
have appeared in print have seemed purposefully designed to
"confirm" the value of one approach over the other. Apparently most arguments concerning the possible value of manualism over oralism should be restricted to the training of "most
prelingually deaf children" (385, p.92) or to prelingually deaf
persons with profound hearing loss (123; 196, p.2) and to the
communication between deaf adults.

Until much more objective data are available, we would
agree with Coats (64) that no one method is superior under all
conditions and that each method performs a definite, essential
function that is more or less successful under varying conditions. Perhaps one method is "best" for the preschool child
and another for the older child, or one method more beneficial
for early language acquisition and another at later stages of
learning. There are also suggestions that the deaf might
profitably use one method in communicating with other deaf
individuals and another method in communicating with other
persons, a situation which, however, would require that the
deaf learn two languages in spite of their difficulty in master-
ing a single language.[11]

[11]It might be argued that if the deaf would limit their oral vocabulary to that of
the language of signs, their understanding by speechreading would increase
immensely.

Orally trained deaf adults do typically communicate by one of the manual methods, in whole or in part, when in the company of non-orally trained deaf adults. In one survey it was found that 60 percent of the orally trained adults had learned signs and finger spelling so that they might communicate with non-oral deaf, but 80 percent stated that when visiting with other orally trained deaf, they preferred to use speech and speechreading (46).

A survey of communication methods used by the deaf in various situations was made by Green (144). Based on incomplete responses from fifty-nine deaf males in a trade school with ages ranging from seventeen to twenty-seven years, the results were as follows:

	At Home	At Work	Socially With Deaf	Socially With Non-Deaf
Completely Oral	27	21	0	18
Combined	16	16	27	3
Manual	9	9	22	9
Reading and Writing	7	13	0	26

A similar finding for hard-of-hearing and deaf employees was reported by Follwell (115). Interestingly, in that survey it was found that more of those interviewed used only speech-speechreading when communicating with other deaf persons than used signs and finger spelling only, but the majority used speech combined with signs and finger spelling.

The so-called combined method (oralism and finger spelling) or the simultaneous method (oralism and the language of signs) have some appeal, but in practice one of the two components usually seems to predominate almost to the exclusion of the other (137, p.206). One argument sometimes advanced is that each child should be given an opportunity with oralism, but if he is not successful with this method, he should be changed to a manual method.[12] The idea is logical, and this

[12]Some state statutes include a clause relating to this subject. For example, Ohio schools receiving state support for classes for the deaf are to use the oral method, but if after nine months the child is unable to learn, he may be transferred to a manual class.

philosophy has some surface appeal, but at what point should failure be admitted, and may it be tempting to acknowledge failure too late, or too soon? Children tend to favor the easiest forms of communication. For instance, if the teacher uses speechreading and finger spelling, most deaf children will probably choose the latter, since it is the quickest and easiest to learn, even though with adequate training they might be quite successful with speechreading alone. Further, it is obvious that training with two methods of communication requires a division of effort which might better be spent in perfecting one method.

One difficulty introduced by using both the language of signs and oralism is that the signs can easily interpose themselves into oral language patterns, the result often referred to as deafisms. Deafisms are oral language patterns that are difficult to eradicate because they are habits of thought. The following is an example of a literal English translation of two persons communicating by the language of signs:

A: Name your what?
B: S-m-i-t-h (spelled)
A: Christian name what?
B: G-e-o-r-g-e
A: Trade your what?
B: Male shoe make
A: School learn you where?
B: School G-l-e-n-v-i-l-l-e
A: Stay you long this place?
B: No, came morning yesterday.

It should be recognized that neither finger spelling nor the language of signs is a complementary procedure with speechreading, but rather either can substitute for speechreading. Simultaneous use of sign language and speechreading is found, but the two represent different languages. The combination of speechreading and finger spelling is somewhat more compatible, but it usually requires that the speech be slowed down drastically, and spellings often don't match the spoken sounds. Where manualism is considered necessary to supplement oralism, it is suggested that a phonetic rather than an ideographic or alphabet form will prove to have the most beneficial long-range application and be a reasonable compromise. This position was taken by Alexander Graham Bell as early as 1888. A next-best solution would be the supplemental use of finger spelling at the early stages of training and its use later only to clarify obscure patterns of spoken English. This alternative is being used in a growing number of schools for the deaf in the United States, particularly in primary classes.

It might be expected that combining speechreading with finger spelling would permit the reception of speech to become less ambiguous than would speechreading alone. This claim is made by many persons experienced with the combined method. However, Block and Kinde (37) had thirty-six normal-hearing college students learn a series of paired-associate picture items under conditions simulating finger spelling, speechreading, and the combination. Learning the combined stimuli required more errors to meet the criterion than learning either of the simple stimuli. Although this experiment did not actually involve finger spelling or speechreading, it can be inferred from the findings that where combined stimuli are used by the child in learning, he is likely to attend to the most meaningful aspect of the compound stimulus.

Total communication or the *total approach* are terms attaining some recent popularity. Behind the use of these terms is the concept that any and all input sensory modalities, as well as communication methods, should be employed in communication with and between the deaf. The oralist suspects that the terms are merely a mask for the older terms of combined or simultaneous method and are used because they suggest a neutrality in the oral-manual argument when, in fact, they appear to be an open door to manualism.

Although studies relating the effects of oralism and manualism are few and usually not well controlled, several bear brief discussion. A significant difference in favor of combined speechreading and finger spelling over speechreading alone was found with deaf high school students for a test of concrete concepts (304). The difference for abstract concepts, however, was not significant. In an early study at the Michigan School for the Deaf with students between the age of thirteen and eighteen years. the orally and the aurally trained students scored higher than manually trained students on language usage, arithmetic reasoning, and arithmetic computations. The manually trained students scored higher on paragraph meaning (204).

The Illinois School for the Deaf formerly segregated its pupils in separate buildings according to the method of communication. One study from this school included students from the fourth through ninth grades, with ages from eleven to twenty-four years (mean age, seventeen years). There were approximately eighty students in each of three groups: manual, oral, and acoustic. I.Q.'s by the Chicago Non-Verbal Examination averaged 99 for the manual, 97 for the oral, and 95 for the acoustic groups. Their reading level, measured with the Gates Test, was 4.1, 4.4, and 6.5, respectively. Ten unrelated sentences were presented by five forms of communication with the following results expressed in percent correct responses (176):[13]

	Manual	Oral	Acoustic
Audition alone	0%	0%	76%
Speechreading alone	9	33	66
Speechreading and audition	10	38	92
Finger spelling	76	75	73
Signs and finger spelling	59	60	62

The influence of early manual communication on the linguistic development of deaf children was investigated by Stuckless and Birch (362). They compared matched pairs of deaf students, half of whom had deaf parents and learned manual communication from an early age and half of whom had hearing parents. In matching, an attempt was made to exclude children with emotional or central nervous system dis-

---

[13]Among the interpretations of these data is one that orally and acoustically trained students **without** special training in manualism learn to perform as well in manualism as manually trained students, but that the reverse is not true.

orders, but the latter are difficult to rule out and may have worked to the disadvantage of the group not having deaf parents. The two groups did not differ in speech intelligibility or in psychological adjustment. In a reading test, word recognition, the Craig Lipreading Inventory, and in a test of written language, the early manual group produced the better scores. The authors suggest these differences are caused by the manual group's ability to manipulate symbols and attach meaning to them earlier. The results of this study do not indicate that manualism is harmful for language, speech development, or even speechreading progress. It should be noted that in this study the early manual group had parents who used manualism early in the child's life, but there was no requirement that the parents of the control group have used oralism early in the child's life. The results, as pointed out by the authors and in spite of misquotation by others, can only be considered as a comparison between two groups of children, one of which learned manualism early in life while the other did not. The results might also be interpreted as showing the need for developing formal oral methods with deaf children earlier than is typical at present. The procedures for matching the two groups and the appropriateness of the statistical manipulation of the data in this study have been questioned (85).

Another study to investigate the effect of manualism on oralism compared deaf adolescents on a nonverbal intelligence test, a phoneme count within speech samples, a face-to-face speechreading test, and the child's manual skills (241). Approximately 71 percent of the children could communicate fluently by finger spelling, as compared to 25 percent who could follow a normal conversation reasonably well by speechreading. Only 7 percent produced fairly fluent speech. The author concluded that profound hearing loss was the cause of poor speech and the tendency to rely on manual communication, but he felt the contention that manual communication causes oral backwardness was illogical. It had previously been found, as mentioned above, that oral training was not a hindrance to learning manual communication (176).

At this point it might be appropriate to make an approximation, even though it is a tenuous one, of the amount of information to be received by speechreading. In one study it was found that 21 percent of isolated words could be correctly perceived by pure lipreading (19).[14] These scores were obtained in the absence of visual distractions and at distances between speaker and speechreader typical of conversations. To this basic score let us add an arbitrary 15 percent for practice and training in speechreading (40, 276, 292), and approximately 20 percent can be added for the verbal context (39). The effects of facial expression of the speaker and the nonverbal context are not well known, but for gestures about 10 percent can be added (31, 306). Although this latter figure is for selected gestures, it might be assumed that the combination of facial expressions, gestures, and nonverbal context typically contributes this quantity of information (7). The interactions of these various factors are not yet clear, but for the present let us consider them additive, an addition which results in a total speechreading score, on the average, of 66 percent. To this can be added *at least* 7 percent for the use of audition by profoundly deaf persons (101, 290) and considerably more for individuals with less hearing loss. In sum, using lipreading plus all those factors known to contribute to speechreading and audition under amplification, the individual with a profound hearing impairment can expect a receptive speech score of approximately 73 percent.[15] For lesser hearing losses the score can be expected to be considerably higher because of increased assistance from audition.

The validity of the formula employed in arriving at this receptive speech score is tentative, but the resulting score does suggest that the receptive portion of the oral-aural approach provides for reasonable understanding, certainly more than its critics would imply. On the other hand, if accurate reception of speech is the goal, then the predicted 73 percent understand-

[14]This approximates scores of 19 percent found with hearing-impaired subjects (*380*), 18.9-23.9 percent found with another group of hearing-impaired subjects (*71*), and 18.3 percent for words obtained with a group of normal-hearing subjects (*20*).

[15]This total approximates the 79 percent auditory-visual intelligibility found with children having 96-110 dB hearing loss (*329*), 76 percent for familiar PB words reported for children having an average hearing loss of 94 dB (*290*), and 72.8 percent for children averaging 89 dB hearing loss (*97*).

ing by the profoundly deaf population still leaves much too high a margin for error. Obviously speechreading plus audition in their cases is not sufficient for precise understanding. Either the addition of tactual stimuli or some form of manualism, such as phonetic signs or the manual alphabet, seems the logical supplement to attain the desired accuracy.[16] As shall be seen in a subsequent chapter, if all consonant sounds are to be perceived by speechreading, what is required as a minimum is a nonauditory means of identifying the presence or absence of voicing, the presence or absence of nasality, and a differentiation between plosive and nonplosive sounds.

Another possibility for assisting in the identification of consonants is a wearable acoustic analyzer that employs integrated circuitry and is very small. Upton (*378*) describes such an experimental device that he uses to supplement speechreading clues. This analyzer includes five very tiny display lamps mounted on an eyeglass lens that respond to voiced sounds, unvoiced fricatives, voiced fricatives, unvoiced plosives, and voiced plosives. Such an analyzer may become practical, but it would not be of value in environments of considerable noise.

Several steps which have been begun, but which remain imperfectly achieved, can be expected to increase the hearing-impaired individual's success in understanding speech: (1) more efforts to detect and diagnose deafness early and improved test apparatus to make an early diagnosis, (2) better training of physicians and nonmedical specialists [17] so that they can recognize the deaf infant and refer him to special programs early, rather than hoping the child will "outgrow" his problem or waiting for treatment until he is of school age, (3) more and better trained teachers for the hearing impaired, (4) more graded day classes for the hearing impaired in or

---

[16]Despite general and usually high claims, the intelligibility and rapidity of communication with any of the manual methods are not well known at this time.

[17]A list of hearing clinics in the United States and Canada may be obtained from the American Speech and Hearing Association or the National Association of Hearing and Speech Agencies. The *American Annals of the Deaf* annually publishes a list of such clinics as well as a listing of day and residential schools for the deaf.

near the child's community and state laws permitting formal education to begin earlier than heretofore, (5) more powerful individual and group hearing aids which also permit greater flexibility in transformation or transduction of the acoustic parameters, (6) the earlier fitting of hearing aids on children along with an earlier beginning of formal and informal training in speech and language, (7) advances in medical and surgical techniques which may permit some deaf to move to the hard-of-hearing category and some hard-of-hearing persons to regain essentially normal hearing, (8) the availability of instruments that permit visual illustration or monitoring of speech intensity, pitch, and other acoustic parameters, and (9) amplifier applications that permit many deaf persons to enjoy listening to radio and television or use the telephone and understand speech at church services and the theater. Certainly these and other developments already available, or those likely to emerge in the future, should remind us to take inventory and to re-evaluate our philosophies and methods of deaf education periodically. Technological developments are underway in many laboratories, and newer medical techniques are appearing. It seems likely that improvements in technology, medical science, pedagogy, and a host of other areas will prove more beneficial to oralism than to manualism.

Our discussion on the subject of oralism versus (or supplemented by) manualism must remain tentative and incomplete. Neither communication technique alone is perfect, and their combination may prove to have as many disadvantages as advantages. The success of oralism-auralism with the prelingually deaf population is substantially below the level required for educational, social, and vocational activities. But, despite the known weaknesses of oralism, manualism in whatever form does not appear to hold as much promise.

The subject of communication for the deaf has been charged with emotionalism and has remained unresolved for a century. Hopefully objective laboratory examination will point to a resolution of the problem and thereby permit the wasted efforts of "proving" the value of one method over the other to be directed toward more profitable work with the communication problems of the deaf. However, in the author's opinion the present status of the "hundred-year war" between the methods will increase rather than abate in the near future.

III
receptive speech by vision

The greater the hearing loss, the more we might expect the individual to depend upon vision for receptive language. The gradually increasing degree of dependency on vision — specifically speechreading — as hearing loss becomes more severe is illustrated in Figure 3-1. The proportion of the relative use of vision and audition for communication as shown is, of course, arbitrary.

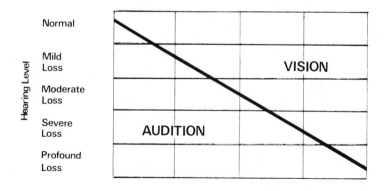

FIGURE 3-1. Relationship between Relative Dependency on Vision and Audition for Reception of Speech as a Function of Hearing Level

As may be noted from Figure 3-1, which is a representation of an idealized relationship between the contributions of vision and audition for speech reception, the person with normal hearing frequently uses vision to supplement audition in communicative situations. Particularly if in an environment with considerable noise or if the speaker talks at a low intensity, the normal-hearing individual calls on his speechreading abilities, even though he may not be aware of doing so. This fact can often be observed at a theatrical production or where a speaker or minister talks in a mumbling fashion, with the result that the audience sits up and carefully watches the speaker for supplementary cues to augment the reception of an inadequate acoustic signal.

Speechreading by normal-hearing individuals has long been known. As early as 500 B.C. priests of India used speechreading in religious ceremonies (236). In 1665 Casaubon, as noted earlier, suggested that the normal-hearing person would find training in speechreading useful (83). Nitchie (266) recommended that normal-hearing teachers of the hearing impaired become proficient at speechreading and that military personnel be taught speechreading to assure more accurate speech reception under combat conditions.

For the hearing-impaired individual, [1] as suggested by Figure 3-1, a mild hearing loss does not preclude the reception of substantially more information by audition than by vision. As the hearing impairment becomes more severe, it can be seen that vision gradually emerges as the lead receptive sense, while audition becomes of less value. For persons with impaired hearing the

---

[1]The term *hard-of-hearing* is used to describe a mild to moderate loss of hearing sensitivity and *deaf* as a severe to profound loss. State school laws differentiate the deaf and the hard of hearing by degree of hearing loss. For instance, in Ohio the hard of hearing, for school placement purposes, must have a hearing loss between 50 and 70 dB and the deaf a loss of 70 dB or greater, in the better ear. More specifically, the hard of hearing can understand speech either with or without amplification. The deaf cannot understand speech by hearing alone, although they may have extensive sound perception. The deaf may hear many sounds when amplified, but they do not hear enough speech sounds to understand connected speech by audition alone. The prelingually deaf child is one who was deafened before the onset of speech acquisition. A few authors restrict their discussion of the deaf to the prelingually deaf with at least 90 dB hearing loss in both ears (for instance, *196*).

relationships illustrated in Figure 3-1 should be interpreted as representing hearing levels with amplification. Just as we observed that the person with normal hearing may need to utilize vision under some communicative situations, it should also be recognized that, unless the individual has a total loss of hearing, vision seldom needs to be the sole receptive sense for speech. The availability of improved and powerful hearing aids usually enables even the individual with a profound hearing loss to make some use of his hearing.

The gradually decreasing function of audition as hearing loss becomes more severe is well known. The following data show hearing loss categories as compared with percent discrimination scores for monosyllabic word tests by audition (101):

Hearing Level	Scores	SD^2
70-79 dB	73%	2.8
80-89	42	13.8
90-99	29	13.6
100-109	14	8.7
110-119	3	1.2

SPEECHREADING: AN ORIENTATION

From the standpoint of habilitation and rehabilitation, the teacher and the audiologist are concerned with building and improving the receptive and expressive language of the hearing-impaired child or adult. In addition to teaching subject matter, the teacher of the deaf — often assisted by the audiologist or speech and hearing clinician — concentrates on helping the hearing-impaired individual to become more proficient in language concepts. Communication tools toward that end include speechreading, auditory recognition, and speech production. Therapy and training programs are built around this triangle, as shown diagrammatically in Figure 3-2.

---

[2]Standard deviation is a statistical measure which when added to and subtracted from the mean (arithmetic average) score approximates the range within which two-thirds of the scores for the group fall.

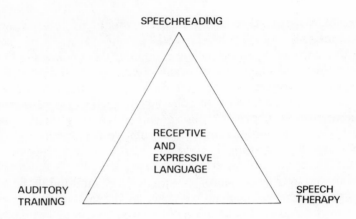

FIGURE 3-2. Improving Oral Communication of the Deaf

It is the author's belief, with some research and much clinical evidence to substantiate the statement, that improvement of skills at any one of the points of this triangle is likely to benefit those at the other points of the triangle. For instance, it has been found that improvement in visual perception of syllables can best be achieved by visual training but that training in one modality shows pronounced transfer to the other modality (307). Auditory training and vibration-sense training with deaf students over an extended period resulted in increased speechreading ability for all degrees of hearing loss (92). With prelingually deaf children there is a significant correlation (r = .63) between speech proficiency and speechreading (119).

Thus speechreading is one avenue through which the habilitation or rehabilitation of the hearing-impaired individual may be directed for improvement in oral communication. We feel that it is a vital avenue. Oral communication, often referred to as oralism, includes the use of a properly fitted hearing aid where appropriate and attention to speech production as well as auditory training in the area of speech discrimination. These habilitative regimens, particularly with the prelingually deaf child, are accompaniments to major efforts toward language development (vocabulary building and grammatical structure) employing reading and writing skills when appropriate. All hearing-habilitative measures are, in turn, but steps toward the ultimate goals of educational progress, social competency, and vocational achievement.

Although speechreading, auditory training, and speech therapy are frequently treated as though they are mutually exclusive subjects and as often as not are taught as such in university training programs, the good teacher or clinician works with all three processes concurrently with every hearing-impaired child or adult. While any class or therapy period may well concentrate on one of these areas, it is our strong opinion that, except for occasional training periods or for testing purposes, the three are not and should not be treated as separate techniques in teaching or therapy. As a matter of fact, it is difficult to concentrate on one area without also involving the other two. Nevertheless, to avoid repetition of a huge clinical and research literature, the present book is concerned primarily with speechreading.

One problem facing the teacher or clinician working with an individual or group having a hearing impairment is the percentage of time that should be devoted to activities stressing speechreading, auditory training, speech correction, and language acquisition. As suggested above, a meaningful prescription or formula to use under all circumstances is impossible. Achieving a reasonable balance of emphasis is complicated by individual and group differences, such as the existing abilities of the individual or group, degree of hearing loss, past training, and other factors. Again, Figure 3-1 suggests that the mildly to moderately hearing-impaired child can, typically, function adequately with audition, and therefore this modality should usually be emphasized more than speechreading. But whether the individual or group is hard of hearing or deaf, speechreading deserves a reasonable amount of class time.

It has been suggested that language typically receives more than its fair share of stress to the detriment of speechreading (44). Figure 3-2 should remind the teacher of the deaf that time spent on speechreading skills assists in developing one important avenue to language and warrants specific and regular attention. For the young prelingually deaf child speechreading should be taught initially and informally as a skill necessary for language development and later used regularly in teaching him subject matter. As a related issue, we feel that those few teachers who present part or all of their speechreading lessons from behind a window are unwise. It is difficult to see the logic in taking away more of an already deficient auditory sense. There are two exceptions to that statement. The first is where the child's speechreading ability is under test, and the second is when the student is not making adequate use of speechreading skills. In the latter instance brief periods with vision alone may be advisable.

WHAT IS SPEECHREADING? Edward B. Nitchie defined lipreading as "The art of understanding a speaker's thoughts by watching the movements of his mouth." Later Nitchie became less interested in the distinctions between fine lip movements and positions and modified his beliefs to such an extent that to him the purposes of teaching lipreading were to train the mind as well as the eye. A similar definition is given by Irene Ewing (103): "Speechreading is a mental activity by which the speech of other people can be understood when the words can be seen but not heard." Anna Bunger came closer to the present-day concept of speechreading by describing lipreading as "the understanding of spoken language while attentively watching the speaker." We note here a broadening of the definition to include all visual clues available to the "hearer." Still, the common concept of lipreading among laymen is much like the seventeenth century description of Dr. John Bulwer: "That subtle art which may inable one with an Observant Eie to Heare what any man Speaks by the moving of his Lips."

Another description of speechreading, to paraphrase Myklebust (257), is that it is a symbol-receiving process by vision just as hearing is by audition and it can either replace or supplement audition in cases of impaired hearing. Although this is a good description, like "visual communication" (286) it is so broad that it would include communication by manualism as well as the Morse Code by blinking lights or semaphore flags. To refer to the process as "visual hearing" or "hearing through the eye" (229) is, in our opinion, merely to confuse the issue with a play on words no more appropriate than John Bulwer's term "Ocular Audition" of 1648. [3]

Today speechreading and lipreading are usually considered synonymous terms, with some preference for the former term by the professional individuals involved in auditory rehabilitation, although the public uses the latter term with greater frequency. Historically, lipreading was concerned almost solely with a visual concentration on the lip positions and movements of the speaker. The newer term, speechreading, suggests that other visual and linguistic clues to supplement observed lip positions and movements are valuable in understanding the spoken signal.

As we shall see and as any speechreader knows, the speaker's lip positions and movements offer incomplete clues to the message. Thus the importance of recognizing and using supplementary clues should be strongly emphasized. On the other hand, the incomplete visual representation of speech sounds is not a valid reason to criticize the usefulness of speechreading as a receptive means of communication — it is merely an explanation for the difficulty of relying on vision alone. The value of speechreading to the hearing impaired can hardly be questioned, as is evident from reports of almost any person who has received any reasonable amount of training and practice in this skill (32, 384). While most such individuals acknowledge that speechreading is an incomplete speech-receptive modality, few deny its value and importance.

That speechreading is a learned linguistic behavior is generally but not universally accepted. Many research studies of speechreading, for example, show a learning effect that needs to be counterbalanced or otherwise accounted for in experimental designs (for instance, 208, 213, 216, 223, 292, 361). Words which are practiced by speechreading them, whether the individuals are deaf or hard of hearing, produce significantly better scores than matched words that are not practiced (237). Normal-

---

[3] A Dr. Plot of England in a publication of 1686 used the term *labiomancy* (literally, divination of the lips) to describe lipreading. Dr. G. de Parrel, of the National Institution for the Deaf in Paris, in 1917 suggested the term *labiology* to refer to the science or method of teaching lipreading but not to describe the process.

hearing subjects trained in speechreading perform significantly better than those without training, but being familiar with the test materials produces scores in an untrained group almost equal to those of the group that has training (301).

THE COMPONENTS OF SPEECHREADING

In addition to watching lip movements and positions, skills which will be discussed in detail in the next chapter, the hearing-impaired individual can use a number of other visual impressions for assistance in understanding the speaker. These visual impressions are also available to the hearing person, but he does not need to depend upon them so much and usually does not cultivate them. Among these supplementary visual cues are the gestures and facial expressions of the speaker as well as situational or nonverbal contextual clues. Linguistic clues are also of great value, and these will be discussed in the next chapter.

GESTURES. Gestures are stylized movements, primarily of the hands and arms, but they may involve the head, torso, or other body parts. In one sense lip and other articulator movements might be considered as phonetic gestures. Gestures are common to all cultures and vary somewhat in type and degree from culture to culture (324). Gestures may simply supplement the speaker's words to add emphasis or clarity, or they may be quite complex and function as the total but brief and limited message of the "speaker" if the context is circumscribed.[4]

Some gestures seem to be universal, and most of them symbolize a general expression rather than specific or well-structured information. One can immediately think of such arbitrary gestures as the nod of the head for "yes" or "I agree" or the

---

[4]The contention that speech is an outgrowth of or development from gesture language is pure speculation. Only where peoples of varying languages occasionally encountered each other, such as in the case of the American Plains Indians, is a well developed sign language found. This appears to have been used mainly for trade and treaty purposes. Because of a vow of silence some early monastic orders used a form of manual communication, and it is probable that the use of manualism with the deaf evolved therefrom.

shake of the head for "no" or "I don't agree," both of which are learned at an early age by both the deaf and the normal hearing child. Other common gestures include those for "come here," numbers represented by raised fingers, "V" for victory (or, more recently, "peace"), an outstretched palm for "give me," and the hands placed so as to suggest large or small, tall or short. Gestures apparently follow less well defined semantic rules than does speech, but most parts of speech are represented, and there are taboo gestures as well.

The difference between gestures and the language of signs is not a clear-cut one. Rather, the difference seems to be more a matter of degree. It might be argued that the language of signs consists predominantly of arbitrary signs, but many gestures are also arbitrary. Gestures, unlike signs, are generally known within a broad culture and tend to be understood across cultures. The primary difference between gestures and the language of signs is that gestures are used mostly to supplement speech while signs replace the spoken signal. Gestures illustrate, emphasize, point, explain, or interrupt; they cannot usually be isolated from the verbal components of speech (324, p.37).

The Jena speechreading method stresses mimetic and gestural components of speech as incomplete clues that have considerable meaning (53), and Haspiel (154) encourages watching body movements and gestures in addition to lip movements. One of the characteristics of a person difficult to speechread is said to be a lack of natural body gesture (226). Pauls (297) states that facial expressions and gestures frequently express more than the verbal content. On the opposing side it has been suggested that any movements on the part of the speaker other than lip movements can be distracting to the speechreader (187). Similarly, unnecessary hand movements have been discouraged when speaking to the person with impaired hearing (152, p.49). One author suggests that a minimum of gesture is an attribute of a person considered easy to speechread (179), and another discourages gestures in working with young children, even those gestures that might be natural (196).

In one study relating to American Indian signs, pictures of the signs were presented to normal-hearing and deaf high school and college students (323). The subjects were required to match the pictures with one-word meanings for the signs. College students obtained higher scores than high school students, and deaf students higher scores than normal hearing students. Although the differences were small between these and other comparisons they were statistically significant. However, an inappropriate statistic may have been employed in these comparisons, and the relevance of the findings to the communication problems of the hearing impaired seems to be minimal.

Little research has been conducted regarding the value of gestures to supplement speechreading. In one study sentences were used within which gestures might provide direct or add supplementary meaning (29). Half of the subjects received the odd-numbered sentences as a speechreading test and the even-numbered sentences as a speechreading test accompanied by gestures. With a second subject group the procedures were reversed. The difference in words correctly understood using a limited number of gestures was statistically significant in favor of the sentences supplemented by gestures. With gestures the scores were double the scores without gestures. This is not to say that any sentence can be understood better by the speechreader if he also receives gestures but merely that where gestures are appropriate, their contribution to understanding appears to be undeniable. In a follow-up study another series of gestures was used, presented either discretely or during the entire sentence (306). In addition, inappropriate gestures were employed. Again, raw scores increased with gestures (from 50 to 70), whether they were discrete or over the entire message. Inappropriate gestures, on the other hand, significantly lowered the scores (from 50 to 25).

Natural gestures are common to verbal communication and should not be avoided. Obviously then, the hearing-impaired child or adult needs to be reminded of the information to be gained from observing gestures, but at the same time he should be cautioned not to expect too much from gestures in the way of specific information. In training or therapy situations we have occasionally observed the use of too many gestures by the teacher at some point this becomes signing or, at best, a game of charades.

FACIAL EXPRESSIONS. Like gestures, facial expressions can also supplement the information received by the hearing-impaired individual. And like gestures, an assortment of facial expressions is typical in communication between normal-hearing persons.

The same limitations as were mentioned for gestures also apply in general to facial expressions. In fact, facial expressions could be considered as a special class of gesture. Moreover, the number of facial expressions is limited compared with the variety of gestures, and facial expressions seem to furnish less specific linguistic information than gestures. As a minimum, facial expression probably offers a clue to the speaker's own psychological state and to his opinions on the subject matter under discussion. Certainly one does not expect to see a person speaking about an unhappy event while smiling broadly or frowning while describing some pleasurable incident.

FIGURE 3-3. "I only wish that everyone communicated with such clarity"

Facial expressions as related to speechreading have received little attention from experimenters. Undoubtedly they, in company with gestures, assist understanding significantly. "Universal" facial expressions probably include happiness, sorrow, puzzlement, shock, surprise, disgust, bitter taste, pleasant taste, sleepiness, and a furtive look. Some of these expressions probably overlap, and undoubtedly other states of mind can be expressed by facial expressions or eye movements.

SITUATIONAL CLUES. In communication we are continually assessing our environmental situation while attempting to identify others around us, their roles, their status, and their group membership. From this assessment we combine observed features and determine the social situation which forms the context of any communicative exchange (324, p.37). The interpretation of mutual roles helps to clarify communication and suggests that speechreading success is enhanced by social achievement (233). Those who are adept at recognizing roles and are aware of the nature of shifting roles have an advantage in social situations (324, p.72). Situational clues include the physical location where the conversation is going on as well as the participants in that conversation. Other useful clues are objects in the environment.

Clues from the situation are mentioned in a few speechreading references, but they seem to be seldom discussed by teachers or clinicians when working with hearing-impaired individuals. This has been referred to as the preparatory set; however, the preparatory set might best be considered the individual's readiness to utilize all clues (286, p.4 and 7).

Situational clues can be considered to be non-verbal contextual clues, and the gestures and facial expressions just mentioned may take on more specific meaning in certain situations. Recognizing situational clues often assists the hearing-impaired individual from the standpoint of increasing probability in successfully guessing the subject matter under discussion — certainly in eliminating some words or phrases or even topics. For instance, the deaf individual can be reminded to be ready to speechread certain vocabulary items when at a restaurant, such as questions by the waitress like "May I take your order?," "Will you have cream in your coffee?," and a host of other phrases that are predictable. Other sets of words and phrases can be expected from a speaker who is a grocery clerk, or a church pastor, or a member of any one of a number of other professions or trades. Because of situational clues we can usually speech-read the football player's comment as seen on television when he drops the ball!

In an investigation of the value of non-verbal contextual clues, Arthur (7) employed filmed test materials. He included gestures, facial expressions, and objects as non-verbal clues. With contextual clues speechreading scores for hearing-impaired and normal-hearing subjects were measurably higher. The value of contextual clues is also pointed out in the findings of a study by Smith and Kitchen (345). They presented unrelated sentences to normal-hearing subjects. Half of the subjects received the sentences after having seen a word that was related to but not a part of the sentence. For instance, the word "migration" was seen just before the sentence "Birds fly south in the winter" was spoken. The mean correct score without the cue words was 32.8 (SD 13.6) and with cue words 40.6 (SD 9.2), the difference being statistically significant.

As suggested above, it is fortunate that the hearing-impaired individual has some supplementary cues and clues available to him in the way of gestures, facial expressions, and situations. Since speechreading, as we have noted, is not a complete receptive speech system, these additional visual and situational clues take on considerable importance. Although they can easily be overlooked by the teacher or clinician in working with the hearing impaired, lesson time spent in rehearsing and discussing them is worthwhile.

With wry humor the poem below describes an incident encountered by a young hearing-impaired man. Fortunately for romance, the young man called upon linguistic and situational clues along with lipreading, but just in the nick of time.[5]

> I looked with longing at her lips,
> To scan the words appearing.
> I could not make out what she said;
> Alas, I have no hearing.
>
> But how I hoped to read those lips,
> To know what she was saying;

---

[5]By Stanley Rose, in *Hearing* 25 (1970): 383.

To guess that enigmatic smile
Around the corners playing.

And as I gazed upon her face
It seemed I saw a pleading.
And then I knew, the words came through:
"Lips are not just for reading."

THE SENSES

Classically the senses have been considered to be visual, auditory, tactile, gustatory, and olfactory. Since we are here concerned with the hearing-impaired population, the sense of audition is, by definition, deficient to some degree. Vision is generally regarded to be the logical substitute, or at least the most important supplement. Yet vision has some decided weaknesses as a receptive sense for language in addition to its limitations in decoding an acoustic signal, a problem that will be discussed in the next chapter.

Of the senses, vision and audition are sometimes set apart and referred to as the distance or lead senses, while the others are called near senses. Audition is certainly the most important lead sense for oral communication. An old Chinese proverb states that a picture is worth a thousand words, but unless those words were previously learned, the picture (that is, the visual impression) is worth considerably less. Audition functions as an excellent sense in almost every environment where man lives and works, but we have already acknowledged that the hearing-impaired individual is, by definition, deficient in this sense. Thus, vision often becomes the primary distance sense for him, or at least shares that primacy with audition. Vision, however, has more environmental restrictions than audition from a communications standpoint. For instance, vision is inoperable around corners or from behind the speaker, and speechreading is virtually impossible in darkness. Audition might be described as the "around the corner and out-of-sight" sense and vision as the "straight-line sense." Visual distractions may be more detrimental to communication than are auditory distractions, as shall be discussed in a later chapter. In addition, we seem to be able to receive speech by audition with much less concentration or attention than is true for the visual modality.

Most of the time the human is receiving an assortment of information through various sense modalities. One might think that he is only hearing, for instance, when in actuality he may also be receiving a substantial amount of supplementary and complementary information by vision or by another sense. Since the hearing-impaired individual receives less, and usually different, information through audition than the normal-hearing person, the cultivation of information processing through other sensory channels becomes increasingly important. Combining vision with audition in hearing aid evaluations, for instance, has been suggested under certain circumstances (87, 298, 340). An audio-visual perception index to predict the social adequacy of speech perception bi-sensorially has been proposed (90).

That audition plus vision allows the hearing-impaired individual substantially better reception and discrimination of speech than either alone is borne out by a number of studies. To our knowledge, the first mention of this in American literature in relation to persons with a profound hearing loss unfortunately may have given the opposite impression. This was a statement by Dr. Max Goldstein[6] to the effect that auditory training did not seem to be useful with children having a hearing loss greater than 90 dB. This same idea is repeated by Frisina (119), who says that the cut-off point where audition contributes to speech-reading is 90 dB. Numerous writings strongly suggest otherwise, but in the meantime valuable time in employing a multisensory approach with the deaf was lost. As a matter of fact, Goldstein (137) clearly presents case histories that show a substantial improvement in auditory discrimination where before training little or no measurable hearing could be found.

Research reports on the addition of tactile stimulation to audition or tactile stimulation plus vision are mostly old, though still in the preliminary stage from a practical application standpoint. Even so, they suggest tactile clues to be a useful supplement for speech reception with the deaf, particularly during training. A good case can also be made for combining all three of these senses in therapy or training situations, and perhaps in daily life, especially for persons with profound hearing loss. The value of the other senses (olfactory and gustatory) is

---

[6]Max Aaron Goldstein (1870-1941) was a prominent otologist, founded *Laryngoscope* journal in 1896, and was instrumental in the establishment of the Central Institute for the Deaf in 1914.

extremely limited in the reception of linguistic information, although they may occasionally assist as situational clues.

One other sense, not mentioned above, is the kinesthetic or muscle sense. This is an internal sense, as compared to the others, which are external. Although not traditionally included among the input senses, kinesthesia plays a prominent part in the Jena method (53). The idea is that if the student says speech drills along with the teacher, important clues from kinesthesia will enable him to understand the speech of others better. Some evidence to support the value of this technique has been found. In a clinical report it was observed that good speechreaders tended to repeat subvocally before writing test responses to speech stimuli (276). In one study responses to filmed materials simultaneous to their utterance were not found to be as accurate as responses made after a slight delay (343). Although using only a portion of the Jena method, Schaffer (335) found that students using the "kinesthetic method" made gains almost three times greater than the control group.

Mlott (237) employed institutionalized normal hearing subjects (mean chronological age 18.2, SD 2.1) and required responses to speechreading tests of oral only, written only, oral and written, and passive. Mean correct speechreading scores to these four conditions were 10.7, 10.8, 12.4, and 8.2, respectively. There were statistically significant differences between the passive and the other responses, and between either the oral only or written only and the combined oral-written conditions. Another experimenter did not find a significant difference in speechreading scores between a written response and a written response following a subvocal response, but the latter produced the highest mean score (21). Nor was there a difference between the speechreading scores for kinesthetic-written and written-only response with memory for digits as seen spoken.

It is surprising that few experimenters have examined speechreading from a motor theory of speech perception. This is an area of investigation that deserves attention. From the limited evidence available it appears that an immediate

response by the speechreader, either vocal or written, is helpful. Making both kinds of responses produces only slight
improvement in accuracy. For best learning the correct
response should immediately be followed by an acknowledgement by the teacher and an incorrect response by the teacher
correcting the error. However, even without confirmation of
responses visual discrimination has been found to improve with
practice (331).

VISUAL AND TACTUAL STIMULI. One of the diagnostic
symptoms of a hearing loss is that the child or adult seems
more aware of tactual, vibratory, and visual stimuli than might
be expected from a person with normal hearing. Likewise, in
audiometric testing it is often found that the person with a
severe sensori-neural hearing loss nevertheless responds well
to stimuli of low frequencies (for instance, 250 and 500 Hz)
when these are delivered by a bone conduction vibrator. The
bone conduction thresholds for low frequencies may be at a
much better level than would be expected on the basis of the
air conduction threshold. In this case the individual must be
responding to vibration rather than to audition. The question is
to what extent the sense of touch or the use of vibration might
supplement vision in the understanding of speech.

The vibration or tactile method of teaching speech and
speechreading was first used in Norway in the nineteenth century. It was rediscovered by Sophia Alcorn and renamed the
Tadoma Method in 1932. Its first use in America was exclusively with deaf-blind children at Perkins Institute. In the
Tadoma Method the child receives clues of speech by placing
the thumb and fingers on the speaker's face and neck so as to
get maximum tactual information (385).

One of the first persons to study the combination of
visual and tactile stimulation in the understanding of speech by
the deaf systematically was Gault (126, 127, 128, 129). In one
study Gault used a subject who was experienced in working
with vibrations communicated to the finger tips. The subject
was tested with lists of monosyllables by speechreading or by
touch and speechreading combined. For this subject vowel
identification improved from 29 percent to 41 percent in the

combined condition, and for six consonant combinations, from 24 percent to 41 percent. More recently it has been confirmed that combining visual and tactile stimuli produces better speech reception scores than does vision alone, but only if the subjects have received practice (92, 177).

Pickett (302) also compared speechreading, tactual stimulation, and combined speechreading-tactual scores. The instrument producing the tactual stimuli was a ten-channel tactual vocoder. The combined stimuli produced better scores than either stimulus separately. It was found that the vocoder provided for better discrimination of sound duration and of the number of syllables than did speechreading. The tactual vocoder is a more complex instrument than is available in most classes or clinics for the deaf, but the employment of an amplified signal through a hearing aid bone conduction vibrator, along with speechreading and in addition to regular hearing aid amplification, might be worthwhile. To our knowledge no clinical or experimental evidence has been presented which combined this simple vibrator with vision alone or both vision and audition. One might assume that receiving speech by blending cues from audition, vision, and vibration would be particularly valuable for the young deaf child who is learning language.

VISION PLUS AUDITION. As early as 1761 Ernaud, and in 1767 Pereira, observed that some hearing remains in almost all cases of deafness and that this residual hearing can be trained to be useful in speech reception (137). Although there is some difference of opinion over the benefit of combining hearing with vision during the early years of teaching the deaf (305, 354, 393), there appears to be little disagreement that using these senses together produces better speech reception and speech discrimination than either alone. Perhaps the primary objection to the multisensory approach during early training is the fear that auditory skills are likely to receive too little stress and speechreading too much emphasis. Whitehurst (396, 397) has long been a champion of auditory training but also a strong believer in combining vision and audition in working with hearing-impaired children and adults. Although a purpose of the present book is to show the value of speechreading, we at no time wish to imply that auditory training and the use of amplification are less important. Ideally, audition and vision will blend to produce perception more complete than either alone would permit.

A large number of investigations have examined interactions between vision and audition. Only a few of these will be summarized. One early study compared the speechreading scores between those students at a school for the deaf who had received auditory training and those who had not and found the scores to be 50 percent and 38 percent respectively (158). Furthermore, only 35 percent of the students who had received auditory training had speechreading scores below 40 percent, while 52 percent of the students who had no such training fell below that score.

Monosyllabic word scores obtained from stimuli presented visually, acoustically under earphones, and by combined vision-audition were examined by Numbers and Hudgins (277). For the deaf children studied the conclusions were as follows: (1) speech discrimination by speechreading was high for the group, (2) students with high scores by hearing alone were just as good or better at speechreading than those who could never understand speech by audition alone, and (3) scores invariably increased with the combination of vision-audition, regardless of the scores attained by audition alone.

In a similar study Hutton (166) presented three multiple-choice discrimination word lists to hearing-impaired subjects. The four test choices had limited phonemic contrast, for instance: am, add, an, at. The results for consonant discrimination follow: 41 percent vision, 64 percent audition using individual or group hearing aids, and 83 percent combined. The results for vowel discrimination were: 45 percent vision, 84 percent audition, and 90 percent combined. Hutton concluded as follows: (1) combined scores were higher than those by either vision or audition alone, (2) there were large differences among the various phonemes in intelligibility as a result of combining stimuli, (3) the most frequently occurring sounds had relatively low combined values, (4) there was no apparent relationship between visual intelligibility and the difference between the combined and auditory vowel recognition, (5) auditory clues were primary determinants in combined vowel recognition, and (6) the subjects varied considerably in the utilization of visual clues in combined stimuli.

Evans (97) found that forty-five of his fifty subjects (average pure-tone loss 89 dB in the better ear, ages nine to sixteen years) produced better combined scores on his filmed Progressive Discrimination Test than they had by speechreading alone. For the entire group the combined scores were 11 percent higher than they had been for speechreading alone and 48 percent higher than they had been for listening alone. In a later study Evans (98) again found a superiority of combined vision-audition with subjects having either a severe hearing loss (mean loss 76 dB) or a profound loss (mean loss 101 dB). Ten of his subjects had hearing levels of 105 dB or worse, and seven of these had higher combined scores than they had for vision alone.

Another study reporting on speechreading plus audition and on each separately was that by Overbeck (290). Subjects were prelingually deaf children between 11 years 6 months and 18 years 11 months of age. I.Q.'s on the Wechsler Performance Scale ranged from 81 to 121 and on the Verbal Scale from 76 to 116. Average hearing loss in the speech frequencies was 94 dB. Familiar monosyllabic words were presented either visually, through a group hearing aid, or combined, with the following average scores: vision 68 percent, audition 12 percent, and combined 76 percent. Overbeck's data permit another calculation. The results for the seven children with the best hearing (average pure-tone level 85 dB) were as follows: vision 68 percent, audition 15 percent, and combined 75 percent. For the seven children with the greatest hearing loss (average level 112 dB), the results were the following: vision 67 percent, audition 4 percent, and combined 74 percent. In this division the number of subjects is small; yet, several conclusions are possible. First, although the scores by audition vary by 11 percent, the speechreading, as well as the combined scores, for these two sub-groups are almost identical. Furthermore, in the sub-group with the greatest hearing loss, the combined score was 7 percent better than that for speechreading alone.

Thus it seems clear that combining audition with vision, even in cases of the most profound hearing loss, is likely to produce better understanding of speech than will speechreading alone.

Many other reports could be quoted to show the improvement in speech reception or speech discrimination by vision plus audition over either alone (1, 90, 92, 96, 99, 102, 165, 166, 167, 175, 176, 232, 260, 282, 310, 311, 328, 330, 331, 406), but one further study will suffice. Krug (198) compared speech discrimination scores employing two tests with three groups of adult subjects. Group I had normal hearing, with ages ranging from twenty-two to thirty-four years. Group II had flat hearing losses of 40 to 75 dB, with an average loss in the better ear of approximately 55 dB within the frequency range of 500 through 2,000 Hz. The types of hearing loss were three conductive, three sensori-neural, and two mixed. Group III had sloping hearing loss of not less than 15 dB, with average pure-tone levels of approximately 55 dB, within the same frequency range, 500 through 2,000 Hz. Types of hearing losses in this group were seven sensori-neural and one mixed. Results are given below for the PAL PB-50 word lists[7] and multiple-choice word tests (34). For audition and combined scores his results at a 15 dB sensation level[8] only are reported.

	PAL PB-50 TEST LISTS			**MULTIPLE-CHOICE TESTS**		
Groups	Vision	Audition	Combined	Vision	Audition	Combined
I	11.0%	85.0%	94.5%	40.3%	83.3%	94.0%
II	9.3	85.0	94.5	36.6	89.8	91.2
III	5.3	64.5	89.0	20.4	68.5	82.9

Unlike the results that are sometimes predicted, Krug clearly presents evidence that persons with normal hearing speechread better than those with impaired hearing and that individuals with sloping and predominantly sensori-neural

---

[7]Phonetically balanced word lists of monosyllables for speech discrimination testing that were developed in the late 1940's at the Psycho-Acoustics Laboratories at Harvard University and later modified at the Central Institute for the Deaf.

[8]Sensation Level (SL) is the pressure level of sound, in decibels, above the individual's threshold of audibility.

hearing losses perform the least well in speech discrimination, regardless of which sense or senses are used. We shall return to this proposition in a later chapter.

In spite of what appears in the foregoing to be overwhelming evidence in favor of improved reception and discrimination of speech by combining vision and audition and the fact that audition almost always provides some understanding, even in cases of profound hearing loss, Myklebust (256, p.51) presents the following hierarchies of sensory organization. As one descends these lists, the informational content for language purposes becomes less.

DEAF	HARD OF HEARING
Visual	Visual
Tactual	Auditory
Olfactory	Tactual
Gustatory	Olfactory
	Gustatory

It seems curious that for the deaf audition is omitted from the hierarchy,[9] even though abundant research shows that unless the hearing impairment is total, significant information can usually be received by audition. For the hard of hearing, on the other hand, it is likely that audition is the lead sense. In both cases this is particularly true if a hearing aid is used. These points seem to be overlooked many times, at least from our frequent observations of children in classes for the deaf and in hearing therapy who are not wearing a hearing aid. At any rate, we can accept the Myklebust hierarchies only if a hearing aid is not used by either the deaf or the hard of hearing.

We would like to suggest that, for the purposes of speech reception and speech discrimination, the deaf and the hard of hearing can best be differentiated based on the use of audition as the lead sense. We believe that audition is the lead sense for the hard of hearing, or in any event that no less

---

[9]For the profoundly deaf Myklebust (p.51-52) notes that audition is of minor consequence, hence it is included after gustation or left out.

information is received through audition than through vision. For the deaf audition typically becomes the second most important sense for the reception and understanding of speech. In these proposed hierarchies it will be seen that the auditory sense for the deaf is placed second, and for the hard of hearing it is either the primary lead sense or else equal in rank with vision. This proposed differentiation between the deaf and the hard of hearing is shown graphically in Figure 3-4.

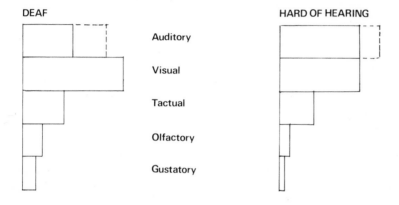

DEAF   HARD OF HEARING

Auditory

Visual

Tactual

Olfactory

Gustatory

FIGURE 3-4. Hierarchies of Sensory Organization

IV
the signal

The person who speechreads must have some mastery of the basic elements and structure of the speech signal he is to understand. The difficult task facing the prelingually deaf child is that speechreading also needs to serve as a vital avenue through which that signal is learned. For our purposes the signal is English, specifically the sounds and rules employed in spoken English. English, like most languages, is based on an acoustic code. The basic units of the acoustic speech code are distinctive sounds or *phonemes*. Unfortunately the phonemes and the alphabet letters used to represent them are not always consistent in English, and particularly among the vowels there are numerous inconsistencies between spellings and sounds.

An example of one alphabet letter that, at least when it stands alone with a vowel, is rather uniform in its sound representation is the letter "t," indicated in International Phonetic Association (I.P.A.) transcription as /t/. The /t/ is a phoneme, even though its production varies somewhat from speaker to speaker and from one sound environment to the next. Notice that even though the initial sound in the word "tack" is released with considerable explosion of air and the final sound in the word "cat" is produced with little or no explosion of air, we will all undoubtedly agree that each of the sounds in question is a /t/. The true test of whether any given sound is a phoneme is to alter that sound and determine whether the typical listener would agree that changing the sound within that word has produced a change in meaning. Depending upon how one wants to count them, as well as some minor geographic differences in usage, there are about thirty-six such phonemes or sound families in General American English.

Spoken language is a rapid succession of syllables consisting of sounds varying in degree of audibility and visibility. In speechreading one cannot depend upon the acoustic code for understanding, but rather one must rely upon the visually contrastive part of that code. Since some of the difference in the acoustic code depends upon voicing and nasality and, as will be discussed subsequently, voicing and nasality cannot be seen, it is obvious that there are far fewer visually distinctive sounds than there are those which are acoustically distinctive. The term visual phoneme, or *viseme*, has been proposed to describe visually contrastive speech sounds (110). We shall use that term since it is appropriate, even though it takes some time to become accustomed to visemic, the adjectival form of the word. A German author uses the term "kineme" as descriptive of the visual landmarks of the phoneme (3).

As has been suggested, there are far fewer than thirty-six visually distinctive sounds, and this discrepancy between acoustically distinctive and visually distinctive sounds is a major stumbling block to speechreading accuracy. Also, there seems to be no significant relationship between auditory intelligibility and the visual identification of the same stimuli (166, 315). On the other hand, one should not overestimate the problems brought about by the fact that there are fewer visemes than phonemes. Inasmuch as there is usually no meaning in an isolated phoneme[1] or viseme, let us discuss the problem as it relates to words. Words that look alike to the

---

[1]Only vowels and continuants can be prolonged or uttered in isolation. In a few instances these serve as words, usually interjections. For example: /o/ (oh), / ɑ / (ah), / ʃ / (sh!) and / ɔ / (aw!).

speechreader are called *homophenes* or *homophenous words*.[2] These words look alike because they contain no sounds between them which are not also visemes. For some obscure reason Mlott (*237*, p.5) defines homophenous words merely as words difficult to speechread, when in fact they are impossible to identify precisely out of context.

There are also words that sound alike, called homophonous words, that the listener must differentiate on the basis of the context of the message or upon other linguistic clues. Words such as *there-their* (and *they're* in rapid conversation), *seem-seam*, *yule-you'll*, *ate-eight*, *bear-bare*, and *two-to-too* sound alike to the listener, and these kinds of words are fairly common. It should be noted that all homophonous words are homophenous, but the reverse if frequently not true. Thus homophonous words can cause some difficulty in understanding on the part of the listener who must differentiate them on the basis of context, and homophenous words will cause even greater difficulty to the speechreader because they are more frequent.

The problem of homophonous words to the listener and homophenous words to the speechreader are not unique in our language. Less often realized is the fact that in reading we have a form of "homophenous" words. For instance, the word *read* can be either /rɪd/ or /rɛd/, *live* either /lɪv/ or /laɪv/, *tear* either /tɪɚ/ or /tɛɚ/, *bow* either /bo/ or /baʊ/, *wind* either /wɪnd/ or /waɪnd/, and *do* either /du/ or /do/ (the musical note).[3] There are other such words, but their numbers are far fewer than homophonous or homophenous word varieties. Again, the precise word is determined by the context. We merely point out that the reader, the listener, and the speechreader all encounter a similar problem in the accurate reception of English. Of course, the speechreader is faced with the much more severe problem of attempting to understand an

---

[2]The concept of homophenous words was introduced at least as early as 1874 by A.G. Bill. Arguments continue as to whether these words look *exactly* or *almost* alike.

[3]The author has not found a term for this special class of words that are homographs but not homophones.

acoustic code that includes differentiating qualities other than those that are readily visible.

Homophenous words increase the probability of a breakdown in understanding by speechreading. They can also cause embarrassing responses. Consider the following dialog between two old friends meeting for the first time in several months.

Mr. Deaf: By the way, how is your brother?

Mr. Hearing: My brother was buried last week.

Mr. Deaf: Wonderful! You must be very pleased about that.[4]

The percent of homophenous words in our language is given by a number of authors, but their figures are seldom based on experimental data. Story (358) felt that 57 percent of speech is visible. Nitchie (271) stated that more than 40 percent of the sounds used in speech have other sounds homophenous to them, while Bruhn (49) claimed 50 percent. "Only one-third of the sounds are visible" according to Saltzman (326), and Pauls (297) and Keaster (181) said 30 percent. Kinzie and Kinzie (191) stated that 50 percent of all speech elements are invisible or indistinguishable, while Cranwill (75) quoted Nitchie as saying that "about 50 percent of the words are homophenous to one or more other words." Muyskens (254) and Wood and Blakely (401) give the smallest percent of distinguishable speech sounds by vision, claiming that only 11 to 17 percent of the movements of speech are visible on the lips.

According to Vernon and Mindel (384, p.92) 40 to 60 percent of the words of English are homophenous, and consequently "the maximum possible comprehension is 40 to 60 percent." Vernon and Mindel do not indicate a source for these percentages or for their statement that anatomical and environmental factors reduce speechreading perception to at most

---

[4]Here the homophenous alternative "married" was mistaken for "buried." In this particular illustration it might be assumed that the speaker's facial expression would have allowed the speechreader to identify the word correctly.

20 to 30 percent. In an effort to determine the number of homophenous words in conversational speech, one author compared the different words found in a sample of 25,000 words used in conversations; 33.1 percent of the 2,507 different words in that sample had one or more words homophenous to them (24). If, on the other hand, the number of homophenous words is tabulated by weighting according to their relative frequency of usage, the homophenous words appearing in conversations is somewhat higher, 48.8 percent. The percentage of homophenous words within more formal speech might be expected to be somewhat lower than it is for conversation. Whatever the precise proportion of homophenous words to non-homophenous words, it is obvious that homophenous words are a major detriment to speechreading accuracy.

The difficulty in differentiating the speech signal by vision is influenced by a number of factors. These are the most important factors affecting the identification of speech sounds: (1) the degree of visibility of the movement, (2) the rapidity of articulatory movements, (3) the similarity of visual characteristics of the articulatory movements between the various speech sounds, and (4) variations in the visible aspects of articulatory movements from speaker to speaker (329, p.72).

An early report on the speechreading difficulty and distinctiveness of speech sounds is given in a book by the American Society for the Hard of Hearing (262), wherein the sounds were given visibility ratings of 1.0, .75, .50, and 0. Doubt has been cast on the validity of those weightings, however (282). An estimate of the relative difficulty of sounds in speechreading, given in percent, is presented by Heider and Heider (157). Interestingly, this study found several substantial differences between voiced-voiceless consonant pairs. Still another table of the relative difficulty of speechreading English sounds is given by Watson (392), who categorized sounds in four levels, from easy to very difficult, as described in general by Nitchie (274). Only within the past decade have the visible distinctions of sounds undergone careful examination. It will be convenient to consider separately the vowels and consonants and examine their relative confusions.

THE VOWELS

For purposes of discussion two major divisions of the acoustic code in English can be differentiated, vowels and consonants. Differences between vowels and consonants and differences within each of these two divisions are primarily acoustic distinctions, but fortunately it is possible to observe visual differences made by a speaker as he is producing the acoustic distinctions. Among other distinctions between vowels and consonants, the consonants can generally be distinguished by more high–frequency components, shorter duration, and lower acoustic power than vowels. These acoustic distinctions may also be reflected in visual differences. Traditionally the

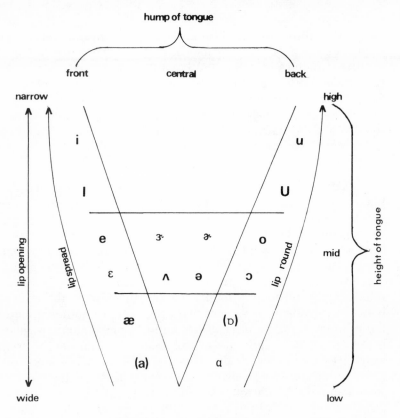

FIGURE 4-1. The Vowel Triangle

vowels are pictured by phoneticians in a triangle according to articulator position as shown in Figure 4-1.

In the diagram of the vowels as shown in Figure 4-1, it may be seen how the shape of the oral cavity is altered in forming the acoustical differences required to produce the vowels. Two of the vowels, /a/ and /ɒ/, are not typically employed by General American speakers, and those persons who do use them usually do not employ one of the adjacent vowels. These two vowels shall be omitted from further discussion. The /ɚ/ and /ə/ are unstressed forms of /ɝ/ and /ʌ/, respectively; for simplicity only the stressed forms of these vowels will be considered.

As suggested by the diagram in Figure 4-1, two major lip and two major tongue positions are involved in forming the varying resonances required of vowel sounds. The overall lip (and jaw) opening is narrow for the vowels shown at the top of the chart, and gradually the lips become more open as one moves through the vowels toward the bottom of the chart. Lip spread, on the other hand, is wide for the high front vowels and gradually becomes rounder as one moves down and around the right side of the triangle. The tongue may be high, mid, or low in the mouth. The hump or bulge of the tongue may be toward the front, in the central part, or toward the back of the mouth. These lip and tongue positions not only create the various acoustic signals but may also serve as useful visual distinctions for the speechreader.

In General American English the /e/ and the /o/ tend to be produced as the diphthongs /eɪ/ and /oʊ/, respectively, rather than being produced as pure vowels. Other common diphthongs are /aʊ/, /aɪ/, and /ɔɪ/. There is no evidence to support the idea that because diphthongs contain two gliding vowels in the same syllable, they are easier to discriminate visually than single vowels, but we suspect that they are.

VOWEL VISEMES. Theoretically there is no vowel that looks like another vowel on the lips. That is, each of the vowels is presumably visually distinctive, each a viseme. However, in rapid speech much of the visual distinctiveness of some vowels disappears. Lipreading methods typically treat vowels each as visemes. Nitchie (274, p.47) discusses the vowels, and he charts some of them as shown in Figure 4-2. It may be noted that Nitchie differentiates vowels both by the shape of the lips and the width of the mouth opening, in general following the variations that were illustrated in Figure 4-1. Nitchie, correctly, discusses the /o/ (as "Contracting puckered movement") and the /e/ (as "Extended-Medium and Relaxed Narrow") as diphthongs. He does not mention the /ɝ/. Although the inference from Nitchie's vowel descriptions for speechreading purposes is that they are readily differentiated, he cautions that several are practically impossible to distinguish except by context.

Width of mouth Opening	Shape of Lips		
	Puckered	Relaxed	Extended
Narrow	u	ɪ	i
Medium	ʊ	ʌ	ɛ
Wide	ɔ	ɑ	æ

FIGURE 4-2. Vowel Classification by Nitchie

The problem of visually differentiating vowels is noted in the Mueller-Walle method (49, p.47): "Theoretically speaking, there are no homophenous sounds among the vowels, although in rapid speech some vowels are difficult to distinguish." The /ɜ/ is referred to in the Mueller-Walle method, and it is also discussed by Kinzie and Kinzie (191) and Ewing (102), among others, but it is often ignored in speechreading methods and studies.

From the arrangement that was depicted in Figure 4-1, it might be predicted that if a vowel is incorrectly identified, the speechreader will probably make the error by perceiving the vowel on the triangle just above or just below the one actually spoken. Or the error might be made between front and back vowels of the same tongue elevation. In one study that examined vowel confusions, subjects were asked to identify which word from word pairs was spoken (406). The two words on the filmed test differed only in the vowel nucleus. The findings from this study are represented in Figure 4-3 by the upper numbers. We have omitted a diphthong that was employed in the study, and the study did not include the /ɝ/. Also omitted are responses amounting to 4 percent or less so as not to clutter the figure. From Figure 4-3 it is clear that where the speechreaders incorrectly identified the vowel, they did in fact most often choose an adjacent vowel. In a few cases, such as the high and mid lax vowels /I/ and /ɛ/, some errors were made toward the central vowel /ʌ/. It seems evident that the speechreader uses lip spread and lip rounding as his major clues in identifying the vowels.

Two of our studies also examined vowel confusions by speechreading. In the first, inexperienced speechreaders were required to identify vowels from among all of the vowels in General American English as they appeared before or after three different consonants in a face-to-face test (17). The responses obtained for the combined initial and final vowel identifications for the three consonant environments are presented in Figure 4-3 by the lower numbers. Omitted from these data are responses amounting to 4 percent or less. Although the two studies summarized in Figure 4-3 differed in the type of stimuli employed (word pairs versus consonant stems to which vowels were added), the relative percentages of identifications and confusions bear certain striking similarities. Clearly the vowels are not of equal visual difficulty, and the /ʌ/ in particular shows a large spread of mistaken identifications.

In a second study on vowel confusions we used word pairs differing only in their vowel nucleus (26). The speechreader needed merely to identify which word from each word-pair was spoken. A confusion matrix derived from this experiment is presented in Figure 4-4. Figure 4-4 does not give error scores but rather confusions found in the visual identification between vowels. For instance, the /i/ and the /I/ were confused 28.8 percent of the time. On the other hand, /o/ and /i/ were never confused. Again, with the exception of the

SPEECHREADING: PRINCIPLES AND METHODS

RESPONSE

STIMULUS	i	I	e	ɛ	æ	ɑ	ɔ	o	ʊ	u	ʌ	ɝ
i	73 73	23 27										
I	46 31	20 28	 15	7 12							19 	
e		5 16	32 31	13 8	36 32						 6	
ɛ		 8	29 29	7 18	42 17	 14					 9	
æ			 10	 7	79 62	7 13						
ɑ					12 8	65 70	10 11				10 	
ɔ						32 5	56 67	 20				
o								71 83	14 	11 9		
ʊ									63 36	 38		 19
u									29 11	41 74		 5
ʌ	10 5	 15	22 	6 7		 7	 6		 9		32 37	 10
ɝ									 12	 16	 8	xx 58

FIGURE 4-3. Percent of Visual Identifications and Confusions of Vowels

Upper numbers from Woodward and Lowell (406).
Lower numbers from Berger (17).
xx = Not Tested.

central vowels (/ʌ/ and /ɝ/), it may be seen that the greatest number of errors in general appear between adjacent vowels as diagrammed on the traditional vowel triangle. Note that relatively few errors appear between front and back vowels or between high and low vowels.

I	e	ε	æ	ɑ	ɔ	o	ʊ	u	ʌ	ɝ	
28.8	5.0	15.0	7.5	5.0	10.0	0.0	2.5	3.8	18.8	3.8	i
	8.8	17.5	3.8	5.0	8.8	3.8	8.8	6.3	26.3	7.5	I
		35.0	27.5	17.5	7.5	2.5	2.5	0.0	25.0	8.8	e
			31 3	25.0	11.3	3.8	6.3	2.5	36.3	3.8	ε
				15.0	13.8	1.3	8.8	0.0	18.8	6.3	æ
					47.5	11.3	5.0	2.5	25.0	2.5	ɑ
						10.0	6.3	1.3	12.5	31.3	ɔ
							17.5	17.5	1.3	1.3	o
								35.0	17.5	45.0	ʊ
									3.8	32.5	u
										11.3	ʌ

FIGURE 4-4. Confusion Matrix of Vowel Errors in Percent

From the data appearing in Figures 4-3 and 4-4, it may be seen that there are degrees of difficulty in visually identifying spoken vowels. Thus it seems logical that the beginning speechreader would be given practice in speechreading and in differentiating those vowels which are most easily contrasted. As he progresses, the student can receive drills specifically designed to help him differentiate the more difficult comparisons. The figures given in this chapter can provide the teacher or clinician with information as to which sounds might best be employed during initial and at progressively more advanced stages of training.

It is also evident from these figures that every vowel sound does not form a viseme and that none are visually identified with complete correctness under conditions of pure lipreading. Some vowels in fact are identified correctly less than 50 percent of the time, such as the /I/, /e/, /ɛ/, and the /ʌ/. Determining vowel visemes is complicated by some non-reciprocal error patterns. For instance, /i/ was incorrectly identified for /I/ much more frequently than the reverse. It should be stressed that in obtaining the data in Figures 4-3 and 4-4, the speaker provided the viewer with no linguistic or other clues and that these figures represent lipreading rather than speechreading scores. For all vowels shown in Figure 4-3 the correct identification averaged 49 percent based on the data from Woodward and Lowell (406) and 53.1 percent based on the study by Berger (17).

From his experiment with vowels Fisher (110) suggested that there are only four vowel visemes: (1) /i, I, ɔI, ɝ/; (2) /e, ɛ , ʌ , ɝ, aI/; (3) /ae, ɑ , aʊ /; and (4) / ɔ, o, ʊ , u/. This limited categorization seems much too stringent.

In some ways the /h/ acts in the capacity of a consonant, but in other respects it behaves much like a voiceless vowel. From the standpoint of visual distinction the /h/ is a voiceless vowel. It has no typical mouth position, but rather it takes the shape of the vowel following it. Since the /h/ has no distinctive movement or position of its own, words such as "ham" and "am" look alike to the speechreader (102, 221). Thus the /h/ presents a special problem to the speechreader in determining its presence or absence in a word. Bruhn (49) agreed that the /h/ cannot be seen but suggested that the speechreader could, nevertheless, distinguish between words that had the /h/ before the vowel and those that did not on the basis of the slightly greater duration of the former. In one of a series of experiments, we found that subjects were unable to differentiate (on better than a chance basis) word pairs that differed only in that one of the words in the pair began with /h/ (23).

CONSONANTS

Figure 4-5 is a consonant chart. Consonants may be categorized and differentiated in a number of ways, but the relationships and differences as shown should serve our purposes. This figure illustrates differences between consonants according to (1) the point of contact of the articulators, and (2) the alteration of the breath stream. In addition, many consonants exist in voiced-voiceless pairs; the voiced consonants in the chart are in the upper part of each square, and the voiceless members are in the lower half of the square.

POINT OF ARTICULATOR CONTACT

	Bilabial	Labio-Dental	Lingua-Dental	Alveolar	Alveo-Palatal	Velar	Glottal
Plosive	b p			d t		g k	ʔ
Continuant	m	v f	ð θ	n l z s	ʒ ʃ	ŋ	h
Affricate					dʒ tʃ		
Glide	w			r	j		

(Left margin label: BREATH STREAM)

FIGURE 4-5. Consonant Chart

The voiceless correlate of /w/ is /ʍ/, pronounced "hw." Some speakers make a distinction in their production of such words as when-wen, which-witch, where-wear, whether-weather, whale-wail, and whirled-world. The distinction between these two sounds has tended to disappear in General American English, and further reference to the /ʍ/ shall not be made. Other categories could be added to the consonant chart. For instance, the /m/, /n/, and /ŋ/ are nasalized, but this classification is not visually observable so it does not help the speechreader. The / ? / is not phonemic in English; rather it is considered a substandard substitution for plosives in some cases, or it is sometimes used in the strong initiation of syllables beginning with a vowel.

The consonants charted in Figure 4-5 do not always retain the exact point of contact of articulation shown, particularly in rapid conversational speech. For instance, many persons produce the /r/ as a lingua-alveolar sound if an adjacent consonant is one produced forward in the mouth (such as in the words "tree" or "art") but as an alveolpalatal sound if the adjacent consonant is produced toward the back of the mouth (for instance, in the words "green" or "arc"). The lingua-dental sounds / θ / and / ð / may, in rapid conversation, become lingua-alveolar sounds or they may be articulated somewhere between those two points.

The fact that the contact point for articulation of the consonants is not invariant at different rates of speech or in different phonemic environments, and certainly not from speaker to speaker, produces additional difficulties in speechreading. In addition, it is obvious that as the contact point for articulation of the sound is further and further back in the oral cavity (moving to the right in Figure 4-5), it can be expected to become less and less visible. Using six visibility categories, Brannon (39) found significant differences in favor of "front consonants," but he found consonant clusters (such as *sk*ill and *bl*own) not apparently easier to speechread than a single front consonant. In one of our speechreading experiments it was found that initial consonant clusters could be identified visually better than could either of the consonants comprising the cluster (21). The ease of speechreading initial consonant clusters is probably caused by the fact that the combination of sounds provides more linguistic as well as visual clues than does a single consonant. It was also found that the front consonants produced better speechreading scores than the back consonants, whether in clusters or not.

Consonants sound different depending upon whether they are in the initial or final position of a word. It might be supposed that they would also differ visually in those positions. On the other hand, in rapid conversation the breaks between words tend to disappear, resulting in long series of sounds strung together almost without pause or distinction between the end of one word and the beginning of the next. This factor is illustrated in two reports. The first showed initial consonants to be successfully discriminated 13.2 percent more often by vision than final consonants (41). A filmed test was used, and the test words were preceded by the item number but were not in context. In contrast, in a face-to-face test with words in a speech context, no statistically significant differences in speechreading scores were found between words from word pairs that contained final consonant distinctions and those that contained initial consonant distinctions (22). Although beginning and final sounds in words may not differ in difficulty of visual perception, speechreaders generally use the beginning rather than the end of an isolated word in making identifications (19).

CONSONANT VISEMES. The consonants presented in Figure 4-5 are called phonemes or sound families, as were the vowels in Figure 4-1. These are acoustically distinctive sounds in the English language although any phoneme has many acoustic variants called allophones. Just as we saw that among the vowels there is a gradation of difficulty in their identification visually, so let us now examine similarities and confusions within the consonants.

The first consonant characteristic to be examined as to possible visual distinctiveness is the voiced-voiceless feature. By definition these sounds differ primarily by the presence or absence of vocal fold vibration. These eight sound pairs are under consideration: /b-p, d-t, g-k, v-f, ð-θ, z-s, ʒ-ʃ, dʒ-tʃ/. A study by Larr (200) dealing with voicing used closed circuit television to determine whether speechreaders could differentiate voiced from silent speech. Sentences were spoken out loud or silently by the speaker, and the subjects indicated whether voice was used or not. The number of sentences correctly identified was 54 percent, a percentage not significantly better than chance would dictate. It should be noted that the speaker in this test either used no voicing throughout a sentence or else vocalized all appropriate sounds. The speechreader, on the other hand, needs to identify voicing variations within a particular word, a task which is more difficult.

In a follow-up to the study by Roback (321), Sahlstrom and Oyer (325) used homophenous words selected so that /p/, /b/, and /m/ appeared in either the initial or final positions. Five males and five females spoke the test words. A strain gauge made of silastic tubing was attached to the speaker's face, coupled to an instrument that permitted a graphic tracing of such factors as these: the number of changes in facial movement during the production of a word, total elapsed time from the onset of the word to each of the changes in movement pattern, intensity of facial movement during the production of each word, and total duration of the word. Significant differences among the three sounds under study were found on one or more of the measurements, mostly in the final phoneme in the word. Although these differences were measurable with the apparatus employed, one cannot conclude from this evidence that voicing or nasality can be differentiated by speechreading.

In another study investigating the possible distinction of voicing by speechreading, word pairs differing by initial or final voicing were presented on a face-to-face basis (23). The subjects were university students learning to teach speechreading. Although 53.5 percent of the voicings were correctly identified, this percentage is not significantly better than chance would give. Thus it appears that the presence or absence of voicing of such sound pairs does not differentiate them as two visemes, and each of the eight consonant pairs mentioned above is reduced to a single viseme. That is, those sixteen phonemes constitute eight visemes.

If voicing is not distinctive to the speechreader, then what does he see that enables him to differentiate the sounds of English? Speechreading method books typically include information about the visibility of and the contrasting distinctions among consonants. In the Jena method there is a discussion of only three categories of consonants based on vision (53, p.18). These are (1) Lips: /p, b, m, f v, w/; (2) Tongue: /r, θ , ð , t, d, n, l, s, z, ʃ , ʒ , tʃ , dʒ /; and (3) Tongue-Palate: /j, k, g, ŋ , h/. Later (p.84) there is the suggestion that some of the consonants within these three categories are visibly different. Pauls (297) follows the same three basic consonant categories as the Jena method, but she refers to them as Parts I, II, and III, respectively.

A more common categorization of consonant visemes is presented in almost identical form by a large number of speechreading books (41, 49, 54, 63, 102, 221, 262, 274, 288, 394). In these books are found twelve categories of consonant visemes:

1. p, b, m	7. l
2. f, v	8. s, z
3. w	9. ʃ , ʒ , tʃ , dʒ
4. r	10. j
5. θ , ð	11. k, g, ŋ
6. t, d, n	12. h

As may be noted, these traditional categorizations of visible distinctions among consonants follow the point-of-contact of the articulators classification that was pictured in Figure 4-5. However, there are some exceptions. For instance, /r/ and /w/ are treated as separate visemes, outside of their expected category. The /l/ and /s, z/ would be expected to be in the alveolar group with /t, d, n/, and /j/ would be expected to be in the alveopalatal group. Although most traditional speechreading books use these twelve viseme categories, there are some differences among them. The / ʒ / is not included in all of the books, and the / ŋ / is often omitted or is not uniformly placed in one of the categories. In addition, it should be recognized that these books generally use these categories, in both discussion and drill, only for visemes in the initial position of words.

The traditional classification of visemes was not seriously challenged until publication of the studies by Woodward and Barber (405) and Woodward and Lowell (406). Basing their deductions upon experimental research with a filmed test of syllables, they concluded that there are only four consonant viseme groups:

1. p, b, m
2. f, v
3. w, r
4. θ , ð , t, d, n, l, s, z, ʃ , tʃ, dʒ , j, k, g, ŋ , h

It is obvious that this classification presents a much smaller number of visually distinguishable consonants than has heretofore been supposed. The Woodward and Lowell formula for classifying consonants as alike or different, however, can be criticized on the basis of the fact that an arbitrary point was chosen for the similar-dissimilar distinction. We have examined their raw data (p.113 ff) and found a number of consonant pairs that they classified as "alike" to have been correctly differentiated between 59.5 and 76.2 percent of the time; in all instances chi square computations show the differences significant beyond the .05 level. Woodward and Lowell may have grouped within visemes some pairs (notably those involving the alveopalatal fricative and lingua-dental sounds) that are merely more difficult to distinguish than are other pairs of consonants. It can also be questioned whether the subjects might have found a response of "different" to be a safe guess inasmuch as only a small proportion of the stimulus syllable pairs were actually alike.

In another part of the Woodward and Lowell series of experiments (p.67ff), consonant confusion matrixes as determined by a filmed test of words are given for normal-hearing and for deaf subjects. Data are presented separately for initial and final consonants, but differences are not striking, except that the lingua-dental sounds were identified more successfully in the initial than the final position. Other than a generally lower score overall for the deaf, the two subject groups did not demonstrate substantial differences in their ability to identify particular phonemes. In Figure 4-6 we have combined and summarized the scores for the deaf and the normal-hearing subject groups for identification of phonemes in both initial and final positions. Omitted from this figure are responses that did not occur to at least 4 percent of the presentations of a given stimulus, but we have combined some of the consonant responses that are reported separately by Woodward and Lowell, and we did not compute responses that were clusters. From Figure 4-6 it will be noted that the linguadental and the palatal fricative sounds each appear to form separate viseme groups, despite their inclusion in Woodward and Lowell's fourth category above. In fact, from Figure 4-6 one might conclude that consonant identification (except for the lack of visual confusion between the continuant and glide palatals) closely follows the classic point-of-contact of the articulators classification and, in turn, the consonant classification in the traditional speechreading method books.

Using a filmed test of multiple-choice words, Fisher (110) cast further doubt on the soundness of the traditional consonant distinctions by vision. He reported consonant confusions resulting when the stimulus word was not among the four choices represented on the subject's answer sheet. Fisher presents consonant visemes that agree, at least broadly, with the categories of Woodward and Lowell. For the initial position he found the following visemes: (1) /p, b, m, d/, (2) /f, v/, (3) /w, r/, (4) /t, d, n, l, s, z, ʃ, j, h/, and (5) /k, g/. For the final position he found the following consonant visemes: (1) /p, b/, (2) /f, v/, (3) / θ, ð, t, d, n, l, s, z/, (4) /ʃ, ʒ, dʒ, tʃ /, and (5) /k, g, m/. Fisher's approach to consonant confusion examination was unique in that it called upon the speechreader to respond to either the initial or the final sound of a spoken word when the four choices available did not actually include the sound. One criticism of this experimental design is that when the subject was to observe initial consonants, his choice may have been swayed by either the vowel nucleus or the final consonant of the word spoken, and for the final consonant he could have been influenced by the initial consonant or vowel nucleus. Fisher's results do not suggest that the lingua-dental sounds form a separate viseme category but the palatal fricatives do in the final position only. His placement of /d/ with the bilabials in the initial position and the /m/ with the velars in the final position seems curious, and perhaps they relate to the criticisms just given or represent sampling errors, since they don't seem logical nor do they coincide with traditional concepts or with other data.

RESPONSE

STIMULUS	pbm	w r	f v	θ ð	tdn lsz	ʃtʃ dʒ	j	kg ŋ	h ʔ
p b m	89.5								
w.r		88.5							
f.v			77.8						
θ ð				65.5	18.5				8.7
t.d.n l s z					62.1	4.3		4.1	7.0
ʃtʃ d ʒ					10.7	76.3			
j				4.0	43.5		32.0	8.5	6.0
k g ŋ					23.4			23.3	29.3
h ʔ	4.0				10.3			5.7	70.8

FIGURE 4-6. Percent of Visual Identifications and Confusions of Consonants (after Woodward and Lowell, 406)

In view of the obvious and significant differences in the reports on visual distinctiveness of consonants, we designed an experiment in which consonants were placed in front of and following three different vowels (22). Subjects were untrained speechreaders in a face-to-face test. The results are given in Figure 4-7 for the initial consonant position and in Figure 4-8 for the final consonant position. For simplification of these figures, responses which occurred to less than 5 percent of the presentations of a given stimulus item are omitted. A comparison of total consonant errors at the beginning and at the end of test syllables, regardless of the different vowel nuclei, showed no statistically significant differences.

The visual intelligibility of consonants seems to be influenced to a considerable extent by adjacent vowels (96a, 299), and limited evidence suggests that consonant identifications are enhanced when adjacent to vowels produced with the mouth open wide (22, 96a). From the scores for all consonant visemes shown in Figures 4-7 and 4-8, one can see that identification occurred with an average accuracy of 54.9 percent for initial consonants and 57.5 percent for final consonants. These scores compare with an approximately 53 percent correct score for vowels. However, in the case of consonants it should be recognized that if the number of phonemes comprising the visemes is considered, the percentage of correct identifications of initial consonants is only 28.7 percent and of final consonants, 23.0 percent. Ewing (103) claimed that a discrimination score of 70 percent for consonants by audition is required for understanding. She stated that the percentage of accurate responses in visual discrimination of consonants is approximately 40 percent, and for good speechreaders, about 60 percent, rates which are below the minimum required for understanding.

Our experimental data for consonants cannot be directly compared with those of Woodward and Lowell (406) because in their study certain consonant response data were grouped and, in addition, they included consonant clusters. Even so, the two studies using syllables do show remarkable agreement on percentage of consonants correctly identified. Further experimental examination of vowel and consonant confusions by speechreading is needed to clarify unresolved differences in the findings of the several studies summarized above.

Although our findings are similar to those of Woodward and Lowell, from our examination of percent-correct-identification and of consonant confusions we have come to a different conclusion. That is, we feel that the traditional classi-

RESPONSE

STIMULUS	p b m	w	f v	θ ð	t d n	l	s z	ʃ tʃ ʒ dʒ	r	j	k g	h
p b m	91											j
w		91										
f v			91									
θ ð				39	16	14	5				10	8
t d n					51	5	8	6	6		6	6
l				5	16	47			7		6	9
s z					25	8	46	9				
ʃ tʃ ʒ dʒ							5	79		5	6	
r				5	15	5		8	53			
j					26		9	16	8	13	16	
k g					24	11		5		8	29	10
h				5	14	7			7	9	16	29

FIGURE 4-7. Percent of Visual Identifications and Confusions of Initial Consonants

RESPONSE

	p b m	f v	θ ð	t n	1	s-z	ʃtʃ ʒdʒ	k g ŋ
p b m	90							
f v		92						
θ ð			38	17	13	16		10
t d n			6	45	12	18	7	10
1				35	36	15		10
s z			5	21	7	32	27	
ʃtʃ ʒdʒ						8	82	
k g ŋ				25	9	7	11	46

STIMULUS (row axis label)

FIGURE 4-8. Percent of Visual Identifications and Confusions of Final Consonants

fication of consonants on the basis of visible distinctiveness is essentially correct. Combining all alveolar sounds, for instance, does not seem to make them more of a viseme group than the independent members. Rather, when one works with the hearing-impaired, it is suggested that the sounds as shown in Figures 4-7 and 4-8 should each be considered as individual visemes, except for the /j/ (which doesn't really become a viseme in any reasonable combination) and the lack of voicing and nasality distinctions. Note that even though some consonants are incorrectly identified more often than they are correctly identified, only in the case of the /j/ is a specific error response found to occur more frequently than the correct response. Further support for this position is given in another report (19), which considered selected sounds in a presentation of isolated words. On the other hand, the hearing-impaired need to be alerted to the fact that some of the consonants are more easily confused visually than others, while some are almost invariably identified correctly.

Again, the teacher or clinician should find this information useful in designing and organizing training materials. It seems appropriate that speechreading instruction should first begin with materials containing as many consonants and vowels of high visual contrast as possible. For instance, the initial speechreading lessons might consist predominantly of words containing the initial consonants /p, b, m/, /w/, /f, v/, / ʃ , tʃ , dʒ /, and /r/, final consonants /p, b, m/, /f, v/, and / ʃ , ʒ , tʃ, dʒ /, and the vowels /i/, /ae/, / ɑ /, / ɔ /, /o/, and /u/. This is not to suggest that only these sounds should be used in introductory lessons, for this would be unduly restrictive and offer a very limited vocabulary. Employing just these sounds would permit the use of only a little over a hundred words of one-syllable length. Gradually the more difficult visual distinctions can be introduced. That is, after initial lessons the speechreader should be taught to discriminate between speech samples in which the visual contrast and redundancy progressively decreases (329, p.285). The speechreader should be alerted to those vowels and consonants that will cause the most difficulty in understanding speech.

As discussed above, traditional speechreading books describe approximately twelve consonant visemes, while Woodward and Lowell have suggested that there are four. Fisher has listed five that vary slightly depending upon whether they are in the initial or in the final position of words.

Our own work suggests that there are twelve initial and eight final consonant visemes. For vowels there are twelve visemes according to the traditional classification, Fisher gives only four, and from the Woodward and Lowell data we infer that there are nine (but they did not test /ɝ/). Our own studies suggest that there are nine vowel visemes. For both consonants and vowels the visemes range from very distinctive to barely distinctive. Regardless of which classification of vowel and consonant visemes one accepts, it is obvious that visually there are far fewer than the twenty-four consonant and twelve vowel phonemes generally regarded as necessary for precise understanding of spoken American English. This discrepancy between phonemes and visemes causes a breakdown in the understanding of the signal by vision.

A comparison of the signal spoken by the normal-hearing speaker and that received by the normal-hearing receiver is illustrated by Figure 4-9. This figure shows in simplified diagrammatic form the message as coded verbally by the speaker and spoken via the vocal mechanism (4). It might also be seen that the sense organs of the speaker serve as a feedback loop by which the speaker can monitor and adjust his speech pattern. After traversing the environment, the signal stimulates the sense organs of the receiver. The brain then receives the signal from the sense organs and decodes it.

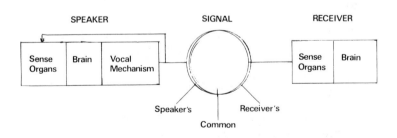

FIGURE 4-9. Normal Signal System

For maximum understanding the speaker and the receiver should have the same signal system. That is, both should know the same language, including dialectal patterns. Both should have a common vocabulary and syntax. Probably no speaker-receiver combination has an identical signal system, but the closer it is, the better the understanding of the speaker's message by the receiver. In the case of hearing impairment the elements of the signal system which the speaker and receiver share is reduced. It has been shown that the phonemes produced by the speaker don't correspond precisely to the visemes perceived by speechreading on the part of the receiver. In addition, the vocabulary of the hearing-impaired child is often smaller than that of the speaker, and the child's knowledge of syntax may be far from ideal. An example of a reduction in common signal in cases of a hearing-impaired receiver is shown diagrammatically in Figure 4-10. Where the speaker has a significant hearing impairment, his feedback loop by audition, as shown in Figures 4-9 and 4-10, is also deficient. This deficiency can account for the unnatural speech often heard from the severely deaf speaker.

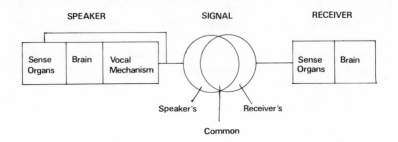

FIGURE 4-10. Signal System with Hearing Impaired Receiver

LINGUISTIC CLUES IN SPEECHREADING

Although many of the speech sounds look alike to the speechreader, there are linguistic clues which can be of substantial help in sound differentiation. For instance, the glide sounds and /h/ do not serve as final consonants and / ŋ / does not initiate a syllable in English. There are no English words beginning with / ʒ /, although that fairly rare sound does initiate syllables in a few words of more than one syllable, and relatively few words begin with /z/. Certain consonant clusters, such as /pg/ and /tf/, do not occur within syllables in English words. These factors are sometimes referred to as constraints. Voiceless consonants, although fewer in number than voiced consonants, occur more often in English. It should also be recognized that some acoustic differences between English sounds, regardless of degree of hearing loss, are likely to supplement visual differences that are difficult, if not impossible, to distinguish. In the previous chapter it was seen that audition plus vision increases speech discrimination, even in cases of profound hearing loss. It is probable that improvement in bisensory reception by those with profound hearing loss is due to small acoustic clues received, such as the distinction between a plosive and a continuant or the recognition of voicing or nasality. In some ways auditory and visual reception are complementary. In auditory discrimination, point-of-contact of the articulator confusions are more frequent than those involving voicing and breath stream modification, while in speechreading the reverse is more nearly the case.

Let us consider an example of the problem the speech-reader encounters, for instance, in trying to determine the meaning of a word that begins with a bilabial sound followed by the vowel /ae/ ending with an alveolar consonant. These are the possibilities, listed in groups:

HOMOPHENOUS	*NEAR-HOMOPHENOUS*
mat mad man	mass
bat bad ban	bass
pat pad pan	pass pal

For some words there may be more homophenous and nearly homophenous words. In the present instance there is no such word as "mal," "bal," "maz," "baz," or "paz." Nor would the plural or possessive of any of these words look appreciably different from the singular form when it can be pluralized by adding a final /s/ or /z/ without adding a syllable.

If some or all of these words look alike to the speech-reader, as do countless other similar word combinations, how can one possibly attain accurate speech understanding by vision? As was indicated above, linguistic clues are a great help, and there are at least three types of linguistic clues available to the speechreader which may guide him through the maze of countless homophenous words. The first and undoubtedly the most important linguistic clue is verbal context, whereby many homophenous words can be predicted by the semantic rules available in the portion of the message that was understood. Linguistic clues from preceding sounds and words are classified as sequential redundancy. Akin to verbal context and also helpful to the speechreader is the redundancy of much of our speech. As much as 50 percent of our language is redundant. There is also usually some conscious or subconscious knowledge of the relative frequency with which certain sounds and words are used (sometimes called distributional redundancy), and variation in word difficulty as it affects frequency and usage can also provide linguistic clues. These factors seem inter-related to a considerable degree. Let us illustrate by using the homophenous and nearly homophenous words that were given in the example above.

Suppose we assume that the speechreader understood the sentence "I saw a ——— talking to her." What was the missing word? Obviously most of the words listed above are not appropriate within that sentence. Only "man" and "pal" can be considered plausible, and since " man" is a much more frequently appearing word (and it is probably more logical in this illustration), the speechreader can quickly come to the conclusion that this sentence must have been "I saw a man talking to her." In other instances one can differentiate homophenous words on the basis of whether the syntax will permit a noun, verb, or other part of speech to complete it, or whether the word must be singular or plural. These are syntactical clues.

In conversation the number of homophenous word alternatives is hardly as simple as in the example above. The word choices the speechreader must consider are usually much more complicated and involve more than a single problem word. The following example more nearly approximates the typical task of visually and linguistically deciphering a sentence:

High	sad	doubt	add	rode	a	letter	do	by	mother
I	sand	down	an	(road)	hey		new	(buy)	
	sat	noun	and	wrote	(hay)		(knew)	my	
		tout	ant	(rote)			to	pie	
		town	(aunt)				(too)		
			at				(two)		
			had						
			hand						
			hat						

This illustration (with homophonous words in parentheses) is a fair example of the problem of homophenous word alternatives faced by the speechreader. Obviously linguistic clues are of major help in focusing on the correct words for understanding in the rapid flow of speech. A number of linguistic clues have been investigated as they relate to speechreading success. To date these studies provide us with a limited number of answers, since the authors do not propose any overall, cohesive linguistic theory. This area of speechreading research affords excellent opportunities to the interested experimenter with the promise of a better understanding of the speechreading process.

The value of linguistic clues in making some differentiations of sentences consisting of homophenous or nearly homophenous words is suggested by the results of a study by Albright and Hipskind (2). They employed English sentences matched to Slurvian utterances. In matching the sentences, they made the consonants and vowels correspond as closely as possible to the nearest viseme in the Slurvian utterances. For example, the sentence "In God we trust" was matched with "Ink ought weed rust." Sixty normal hearing college students saw the sentences as presented by videotape, and the viewers were able to speechread the English sentences significantly better than they could the Slurvian utterances.

The visual perception of the verb in a sentence was considered by one writer to be the most important factor in

CARL A. RUDISILL LIBRARY
LENOIR RHYNE COLLEGE

successful speechreading (132). Pronouns and verbs are reported to be the easiest to speechread, followed by nouns, adverbs, adjectives and prepositions, but only averages are provided as evidence for such ranking (368).

Speechreading difficulty is claimed to increase gradually as sentence stimuli increase in number of words or syllables (250, 368). Phrases are easier to speechread than words or sentences (367). Declarative sentences tend to be more difficult to speechread than interrogative sentences according to one study (368). Kernel sentences were employed in a speechreading test in another experiment (337). These were transformed into seven sentence forms: negative, query, passive, negative-query, negative-passive, query-passive, and negative-query-passive. Subjects were normal hearing university students. The results showed that the passive sentence was relatively easy to speechread, while the negative construction was relatively difficult. These results parallel those previously found with an auditory task.

Further evidence relative to the speechreading difficulty of sentences varying in complexity is given by Hannah (150). She employed kernel sentences that were first transformed by the application of one or more transformations and were then embedded one within another and/or conjoined. Thirty normal-hearing college students viewed the sentence stimuli by videotape. Results indicated that ease of perception followed a hierarchy from the kernel sentence or one with a single transformation to the conjoined and then to the even more difficult embedded sentence. Within the embedded sentence types the verb complement seemed to be the easiest to perceive, with the comparative, relative, and noun complement following in that order. Clearly, the stimulus sentences for speechreading training or testing can be made more difficult by either adding transformations to a kernel sentence or by inter-relating two sentences by conjoining or embedding.

As the number of word choice alternatives increases, the discrimination task might be expected to become more difficult. Using normal-hearing subjects in varying degrees of background noise, Sumby and Pollack (364) employed test vocabularies of 8, 16, 32, 64, 128, and 256 words. They found that test vocabularies above 64 words did not decrease scores for audition and vision combined, but scores for vision alone decreased as test vocabulary size continued to increase. For instance, by vision alone the mean score for the 8-word vocabulary was 80 percent but for the 256-word test vocabulary the score was 40 percent. For these normal-hearing subjects the contribution of vision to intelligibility was small at high signal-to-noise ratios because audition alone provided good intelligibility.

Taaffe and Wong (368) found speechreading differences in word intelligibility related to word length, but curiously they used the number of letters rather than sounds for their length criterion. They reported that three-letter words were easier to speechread than words of one or two letters, but above three letters the words became more difficult to speechread. It should be recognized, however, that the English language contains numerous instances of words with the same number of phonemes but different numbers of alphabet letters.

Speechreading scores for words have been found to improve significantly from monosyllabic words to trochees and from trochees to spondees (96a). Brannon (39) did not find a significant difference in the speechreading difficulty of PB words and spondees, but when words were presented in sentences, the scores increased from about 32 percent to 50 percent. It was felt that the context offered by the sentence was the reason for this increase, but Brannon cautions that the words used in isolation were not the same as those used in the sentences. That scores for speechreading words in context show a significant improvement over those for speechreading words in isolation was also found for Spanish (333), but in a Japanese study it was concluded that speechreading of connected discourse is too difficult to test (334). Although the context offers the speechreader clues above those of the word in isolation, a redundant context was not found to increase speechreading test scores (18). Sentence difficulty and sentence familiarity are not independent in speechreading, as evidenced by correlations ($r = .31$ and $.34$) that are statistically significant (210, 211).

Franks and Oyer (117) examined by means of a filmed test the effect upon speechreading scores of the familiarity of words as determined by a frequency count for printed English (373). The answer sheets contained the initial consonant stem of monosyllabic test words. It was concluded that the familiarity and number of rhyming alternatives were contributors to speechreading accuracy, but word familiarity, as such, was not an important factor.

The effects of frequency of word use and word length on speechreading performance were examined directly in one study (20). An equal number of one-, two-, and three-syllable words were employed, half of which appeared frequently in conversational speech and half of which appeared less frequently. The scores for recognition by speechreading of frequently used words were better than those for recognition of infrequently used words by a statistically significant margin. One-syllable words produced the lowest speechreading scores. Three-syllable words of the familiar variety were identified better than two-syllable words, but unfamiliar two-syllable words were recognized more frequently than unfamiliar three-syllable words. It may be seen that frequency of word usage and word length as measured in syllables are inter-related. Although speechreading methods typically employ monosyllables in early lessons, it seems advisable to include as many two-syllable and three-syllable words of the familiar type as possible in the initial lessons. In the very first speechreading lessons a limited vocabulary of words with varying syllable lengths provides the student additional clues and is helpful in giving the novice initial successes.

Words of one and two syllables were found by Fisher (110) to be reciprocally confused, but words of one or two syllables were seldom confused with words of four syllables. He suggests that as part of homophenous classifications word length be included: words of one and two syllables, and words of three syllables or more. In contrast, other researchers have found that speechreaders are fairly accurate in identifying words by syllable length (18, 96). Where misidentifications do occur, the response is usually to a word having one syllable more or one syllable less than the stimulus word.

Repetition—with up to five presentations of stimulus words—was examined as a speechreading variable with normal-hearing subjects (265). Repetitions produced slightly better scores, but when compared to a single presentation, the differences were not statistically significant. In a similar experiment no significant differences were found in speech-reading scores whether the stimuli were spoken one, two, or three times (22). From these results it does not appear that several repetitions of words or sentences, as is practiced by many clinicians and teachers of the deaf, will give significant assistance to the speechreader. While repetition of drill materials at the early stages of speechreading may be of some value (for instance, a full-face presentation and then one at a slight angle), this should be minimized at later stages of training, since the speechreader will not find such repetitions common in daily communicative situations. These findings also emphasize the wisdom of the speaker's using synonyms or paraphrases when repeating misunderstood messages.

From some of the assorted studies on the effects of linguistic factors on speechreading, a few suggestions for the teacher and clinician emerge. In addition to making use of the relatively visible speech sounds, the student will be assisted in the initial speechreading lessons if the lesson materials consist of relatively short sentences in declarative form. The vocabulary used, particularly for key words, should be limited in size. Drill on word lists does not seem profitable. Preferably, key words can be stressed by placing them in short, varied, meaningful sentences. The vocabulary chosen for early speech-reading lessons should consist of highly familiar and useful words and, where possible, words of two or more syllables. When phrases or sentences are repeated, slight rewording or paraphrasing will be helpful.

POSSIBLE DIRECTIONS OF INQUIRY. In reading this chapter in particular, the reader may have noticed two peculiarities in the discussion. These peculiarities in turn relate to and reflect the past research on speechreading. First, although speechreading is basically a visual process, it is almost invariably described in auditory terms. Even though one must speechread an auditory code, surely it is time to take a fresh look at the speechreading process in visual terms and only then relate it to audition. Second, unlike the study of other senses, the visual recognition of speech is typically dealt with almost solely as a peripheral process rather than any attempt being made to develop an understanding of the central processes involved, if only in a theoretical model.

Is it not probable that there are persons with "speechreading aphasia" (257, p.335), or that there are a number of barely visible differences important to speechreading success (such as visual memory for movements), or that after appropriate training some central process might permit a perception of gradually smaller differences by vision? Is it possible that the distinctions between voiced-voiceless or nasalized-nonnasalized sounds could be taught to the speechreader? These are but a few questions that might be answerable if experimenters were to take a new and broader look at speechreading as a unique process.

A first step in making a logical analysis of the speechreading process would be to develop a more precise psychophysical distinctive feature characterization of speech patterns by vision independent of auditory distinctive features. Next would be the task of attempting to determine how the visual system categorizes these features. Subsequently the transformations between the output of the visual system and both the motor and auditory systems could be discussed and applied to training. Without determining and understanding the progression of levels of signal analysis, the speechreading processes are likely to remain mixed and obscured with other processes.

Finally, experimenters and casual observers who report on speechreading matters will need to use much greater care in their measurements and descriptions. As will become obvious in the next several chapters, many of the factors relating to speechreading are poorly understood. Worse yet, different investigators have produced sharply conflicting findings. Undoubtedly some of the confusions and discrepancies are due to hurried and slipshod experimental efforts. More likely, however, the experimenters have not recognized the need to choose more carefully and specify controls over their test materials, subjects, speaker, or environment.

V
the speechreader

There are many complex variables involved in the successful learning and use of speechreading. Some of these factors are not clearly understood at the present time, and perhaps others have not been recognized, much less isolated and analyzed. It is appropriate to consider some of the known and the presumed variables and factors involved in the speechreading process. In an attempt to cover these in an organized and meaningful manner, we have already discussed verbal and non-verbal clues as well as various aspects of the speech signal. Also of importance are the characteristics of the person doing the speechreading, as well as the person to be observed, and the environment in which speechreading may be or may need to be accomplished. In this chapter pertinent behavioral characteristics and abilities as they relate to the speechreader himself will be reviewed. Among these are visual acuity, attention, intelligence, age, education, hearing loss, other communication skills, and non-verbal visual perception.

Understanding the factors relating to the speechreader as they affect speechreading proficiency is particularly important. In comparison with the signal, the speaker, and the environment, the speechreader's behavior is usually more amenable to modification and improvement. The hearing-impaired child is usually available in the classroom for a protracted period of training. Therefore, those factors relating to his skills which can be improved should receive emphasis, and those factors that do not seem closely related to speechreading success should receive little if any classroom attention. Other characteristics of the speechreader that may not be readily alterable should, nevertheless, be understood, if for no other reason than that they afford information on which the teacher can base his expectations for the student. Further, with better understanding of those speechreading factors most important in the development of the speechreader, we may be able to develop simpler and quicker, as well as more indirect, methods for modifying speechreading habits and behavior.

VISUAL ACUITY. Visual acuity refers to the ability of the eye to distinguish fine details. Obviously a blind person cannot speechread. Yet we know of individuals with considerable reduction in visual acuity who seem to speechread very well. It is logical, therefore, to question what the relationship between speechreading and visual acuity might be. This relationship is particularly important, since visual deficiencies are much more common among deaf children than among normal-hearing children (257, p.323). Since most investigations of speechreading have used subjects with normal or corrected vision, useful information on this factor cannot be gleaned from many past studies.

Goetzinger (135) found no significant relationship between speechreading performance and visual acuity, nor did he find differences in speechreading scores between binocular, monocular dominant eye, and monocular non-dominant eye vision. Evans (97) used a filmed speechreading test with prelingually deaf children. He included visual acuity measurements, as tested with the Snellen chart, and found a small, statistically non-significant correlation between visual acuity and speechreading performance. Curiously, the small difference was that of higher scores from the subjects with poorer vision.

Visual acuity in relation to speechreading proficiency was also examined by Lovering and Hardick (216). They employed five female subjects whose visual acuity was reduced by optical lenses from 20/20 to 20/40, 20/60, 20/80, and 20/100. Test materials consisted of filmed sentences which were required to be correctly speechread word for word. Results showed that speechreading scores improved significantly from 20/100 to 20/80, from 20/80 to 20/60, and from 20/60 to 20/40, but not from 20/40 to 20/20. Hardick et al. (151) also found a significant relationship between visual acuity and speechreading as based on the Utley filmed test of sentences (but not, strangely enough, on the word or story tests). However, these findings can be questioned because nine of the sixteen subjects scored alike on the optometric test criterion, such a large number of tied ranks weakening the statistical comparisons. Also the subjects sat from four to twenty feet from the screen, and if visual acuity were an important factor, this difference in distance might have been a confounding variable. None of the foregoing experiments apparently controlled for near vision, an omission which might be expected to contaminate subject criteria by introducing alterations of visual acuity.

However, these results were essentially confirmed in another study which involved video-taped test materials shown life size (133d). The twenty-four subjects were tested for both near and far vision and then fitted with lenses altering the visual acuity from 20/20 to 20/40, 20/60, and 20/80. It was found that the change from 20/20 to 20/40 vision reduced speechreading scores by only 4 percent, but from 20/40 to 20/60 and from 20/60 to 20/80, the scores dropped 12 percent for each reduction in visual acuity.

There is no reason to believe that visual acuity as measured with the Snellen chart should be directly related to the task of speechreading. Speechreading apparently requires the quick differentiation of rapid articulator movements along with the use of linguistic and other clues, while the Snellen chart simply requires reading small print. To predict speechreading performance on the basis of visual acuity would seem to be much like predicting auditory speech discrimination on the basis of pure-tone hearing sensitivity.

Until good evidence to the contrary is produced, we would expect anyone with vision sufficient to see the articulators of the speaker to be able to speechread, so far as visual acuity requirements are concerned. The limited evidence available suggests that 20/40 vision is sufficient in most conversational situations. For successful speechreading the articulators of the speaker need to be seen; but more importantly, differences in movements and positions of the articulators must be seen. Related to visual acuity is the distance between speaker and speechreader and the lighting on the speaker. These factors will be discussed in a later chapter. Inasmuch as gestures and situational clues have been found to contribute to speechreading success (and some schools combine oralism with a form of manualism), it might be assumed that peripheral vision would be important to the speechreader. Visual acuity at 20° azimuth, for instance, drops to about one-tenth that at 0° (329). This area deserves further research.

ATTENTION, ATTITUDE, AND MOTIVATION. Presumably a number of psychological factors such as attention, attitude, and motivation on the part of the receiver are important to any successful communicative task. It might be supposed that speechreading requires more attention to the speaker and better motivation on the part of the speechreader than does understanding of speech by audition, since only the unidirectional visual clues from the speaker can be used for understanding. Motivation has been difficult to define, much less to measure. It was discussed by Nitchie (266) as a "spiritual" factor, and the Kinzies (191) apparently referred to the same thing as "willpower." Milesky (233) called it motivation or drive and stated that it "cannot be tested, although this perhaps is one of the most important factors in lipreading ability."

In an attempt to estimate the effect of motivation on speechreading performance, one experimenter employed normal-hearing university students as subjects and offered monetary awards for the highest speechreading test scores

(18). Although the monetary-award condition produced slightly higher mean speechreading scores than the no-award condition, the difference was not significant. However, the number of attempts to respond to the test stimuli was significantly greater under the monetary award condition than under the no-award condition. It might be speculated that the speech-reader achieves a certain proficiency with "normal" speechreading effort and that with added motivation he may be more willing to try to guess what was spoken, an added effort which will produce only a slight improvement in his speechreading achievement. With hearing-impaired adults Falconer and Mefferd (105) also found that good speechreaders made more guesses than poor speechreaders. They considered decreased reaction times on a visual-motor task as indicative of high motivation and found good speechreaders to have lower reaction times than poor speechreaders.

Level of aspiration seems to be related to motivation. With prelingually deaf high school students, a strong relationship has been found between speechreading and level of aspiration when performing a motor task, but not with degree of adjustment as measured by a personality inventory (408). Level of aspiration was included by O'Neill and Davidson (285) in their study on speechreading. Normal-hearing subjects with no speechreading training and deaf students were given a filmed speechreading test and the Rotter Level of Aspiration Test. In the latter test the subject predicts his future motor performance based on knowledge of his past performance on the test. Results showed a non-significant correlation between speechreading and aspiration for both the deaf and normal hearing subjects. Further inquiry into motivation and level of aspiration is warranted, especially with assorted age groups from deaf and deafened populations. In particular, it is sometimes claimed that the adolescent deaf become poorly motivated in their academic work and have a low aspiration level.

Good speechreaders appear to have a more positive attitude toward others and toward themselves than do poor speechreaders (148). Whether this positive attitude is a result of speechreading success or is instrumental in achieving it remains to be determined. On three of the ten subscales of the

Zimmerman Temperament Survey, statistically significant correlations were obtained with speechreading performance (399). Myklebust (252, p.255) presents evidence of a relationship between degree of speechreading skill and the extent of depression and hysteria. He suggests that treatment of the hysteria and depression might be more rewarding in these instances than speechreading training. It has also been suggested that speechreading therapy with adults should focus on reducing their anxiety in communication situations as well as on improving their communication skills (280).

Thirty-nine hearing-impaired veterans (aged thirty-five to thirty-seven years with hearing loss in the better ear 35 dB or greater) were divided into two groups according to speechreading scores from a face-to-face test (105). They were then given the Eysenck Personality Inventory as an estimate of extroversion-introversion and neuroticism-stability levels. Good speechreaders were more introverted and less neurotic than the poor speechreaders, the former being an unexpected finding. Getz (131) found well-adjusted deaf students to rank higher in both speech and speechreading ability than maladjusted deaf students, but only the difference in speech ability was statistically significant.

Non-significant correlations were found between scores from a filmed test of speechreading and the Rotter Incomplete Sentence Test, the Rorschach Test, the Knower Speech Attitude Scale, and the Knower-Dusenbury Test of Ability to Judge Emotion (281). Subjects were normal-hearing young adults. However, when deaf children were tested, a significant positive correlation ($r = .47$) was found between speechreading and desirable attitudes toward speech and speechreading as obtained with a questionnaire (72.).

That concentration over a long period of time may not be a vital factor in speechreading success can be inferred from the results of one study (119). In a test that required the maintenance of visual attention over an extended period of time, a non-significant difference was found between good and poor speechreaders and between adult deaf and normal-hearing subjects. On the other hand, speechreaders frequently report that they become fatigued from the concentrated visual attention required for their task, and beginning speechreaders typically make this complaint.

Perhaps the speechreader builds up tensions as he attempts to understand the speech of others, but he would achieve understanding as well or better if he could relax in his receptive communicative tasks. It has been suggested that the speechreader must be alert without being tense (53). Evidence of fatigue while speechreading is presented by Arakawa and Furumaya (6). They measured the influence of speechreading on eye fatigue with junior high school deaf students. The criterion for eye fatigue was eyeblink rate, which was measured before and after ten-minute speechreading sessions. Fatigue, as manifested by increased eye-blink, was found after speechreading; indeed it was found to be greater after speechreading than after reading. Eye fatigue also increased as lighting decreased.

INTELLIGENCE. Numerous studies have investigated speechreading in relation to I.Q., mental age, and educational achievement. In one of the first studies comparing I.Q. and speechreading scores, Pintner (303) compared face-to-face speechreading scores to scores on his own non-language intelligence test, using a large group of deaf children. The students in the study were the three most advanced classes in several schools, with ages ranging from twelve to fifteen years. The results suggested that after a certain minimum level of intelligence is exceeded, intelligence as measured by non-verbal scales is not a significant factor in speechreading proficiency.

With her filmed test of speechreading, Reid (317) found non-significant correlations (r = .07 and .17) between speechreading and I.Q. for female subjects in two schools for the deaf. The correlation between speechreading and the Standard Achievement Test was somewhat higher (r = .29). A non-significant correlation between speechreading and intelligence for normal-hearing pupils in grades six, nine, and twelve is also presented in another report (61), and a low correlation (r = .14) was found between speechreading scores and the Goodenough Draw-A-Man Test scores (71).

A moderately high correlation between speechreading and intelligence (r = .55) as measured by the Wechsler-Bellevue Performance Scale has been reported with normal-hearing young adults (281). On the other hand, Simmons (341), with one live and two filmed tests, found much lower correlations (r = .13 and .25) between speechreading skill and performance on the total Wechsler-Bellevue Test. However, three of the performance sub-tests (picture arrangement, digit symbol, and block design) correlated significantly with speechreading on two or more of her speechreading tests. In particular, Simmons found that the relationship between speechreading and the verbal I.Q. parts of the test was small.

When normal hearing university students were tested, O'Neill and Davidson (285) found a weak relationship between their scores on a filmed speechreading test and on the Wechsler-Bellevue Adult Intelligence Test, verbal concepts scale. Verbal intelligence was found to be a poor discriminator of speechreading performance among hearing-impaired veterans (105). Non-significant relationships are also reported between speechreading and intelligence (251), between speechreading and a performance I.Q. test (395), and between speechreading and a verbal I.Q. test (174).

Two groups of hearing-impaired children were divided by Evans (97) on the basis of I.Q. as determined by the Wechsler Performance Scale. The high I.Q. group (mean I.Q., 114) and the low I.Q. group (mean I.Q.: 93) did not differ significantly on scores of speechreading, audition, or audition and speechreading combined. In a later study with prelingually deaf children, Evans (98) found a small but significant relationship (r = .38) between speechreading scores from a filmed test and I.Q. as measured by performance sub-tests of the Wechsler Intelligence Scale for children. The subjects had a mean age of twelve years six months and a mean Wechsler Performance I.Q. of 103.5. Evans stated that the relationship appeared to be stronger with students having an I.Q. over 100, a finding which contradicts those of Pintner mentioned above.

Craig (74) reported a significant relationship between speechreading and mental age with deaf children. In another study adults with lower I.Q.'s were found to progress less in a four-week speechreading training program than those with higher I.Q.'s, but differences were not statistically significant (*381*).

As may be inferred from the foregoing, the relationship between speechreading performance and intelligence reported in most studies seems to be small. Teachers and clinicians frequently observe marked individual differences between a person's ability to master speechreading and his ability to master other subjects (*375*). On the other hand, it seems illogical that intelligence would not play an important part in any language skill. The reason for the lack of significance found in many of these studies may be that they typically employed subjects who were within a narrow range of normal intelligence. It is likely that, had a broader range of I.Q.'s been employed, a stronger relationship would have been found. We speculate that speechreading requires some minimal intelligence but that intelligence above that level is probably not a significant factor in speechreading proficiency. Indeed, when subjects having I.Q.'s from 30 to 79 were tested, differences in speechreading scores were found to be significant at the .01 level (*344*). Speechreading performance was found to improve as I.Q. increased.

It is also reasoned that the I.Q. tests are usually heavily loaded with items which require analytic reasoning ability (*171*). Assuming that speechreading is a synthetic process, one should not expect a close relationship between I.Q. and speechreading proficiency. However, where the I.Q. test includes a number of verbal sub-tests, it should correlate better with speechreading performance. In general, but not in all cases, the studies comparing speechreading to verbal I.Q. have shown higher correlations than have I.Q. tests of a broader base. On the basis of his study with deaf children, Evans (*98*) concluded that speechreading capacity can be reasonably well predicted (r = .65) by combining three variables: visual recognition, intelligence, and hearing level.

One other study may be appropriately discussed here. In an effort to show the advantages of speechreading training,

Hofsommer (162) found that the I.Q.'s and classroom attitudes of students who underwent such training improved significantly compared to those of students who did not. Unfortunately, the design of the study is questionable and probably shows, rather, that students who are better motivated or whose parents are more interested in their child's verbal output are more likely to improve their Binet I.Q. score after speechreading training.

AGE. The relationship between intelligence and speechreading scores, as was seen above, *appears* to be small. These weak correlations may reflect the select populations studied, and they also may very well represent the use of relatively insensitive speechreading tests which do not readily separate degree of proficiency in speechreading. Also perhaps there is a linear relationship between I.Q. and speechreading up to a certain point, above which a plateau is reached. This theory may be related to and account for the reported finding that after the age of about eleven years, there seems to be a leveling off of increased improvement in speechreading performance, regardless of the intensity or number of years of training in speechreading.

Evidently, the first to report an age plateau in speechreading was Heider (158). In his comparisons of speechreading with a number of other factors, he noted that children who had entered schools for the deaf after ten years of age, even though they might have considerable residual hearing, nevertheless did not seem to become proficient at speechreading. He felt the cause was that these children often lacked systematic drill in the fundamentals of speechreading. More recently, Evans (98) reported that speechreading scores increase rapidly between the ages of eight and eleven years and then begin to plateau. A profile consisting of such factors as mental age, social maturity, vocabulary, and several other abilities was found to be a good prognostic indicator of speechreading proficiency for young deaf children, but the profile was not valid for children over twelve years old (233). These reports concern children in schools for the deaf, and it remains to be seen whether the findings are pertinent to other populations of hearing-impaired individuals. Certainly clinical and research evidence supports the hypothesis that speechreading is a learned linguistic behavior, but it may be that for the pre-lingually deaf child there is a "speechreading readiness age," just as there are other readiness ages. Perhaps working with deaf children after that readiness age produces less progress than if the formal training program is instituted at a younger and more propitious age.

Evans (97) also compared speechreading scores between two slightly older groups with mean ages of 10.9 and 14.4 years, respectively. No significant differences were found between the groups on the auditory test, but the older subjects' scores were significantly higher on the vision and combined vision-audition tests. When she considered normal hearing elementary students, Utley (380) found a relationship between speechreading and experiences in life rather than age, and when hearing-impaired and normal-hearing subjects ranging in age from ten to seventy-eight years were studied, Keil (183) found a significant negative correlation between age and speechreading for both males and females.

As for comparisons between speechreaders of other ages, with a face-to-face speechreading test Brannon (39) did not find significantly different scores between normal-hearing high school students (ranging in age from 16 to 21 with a mean age of 17.4 years) and normal-hearing college students (ranging in age from 17 to 49 with a mean age of 25.2 years). In similar populations of normal-hearing male students, another study likewise found non-significant differences in speechreading scores (29).

Speechreading ability improves from the second to the third decade of life, and then the ability declines, according to Farrimond (106). Scores of subjects over sixty years of age were about one-half those made by the thirty to thirty-nine year old group, and differences were significant even when average hearing loss was held constant. In contrast, the possibility of a speechreading plateau a decade younger is suggested by Goetzinger (135). He found significant differences in favor of the younger aged subjects between those in their twenties versus those in their thirties. He also reports a follow-up study that found these same differences, but in another investigation with subjects of the same approximate ages a significant difference was not found, although the highest mean score was from the younger subjects (26). Coscarelli (70) reported that younger hearing-impaired subjects (nineteen to thirty-nine years old) had significantly higher speechreading scores than older subjects (forty to sixty years old).

A number of other studies have included correlations between age and speechreading. Conklin (65) did not find a significant relationship, but his subjects were in a narrow adolescent age range, and for inexperienced college-age speechreaders a non-significant correlation (r = .12) is reported (22). Heider and Heider (157) found a low correlation (r = .19) between speechreading and age for children between eight and seventeen years, and Reid (317) reported the same correlation for subjects between ten and twenty-two years of age. Logan (212) found that older normal-hearing subjects (mean age of 69.6 years) performed worse on a filmed speechreading test than did younger subjects (mean age of 22.1 years), but the difference was not statistically significant. Moreover, the younger subjects had significantly better scores on a test of visual memory.

Utley (380) obtained a correlation of .38 between age and test scores from her total filmed test, and with the same test a correlation of .51 was obtained between speechreading scores and age for subjects from 9.9 to 19.1 years (160). Low negative and non-significant correlations (r = -.19 to -.25) between age and speechreading for subjects having a mean age of 47.1 years (SD 9.6) are reported by Simmons (341). Older adult subjects were found to progress less in a four-week speechreading therapy program than did younger subjects, but the difference was not statistically significant (381). Craig (74) reported a significant relationship between speechreading and age for deaf children ranging in age from six years, eight months to sixteen years, six months.

From the foregoing it may be seen that a relationship between speechreading performance and age does not clearly emerge from the various reports. Obvious discrepancies between many of the studies remain to be reconciled. Plateaus in speechreading performance, at several age ranges, have been suggested, but evidence is not convincing. Our tentative judgment at this point is that speechreading proficiency will improve as the individual matures, presumably until language itself ceases to improve or begins to deteriorate. However, it does seem likely that the rate of improvement in proficiency is not as steep at the older ages as it is in childhood.

A better understanding of age as related to speech-reading is needed, particularly at younger ages. In Chapter 1 a brief history of some of the earliest efforts at pre-school education of the deaf was presented.[1] A popular dictum of oralism is that the deaf child requires early and constant exposure to speech, and ought to be encouraged persistently to use speech. Parents should begin speechreading training on an informal basis with the child as soon as deafness is discovered, ideally before the age of two years (222). Another author states that linguistic development of deaf children can and should be promoted by special training from the age of two years so as to minimize delay in social, emotional, and intellectual development (99). Pre-school deaf children can be trained to attend to the speaker's face, but special prompts to achieve this attention or expand its length have not proved fruitful (16).

Most educators of the deaf stress the need for beginning informal and formal training with the prelingually deaf child early, but evidence that such training produces a permanent gain for the child is meager. Lane (199) reports a survey on pre-school training of deaf children that began when they were two years of age and older. It was concluded that deaf children who entered school at nursery school age showed less gap between mental ability and educational achievement and were later able to attend public high school in greater numbers than children beginning schooling when older. On the basis of subjective evidence it was also concluded that the deaf children beginning training at nursery school age could speechread better, developed larger vocabularies, and attained better speech skills than other deaf children. From a population of forty-nine deaf children in a residential school, Fiedler (109)

---

[1]For further history of pre-school deaf education, see the article by Guthrie (147).

compared the twelve judged by their teachers to be "very good learners" to the twelve judged to be "very poor learners." Among the differences found was that the good learner group included more children who had had intensive teaching in their home before school age or who had attended a pre-school class.

Owrid (291) found that children who had received home training before admission to classes for the hearing-impaired, whether they were deaf or hard of hearing, had bigger vocabularies and better linguistic concepts than children who had received no home training. On the other hand, Craig (74) did not find that pre-school trained deaf children achieved better speechreading or reading scores than did matched deaf children without pre-school training. Craig did not conclude that pre-school training is inadvisable but rather that the existing goals, admission policy, and educational program are in need of re-evaluation.

EDUCATIONAL BACKGROUND. In addition to intelligence and age, it is important to consider speechreading from the standpoint of educational placement and other factors related to schooling. We would like to know, for instance, the possible differences between day school and residential school training. We would like to know what differences can be attributed to when formal training began and whether the primary mode of communication in the school was oral-aural, manual, or some combination of these. An unknown but important ingredient in the education of the child is the quality and quantity of the teacher's training as well as her classroom attitude and her dedication to the method of communication being employed.

Whether a child is educated in a day or residential school often depends to some extent on the availability of and distance to the several types of schools. It might also be indirectly related to the degree of hearing loss, age of onset of the loss, and whether the loss was hereditary. Some of these factors, in turn, also seem to be at least partially involved in speechreading proficiency. Nor can speechreading ability be isolated from important but difficult to quantify factors, such as speechreading opportunity and motivation.

Pintner (303) found that day school students scored higher in speech intelligibility and speechreading than did residential school students, but the reverse was true for scores on his intelligence test. Day school students had better hearing sensitivity and a later onset of deafness than did the residential school students. Pintner also reported correlations between speechreading and educational achievement to be higher for the day school than for the residential school students. In a more recent report day school students were also found to speechread significantly better than residential school students (118). With the nationwide increase in day school classes for the deaf within hearing schools and in many cases their integration into hearing classes part time, it is important to obtain better information on the communication skills of these children. We suspect that the oral communication skills of these children will be superior to those from the older day-school programs and higher still than those from most residential schools.

Length of training or of schooling and grade placement may be important variables in speechreading. A low correlation between speechreading ability and length of training in schools for the deaf is reported for children (317) and for adult hearing-impaired subjects (70). But Cavender (61) found a significant correlation between speechreading and grade placement. Using the Utley test with school-aged children, Heider (160) reported a correlation of .51 between speechreading scores and the number of years in school. For deaf children from eight different grades, Nakano (259) found a correlation of .54 between speechreading scores and length of training.

Jackson (170) reported a significant relationship between speechreading and grade placement for deaf children, the higher grades producing the better speechreading scores. Utley (380) also obtained a fairly high correlation (r = .55) between scores on her total test and grade placement. In an experiment with normal-hearing college age and older subjects, a nonsignificant relationship (r = .25) was found between speechreading and educational level as measured by number of years of school completed (26). Falconer and Mefferd (105) found that their adult hearing-impaired subjects with high speech-reading scores averaged about two years more of education than did the subjects with low speechreading scores. It may be noted that a moderate relationship appears in most of the reports comparing speechreading proficiency with length of training or with grade placement.

Educational achievement has been compared to speech-reading performance in a number of reports. In the early study by Pintner (303) a small but statistically significant relationship was found between speechreading scores and his own educational achievement test. Utley (380) reported a correlation of .64 between total achievement scores and her filmed speech-reading test, and the Heiders (157) also obtained a fairly high relationship (r = .51) between speechreading and educational achievement. For normal-hearing inexperienced speechreaders of college age, a non-significant relationship (r = .09) between speechreading and accumulated grade point average has been reported (22). From the various efforts to relate school achieve-ment with speechreading performance, it may be seen that a substantial relationship emerges, at least in most studies in which the subjects have had impaired hearing. Educational achievement, grade placement, and number of years in school would seem to be inter-dependent. Their relative importance to speechreading performance is not entirely clear from available evidence, but reported correlations, as noted above, are moderately high for the most part.

HEARING LOSS. Speechreading has been compared with degree of hearing loss and age of onset of hearing loss. We have found no studies comparing speechreading proficiency to type of hearing loss or to threshold contour of the loss, except as may be inferred from the experiment by Krug (198) mentioned in Chapter 3.

In his study of four hundred deaf children, Pintner (303) found indications of a relationship between the age of onset and degree of hearing loss and the degree of speech intelligibility, but the relationship between these measures and speechreading was less clear. Based on low correlations (.10 and .11) between Part I of her test and age of onset of hearing loss, Utley (380) concluded that speechreading skill could not be predicted from age of onset of deafness. Unfortunately, published reports do not always clearly describe the range of the ages of subjects at the time of onset of their loss or the duration of the loss. Comparing the duration of hearing loss (mean duration of 18.1 years, SD 15.0) to speechreading, Simmons (341) found correlations between .29 and .51; the latter correlation, in which a live test was used, was significant beyond the .01 level. Coscarelli (70) did not find a significant relationship between speechreading test scores and length of speechreading training among hearing-impaired adults.

Data comparing degree of hearing loss with speechreading are much more plentiful than are those relating to onset or duration. In Heider's (156) study of deaf children, speechreading correlated significantly with degree of hearing loss (r = .40 to .60), favoring the individual with better hearing. Cavender (61) found that hard-of-hearing subjects scored higher on speechreading than did matched normal-hearing subjects, and hearing-impaired young adults were found to score significantly higher on a filmed speechreading test than normal-hearing young adults (395). But Metz (232) found a non-significant correlation (r = .34) between hearing loss and speechreading of monosyllables, and others have not found significant differences in speechreading scores between hearing-impaired and normal-hearing subjects (70, 183). Costello (71) reported a difference between speechreading scores of deaf (mean hearing loss of 106.7 dB) and those of hard-of-hearing (mean loss of 80.4 dB) subjects significant beyond the .01 level for words and beyond the .05 level for sentences, both in favor of the hard-of-hearing children. Erber (96) reported similar findings for groups of children having approximately the same degrees of hearing loss.

With one live and two filmed speechreading tests, Simmons (341) found low and non-significant correlations (r = .21 to .33) between speechreading and hearing loss (mean average loss 43.9 dB, SD 21.1). From the data presented by

Overbeck (290), we saw in Chapter 3 that speechreading scores for familiar PB words was 68 percent. The scores of the seven children with the smallest average hearing loss by pure-tones (85 dB) averaged 68 percent, while the scores of the seven children with the greatest average loss (112 dB) averaged 67 percent. In this small sample of prelingually deaf students who obviously had had good speechreading and auditory training instruction, the speechreading scores were similar, regardless of amount of hearing loss, ranging from severe to profound.

Evans (97) also compared the speechreading scores of children with severe hearing loss to those of children with profound hearing loss. Children in the first group (mean loss of 76 dB) scored significantly better than those in the second group (mean loss of 101 dB) on both auditory and combined auditory-visual tests, but visual scores were not significantly different, even though the lesser hearing loss group had the higher mean speechreading score. In a later study with prelingually deaf children, Evans (98) reported that speechreading scores on his filmed test declined gradually as hearing loss increased. Craig (74) obtained low but statistically significant correlations between speechreading and degree of hearing with deaf children; with speechreading and the use of the auditory trainer combined, the correlations were somewhat higher.

Lowell (217) compared speechreading scores with average hearing loss in the better ear, the best single speech frequency, and the dissimilarity between the two ears. The correlations were -.22 for the best ear average, -.18 for the best single pure-tone frequency, and .13 for the measure of dissimilarity between the two ears, all of which are significant beyond the .05 level, even though quite low. Thus persons with the least hearing loss and with the greatest dissimilarity between the two ears scored highest in speechreading. The latter finding may simply reflect the possibility that the more dissimilar the two ears are in hearing sensitivity, the more likely that one ear will be in the milder hearing loss range. Correlations between speechreading and speech discrimination (mean discrimination scores of 58.7 percent, SD 20.2) were found to range between -.001 and -.36, none of which were statistically significant (341).

In an autobiographical reort it is claimed that a totally deaf person finds it easier to learn to speechread than does the person with some hearing because the latter tends to concentrate on listening at the expense of looking at the lips (*300*). This belief appears to have some currency with the layman, but as can be seen above and from considerable other data, the opposite is more nearly true. Although it may not seem "fair," persons with normal or nearly normal hearing can with minimum instruction usually speechread with equal or greater precision than persons with a substantial hearing loss. One practical application of this information is that a person with a progressive hearing loss should ideally begin speechreading training long before the loss becomes severe.

The normal-hearing individual shares an equal capacity to speechread with the hearing-impaired individual. Nor is there any reason to believe that the normal hearing and the deaf speechread by a different process, but it is merely that the deaf are daily more dependent upon visual reception of speech. The use of normal-hearing subjects in most speechreading research, therefore, appears to be valid[2] and has the advantage that they are usually more readily available and more numerous. Either the experimenter can block out auditory clues entirely, such as by speaking from behind a window or by using a masking noise background, or hearing and vision can readily be mixed in varying degrees to examine interactions.

It would be helpful to obtain large numbers of scores and more long-range speechreading data from several tests with various age, degree of hearing loss, and experience groups. At present such data are lacking. The largest and most varied populations as they relate to published speechreading scores are those presented in Figure 5-1. In this figure speechreading scores are shown for three degrees of hearing loss and for several grade placements (*217*). From this figure it may be seen that speechreading scores on one filmed test (*366*) show a tendency to be highest for normal-hearing persons and lowest

---

[2]The author has a collection of rejection notices from journal editors who are not of the same opinion!

for the deaf. However, the normal-hearing elementary school students scored lower than their hearing-impaired counterparts, and the deaf teachers of the deaf scored higher than did teachers of the deaf with normal hearing.

Subjects	Normal Hearing	Hard of Hearing	Deaf
Elementary School[a]	13.8%	43.1%	38.0%
High School[b]	37.6	38.1	25.8
College	51.5	—	44.9[c]
Teachers of the Deaf	57.2	—	67.9

[a]Grades 3-6.

[b]Grades 7-9 public schools and Intermediate and Upper in residential schools.

[c]Gallaudet College students.

FIGURE 5-1. Mean Speechreading Scores by Degree of Hearing and Grade Placement (from Lowell, 217)

The information shown in Figure 5-1 seems to indicate that speechreading scores deteriorate from elementary to high school ages. However, the elementary school students took only the first half of a test that becomes progressively more difficult, this fact probably explaining the apparent discrepancy. The large difference in mean scores between the normal-hearing elementary school students and the hearing-impaired students might be accounted for by motivation, but if this explanation is correct, the same motivational differences could be expected to operate at the higher grade levels. Trying to compare the degrees of hearing loss, grade placement, and possible motivational differences in the populations presented in Figure 5-1 could also be confounded by language abilities; but if this is the problem, it must be obscured by other uncontrolled factors.

OTHER COMMUNICATIONS SKILLS. Inasmuch as speechreading is a receptive speech skill, it might be expected to be closely related to other communications skills, such as the child's speech intelligibility and his reading ability. For instance, it has been concluded that speechreading success is largely dependent upon learning opportunity and language facility (217). Deaf children who are superior in one aspect of language (writing, speaking, reading, speechreading) tend to be superior in all other aspects (134, 257). Also hearing-impaired adults with high vocabulary test scores produce significantly higher speechreading scores than do those with low vocabulary scores (106). The value of using several avenues to receive speech and the inter-relation of these avenues is pointed out by Scherer (336), who concluded that reading comprehension was most effectively learned when children see the printed word and its picture representation.

Using his face-to-face speechreading test with deaf children between the ages of twelve and fifteen years, Pintner (303) found a high correlation between speechreading and his test of educational achievement. Since that test was heavily dependent upon language, knowledge of words, word forms, and sentence structure, Pintner felt that these factors were of great importance to success in speechreading. The relationship between speech intelligibility and speechreading was also high, particularly for the students from the day schools; the day schools included more students with a lesser degree and later onset of hearing loss than did the residential schools. Goodman (138) also believed that language ability was important to speechreading success, as was the ability for abstract thinking.

A correlation of .53 between reading and her speechreading test scores was obtained by Utley (380). Others have reported a significant relationship between speechreading and reading scores (71, 74, 157). Using a face-to-face and two filmed tests, Simmons (341) found low, non-significant relationships (r = .02 to .04) between scores from the Iowa Reading sub-tests and her live-interview speechreading test; however, the Key Words sub-test correlated significantly with the two filmed test scores, and the Sentence Meaning sub-test correlated highly with one of the filmed tests. Simmons' subjects were hearing-impaired adults who had no formal speechreading instruction. O'Neill and Davidson (285), using normal-hearing university students, found a non-significant relationship (r = -.03) between reading and speechreading scores.

For deaf high school students Lowell (217) reported a correlation of .50 between scores for speechreading and the Gray-Votaw-Rogers vocabulary sub-tests and a correlation of .37 between scores for speechreading and reading comprehension. For the same subjects the correlations between speechreading and the California sub-tests were .58 for reading comprehension, .67 for reading vocabulary, and .68 for language usage. In a Japanese study with deaf adolescents, a correlation of .74 was obtained between speechreading scores and reading comprehension (334). Thus reading and speechreading skills show a moderate to strong relationship in most of the reports published on this subject. A number of cognitive abilities were found related to speechreading by Taaffe (367). Among those of greatest importance were fluency, flexibility, spatial depth perception, visualization, reasoning, memory,, and perceptual cognitive abilities. Taaffe concluded that facility with language is a necessary, but not necessarily sufficient, prerequisite for speechreading success.

SYNTHESIS AND ANALYSIS. An assortment of verbal and non-verbal visual perceptual tasks has been employed in an effort to relate "synthetic" and "analytic" abilities or personalities to speechreading proficiency. Synthesis seems to be related to, but not the same as, closure, which is the ability to perceive an incomplete figure or movement as a whole. The synthetically oriented person presumably lets his mind fill in the portions of the overall message that he does not clearly see. Thus this person is believed to make greater use of linguistic clues when visual clues are insufficient for meaning. The analytic person, on the other hand, presumably tries to see every position or movement of the articulators in detail and therefore does not learn to speechread so readily because conversational speech probably moves too rapidly for this process to be efficient. Differentiating the synthetic from the analytic person has been the goal of many research studies in speechreading. Minimal hard evidence has been obtained, even though speechreading methods are often categorized or referred to as being primarily either synthetic or analytic in orientation (348, p.10).

Perhaps the synthetic orientation can be illustrated by Figures 5-2 and 5-3. On glancing quickly at Figure 5-2, most readers will probably not notice that either the sign in front of the house doesn't make sense or the letter "F" in the word "FOR" is missing. We might expect the person who notices the missing letter to be analytic and the person who subconsciously fills in the missing letter to be synthetic, since the letter is required for meaning.

In Figure 5-3, on the other hand, a quick reading of the words probably did not reveal to the synthetically oriented person that there was an extra word, that the word "THE" appears twice. We suspect that most readers, on glancing at Figures 5-2 and 5-3, will either "add" the missing letter or "subtract" the un-needed word, as the case may be. [3] Whether

FIGURE 5-2.

[3] In an informal survey of one hundred normal-hearing university students, it was found that 39 percent noticed the missing letter in Figure 5-2 but only 12 percent noticed the added word in Figure 5-3.

FIGURE 5-3.[3a]

these two specific illustrations are actually pertinent to synthetic-analytic ability, however, remains unanswered, since we have not, in turn, related them to speechreading or to any other skill that might be presumed to involve synthesis or analysis.

The first published study to investigate the matter of analysis and synthesis as it relates to speechreading was by Kitson (194), who compared the ranking of adult speechreaders with their ranking on a sentence completion task. The resulting correlation was .65. On the basis of a similar test Gopfert (139) concluded that synthetic ability should be dominant for successful speechreading.

Simmons (341) suggested that synthetic ability may be necessary for success in speechreading but that a satisfactory means of measuring it has yet to be found. Using adult hearing-impaired subjects, she found low and non-significant correlations between one live and two filmed speechreading tests and both a picture completion test and a mutilated word test. Correlations between speechreading and a fragmentary sentence test (r = .40 to .44) were significant beyond the .05 level with the filmed tests but not significant (r = .06) with the live test. Speechreading scores and several auditory tests of distorted and interrupted speech were not found to be significantly related (401).

Persons familiar on a conscious level with the rules of a language seem to be able to predict succeeding letters and words of a message better than chance would allow. Again this ability may show a synthetic orientation. Using deaf high school students as subjects to examine this hypothesis,

[3a]From *Science Puzzlers* by Martin Gardner. 1960. Permission of The Viking Press, Inc.

Worthington (*408*) found no significant relationship between scores from a filmed speechreading test and scores from the Rotter Sentence Completion Test. In a follow-up study Tatoul and Davidson (*370*) divided university students with normal hearing into good and poor speechreading groups as determined by a filmed test (*366*). The subjects were next given twenty sentences one by one from another form of the same speechreading test and were told a key word within each of the sentences. The task was then to predict the sentence, one letter at a time. Mean scores for the letter prediction task between good and poor speechreaders were almost identical, the difference not being significant; the correlation between speechreading and letter prediction was .27. Johnson (*174*) modified the letter prediction test by giving the subjects a key word within a sentence and then requiring the prediction of the letters of the remaining words. The correlation between the score for this test and a speechreading test score (r = .42) was not statistically significant.

In a more abbreviated letter prediction test which employed two seven-letter words, no significant relationship with speechreading (r = .07) was found (*26*). Bode et al. (*38*) reported a weak but statistically significant relationship (r = .39) between speechreading and the completion of printed sentences distorted by the omission of every third letter. Using normal-hearing subjects, Coscarelli (*70*) found a significant relationship between the scores on a live speechreading test and the scores on tests of words with vowels omitted, a word completion test, and a visual closure test. However, when hearing-impaired subjects were tested, the only significant relationship was to the visual closure speed test.

In summary, attempts to relate linguistic-synthesis ability to speechreading have proved elusive. Perhaps synthetic ability is merely the combination of a willingness to guess plus a good knowledge of linguistic rules, or a keen sense of observation of situational and other clues, or a similar related group of factors. It also seems possible that at the initial stages of speechreading the employment of analysis is important, but with progress in speechreading skills synthesis becomes more important.

NON-VERBAL VISUAL PERCEPTION. Like the efforts to relate assorted language factors to speechreading performance, there have also been studies that compared speechreading proficiency with non-language visual perceptual tasks. Heider (159) found that the "integrated type" of child (the good speechreader) usually sorted geometric forms by color, while the more "rigid and analytical" child (the poor speechreader) was more apt to sort the forms by the shape of the form itself. These results were considered to relate to synthetically and analytically oriented students.

A significant correlation (r = .48) between a visual recognition of designs test and a filmed speechreading test has been found (98). The subjects were prelingually deaf children, aged eight to eleven years. A significant correlation (r = .39) has also been reported between speechreading scores and scores on the Hanfmann-Kasanin Test involving non-verbal concept formation shown in the sorting of blocks (285). Costello (71) reported non-significant correlations (r = .30 and .31) between the Knox Cube Test (which is a test of memory for movement) and speechreading performance with deaf and hard-of-hearing children, but she did find a significant relationship between speechreading skill and the ability to arrange picture sequences depicting social situations. The latter finding is a confirmation of the importance of using situational clues in speechreading, as discussed in Chapter 3. A non-significant correlation between speechreading scores and the Knox Cube Test is also reported by Goetzinger (136).

Speechreading scores from a live test were compared with scores on the Gottschaldt Test by Bennett (15). The Gottschaldt Test involves the ability to extricate a simple geometric design from a more complex one. Speechreading correlated significantly with Form A of that test (r = .54) but not with Form B. In contrast, Cutting (78) found a significant correlation between a filmed speechreading test and Form B (r = .28) but not Form A. Goetzinger (136), however, compared filmed and live speechreading test scores of deaf subjects with Gottschaldt Test scores and found no significant relationship to either Form A or B.

Good and poor speechreaders from a school for the deaf were employed by Tiffany and Kates (375). The subjects' task was to determine the non-verbal concept common to a series of cards. Guessing was not penalized, and the number of guesses by each sub-group did not differ. But poor speechreaders more frequently repeated incorrect choices and required the most time to make choices before attaining the concept. From this evidence it appears that good and poor speechreaders make a similar number of guesses in arriving at a concept but that poor speechreaders repeat previous errors more often and require more time to make a decision.

Using hearing-impaired adults, Simmons (341) compared speechreading scores obtained from two different filmed tests and the results of an interview to two visual memory tests. The first visual memory test was the Object-Picture Span, which tests the ability to recognize quickly and remember a group of objects. This test was significantly related ($r = .42$ to $.57$) to both of the filmed tests and the interview test of speechreading. The second visual memory test was concerned with a line of printed digits, and the results of this test did not have a significant relationship ($r = .04$ to $.38$) with any of the speechreading tests. Why memory for pictured objects should and for printed digits should not correlate highly with speechreading scores is not evident. Another researcher has reported an insignificant relationship between speechreading and memory for objects (78). Conversely, in another study significant relationships between speechreading scores and both a visual digit span test and a spoken digit span test are reported (71), and a significant correlation is also reported between speechreading and a combined score of visual memory span and visual perception (395).

Short visual memory was examined in the early pioneer study by Kitson (194). He used words, sentences, and the letter "a" appearing various numbers of times, all of which were shown tachistoscopically. The correlation between scores on this test and the relative proficiency of the speechreaders as determined by the group's teacher was .67. In another study Mahaffey (223) used three different exposure times and three different but brief amounts of training with the tachistoscope. Subjects were normal-hearing high school students. All experimental groups improved in speechreading over the control group, as measured by a filmed test (*380*). Mahaffey found the optimum conditions were those of a fifteen-minute instruction period with the tachistoscope and a 1/15-second exposure time. The use of the tachistoscope has been recommended as a training device to improve attention span for speechreading proficiency (*407*). However, O'Neill and Davidson (*285*) found no significant relationship between visual memory span and speechreading proficiency. A relationship between identification of lip configurations as shown tachistoscopically and speechreading test scores is reported, but training in visual perception with this instrument did not significantly improve speechreading (*116*).

Several teaching ideas for developing attention span by using visual aids are discussed by one author (*12*). Practice with flash cards, filmstrips, and slides is felt by some teachers to help increase the student's visual attention span. O'Neill and Oyer (*286*, p.52ff) also recommend the use of visual materials to improve visual perception, increase attention span, and develop concentration. Mentioned are abstract figures, scrambled sentences, and the use of embedded figures in a background, but evidence that these activities might be related to or help speechreading proficiency is not presented. Since speechreading is a skill heavily dependent upon the rapid perception of quickly changing movements, training designed around visual stimuli that are stationary—even though shown only briefly—seems not to be a profitable approach.

RHYTHM AND PITCH. It is, perhaps, fortunate that the English language makes limited use of pitch changes, and although incorrect stressing might be distracting to the listener, it seldom seems to cause a substantial breakdown in communication.[4] Speechreading methods do not typically mention that the stress patterns for words of more than one syllable may supply visual clues, but the suggestion that visual recognition of rhythmic patterns in phrases and sentences is possible can sometimes be inferred (for example, *102*, p.46-47).

---

[4] A limited number of English words change meaning with alternative stress, for instance: ADdict-adDICT, CONcrete-conCRETE, CONtent-conTENT, DEcent-deSCENT, and DEsert-deSERT.

The Jena method strongly emphasizes rhythmic drill during speechreading training (53), but the drills presented seem intended more to make the speech of the hearing im-paired natural than to be used by the speechreader in understanding what he sees. In an experiment designed to examine the possibility of perceiving stress patterns by speechreading, equivocal findings resulted (23). When correctly and incorrectly stressed two-syllable words were presented to speechreaders, there was no significant difference in scores. However, the spoken numbers "one, two, three" produced with various stress patterns were identified by stress pattern significantly better than provided for by chance. The normal-hearing subjects in this experiment reported that the task was difficult, and they were unable to explain how they arrived at their decision. Since stress changes all three significant parameters of syllable production (intensity, duration, and frequency), it is possible that some visually detectable clue is available to the speechreader. In another study the error responses made by subjects for both two-syllable and three-syllable words suggested that stress patterns were identified more often than by chance (19).

Pitch changes in English seem to be less meaningful and useful than are stress patterns. Like stress patterns, however, pitch changes often add subtle meaning to the message. In particular, in many English utterances there will be a downward pitch for emphasis and a rising pitch for questions. Speechreaders appear to be able to determine the terminal pitch contour of sentences on better than a chance basis (111).

It has been suggested by linguists that the native speaker of a language uses a limited number of specific and well-recognized prosodic patterns that contain subtle clues to meaning. For the speechreader the word and nuclear stresses [5] may contain significant clues. The effect of nuclear stress variation on speechreading performance was examined by Hannah (149) with inexperienced speechreaders. Relatively visible, less visible, and idiomatic sentences were presented to

[5]Nuclear stress refers to the peak of pitch and loudness on one element of a total utterance which determines the intonation and stress pattern for the remaining elements.

the subjects by an American speaker and by a speaker with a foreign accent. Predictably, the idiomatic materials produced the best speechreading scores, the visible sentences next, and less visible materials the poorest scores. Sentences spoken by the foreign speaker produced lower speechreading scores, but the effect on the idiomatic materials was minimal. It is suggested that the beginning and the more advanced speechreader will make different use of nuclear stress clues, with only the experienced speechreader gaining an indication of subtle changes in meaning. As indicated previously, the speechreader might be trained to recognize that the constraints of the language provide significant clues to understanding. The constraints of stress placement may offer subtle but important clues in this respect.

The question of correct perception of stress or pitch patterns by speechreading needs further experimental investigation, but that rhythm and speechreading are related seems clearer. The best speechreaders follow rhythm patterns most easily (158). A comparison of rhythm perception with speechreading scores was made by Simmons (341). For the Seashore Rhythm Test A, which is the easier part of that test, there was a significant correlation (r = .46 and .47) with two filmed speechreading tests but not with the live test (r = .31). The Seashore Rhythm Test B did not significantly correlate (r = .03 to .30) with any of the three speechreading tests employed by Simmons. Perhaps related to rhythm skills is that of demonstrated gymnastic proficiency, which correlated .54 with speechreading proficiency (157).

SEX OF THE SPEECHREADER. Inasmuch as females tend to score better than males on many language tests, it might be assumed that female speechreaders will be superior to male speechreaders. Although many studies report on sex differences of speechreaders, they often fail to include statistical significance. In other cases females have been found to score higher than males, but the difference does not reach statistical significance.

McEachern and Rushford (231) found no significant difference in speechreading scores between males and females, and Craig (74) found very low and non-significant correlations between sex and speechreading among deaf children. Using a live speechreading test, Brannon (39) found that females had higher mean scores than males (44.2 percent versus 42.2 percent), but the difference was not statistically significant. Likewise, Evans (98) found speechreading scores from his filmed test to be, on the average, higher for girls than for boys, but the difference was not statistically significant. Others have reported higher but statistically non-significant differences in speechreading proficiency in favor of females (30, 61, 218, 257, 366, 367, 368).

Several studies, on the other hand, have reported the superiority in speechreading by females to be statistically significant. Costello (71) found a significant difference in favor of females among both deaf and hard-of-hearing children when they were speechreading sentences, but the difference was not significant for speechreading words. Aylesworth (8) found a significant difference in speechreading performance in favor of females, as did Keil (183) for both hearing-impaired and normal-hearing subjects and Frisina (118) with deaf children.

As is true for many other language measures, females score higher on speechreading tests than do males. From the studies mentioned above, the reader may note that in a number of instances a significant difference in speechreading performance was found, while in others the females had higher mean scores than did males but statistical significance was not reached.

Other possible sex differences in speechreading, as well as those related to age and degree of hearing loss, were examined by a questionnaire sent to hearing-impaired persons sixteen years old and older (25). Several potential sex differences emerged from that inquiry. For instance, males considered groups of two or three persons as a more difficult situation in which to speechread than did females. The explanation for this difference might be that hearing-impaired males are less often in small group conversations than are females and, rather, are in one-to-one communication more often and watch television more than do females. It was also interesting to note that males and females responded similarly concerning the difficulty of speechreading male speakers, but male respondents found female speakers more difficult to understand than did the female respondents.

VI
the speaker

In auditory communication the rate and loudness of speech, as well as the articulatory precision of the speaker, are among the critical variables that are important to listener understanding. The speechreader is more dependent on the speaker and upon speaker cooperation than is true in typical auditory communication. Some of the speaker variables mentioned in the speechreading literature as being of possible importance are these: the visibility of the speaker, the rate of speech, the amount of lip movement of the speaker, speaker familiarity, and the sex of the speaker. Speaker differences, such as those just enumerated and perhaps others, are surely substantial, and they undoubtedly play an important role in speechreading success (358).

Because the speechreader needs to converse with many persons, some of whom will be strangers to him, he cannot expect each speaker to modify his speech behavior to facilitate visual understanding. However, the teacher, family members, and others who frequently communicate with the speechreader can be instructed to employ certain kinds of speech behavior that will make speechreading easier. Also the speechreader can be alerted to those persons who are likely to be easy to speechread and those who will prove to be difficult. For these reasons it is important to understand what factors of the speaker's behavior contribute to his being readily understood and what qualities might make understanding difficult.

We can note certain general indications of speaker differences on speechreading performance from some of the published research. For instance, in one study speechreading differences were found among four speakers (two males and two females), and these differences were significant in five of seven test sounds (117). Using six speakers (three males and three females), another study also found significant differences among speakers (337). Speaker differences are also suggested in the results of other reports (265, 367).

In contrast to the foregoing, Reid (317) reports intercorrelations of .83 among speakers, suggesting that all three of the speakers in her filmed test were closely related in the ease with which they could be speechread, in spite of their different educational and speech backgrounds. Similarly, another researcher found no significant differences among speakers or among several presentations by the same speaker (8). In another study the difference in speechreading scores produced by two speakers was small and not statistically significant (96a). Speakers considered to be easy, somewhat easy, and difficult to speechread were employed by Mlott (237). He does not specify how the degrees of difficulty were determined, except that four qualified "graduate lip readers" made the decision. The speaker easiest to speechread tends to be the most intelligible auditorally (281), which suggests that precision in articulation is an important characteristic to both.

An evaluation of the ease with which students can speechread teachers or clinicians is discussed by Dyer and Berg (91). They used a checklist and had speechreaders rank on a five-point scale such speechreadability factors as the following: lip movements, mouth opening, eye contact, expressive face, and use of gestures. It should be helpful for each teacher of the deaf and each clinician to have students make such a ranking so as to determine if there are any factors at work that might be hindering the students' understanding of the teacher as speaker. Further, a videotape from a lesson or therapy session could be made, and the teacher or clinician could study this tape for self-evaluation.

VIEWING ANGLE OF THE SPEAKER. Two major variables regarding the speaker have been mentioned in several reports: the angle of viewing the speaker and the amount of speaker visible to the speechreader. One writer (289) stated that he could often speechread profile easier than full-face, but most teachers believe that profile speechreading should not be practiced until the individual has achieved some success in the front view (or 0°) position. For instance, it has been recommended that speechreading be practiced first at 0°, then at 45°, and finally at 90° (154). It has also been suggested that during training the class members be rotated within a semicircle to allow the individuals to see both the teacher and fellow class members from several angles (372). Practicing from several different angles has been recommended (288, 360).

Larr (201) compared the speechreading scores of normal-hearing young adults on parts of a test utilizing a televised speaker filmed at three different angles: front view (0°), a 45° angle, and profile view (90°). The 45° viewing angle produced slightly better speechreading scores than the other two angles did, but whether this difference was significant is not reported. In another study speechreading scores between front and 45° angle viewing of a filmed test were compared, and no significant differences for total scores or scores by specific sound comparisons were found (406). Highest speechreading scores were reported from a 45° angle by Nakano (259), and the lowest scores, at 90° by Wurtemberger (cited in 13). Another researcher found the highest speechreading scores at 45° (22). However, the scores at 0° and 45° were not significantly different, but both of these angles were significantly superior to the 90° angle. In contrast, Neely (260), using normal-hearing subjects in noise, did find a significant difference in speechreading scores between 0° and 45°, with the best scores at 0°; however, like the other studies the lowest scores were at 90°.

Only one study to our knowledge has reported on the vertical viewing angle in speechreading (27). The two vertical viewing angles compared were that of a child sitting speech-reading an adult speaker standing (35°) to that of an adult sitting speechreading an adult speaker sitting or that of both speechreader and speaker standing (0°). No significant differences between these two vertical viewing angles were found, but the 0° angle produced slightly higher scores.

SPEAKER IMAGE. How much of the speaker is in view might be an important variable in speechreading. Reid's (317) test film showed the upper part of the shoulders and the lower three-fourths of the speaker's face. Most other test films have used a head-and-shoulders view of the speaker (8, 57, 117, 176, 232, 344, 366). A waist-up view has been used in several test films (33, 380). Cancel (58) presented a videotaped sentence test wherein the key word was shown in a close-up view of the mouth following a larger image of the speaker saying the entire sentence.

It has been found that the more of a speaker visible, the easier he is to be speechread (356). Larr (201) compared the speechreading scores obtained when subjects were shown four images of the speaker: upper torso, head-and-neck, head-only, and lips-only. Optimum image seemed to be the head-and-neck or the upper torso, with lips-only being the most difficult. Inasmuch as Larr reports that the subjects' scores improved by 33 percent from the first to the last section of his experimental test and since he does not report on a counterbalancing of conditions, it is not clear whether true differences caused by the viewing angle or the image of the speaker should be inferred.

Presenting normal-hearing subjects with a video-taped speechreading test, Greenberg and Bode (145) examined consonant identifications as seen full-face or only the lips down to the upper laryngeal area. Significant differences in favor of the full-face image were found. In a similar experiment employing three theatrical masks with increasingly large openings around the mouth, it was found that speechreading scores improved as greater amounts of the face were observable, but differences

between the three amounts of image seen were not significant
(27).

As we saw in a previous chapter, gestures, and presumably facial expression also, add clues for the speechreader.
It is probable that the smaller image of the speaker merely
rules out or minimizes these useful clues and makes the task
more that of lipreading than of speechreading. At any rate,
from the studies that have examined viewing angle and
speaker image, it seems certain that the teacher will enable
the students to obtain maximum speechreading results if she
sits or stands so the class is watching at a horizontal angle of
between 0° and 45° and a vertical angle of as close to 0° as
possible. Certainly horizontal viewing angles of up to 45°
should not be avoided in speechreading training, since they
appear to be as conducive to speechreading success as the 0°
angle, perhaps even presenting the easiest view. As for image
view, the teacher should be positioned so at least the head and
shoulders are clearly observable to the students, and it seems
likely that a waist-up view has some advantages to the speechreader.

AMOUNT OF LIP MOVEMENT. The effect on speechreading of the amount of the speaker's lip movement or
possible mouth distortion has not been examined with
thoroughness. One study suggested that normal rather than
tight lip mobility and grim rather than smiling facial expression
effected better speechreading scores more than did the degree
of facial exposure, but these differences were not statistically
significant (356).

The question of whether the speaker should overemphasize speech rate and lip movements has often arisen in
meetings of teachers of the deaf. When a layman talks with a
hearing-impaired person, he often talks more loudly and slowly
than usual, a habit which tends to overemphasize movements
of the articulators. From personal experience one speechreader stated that an expressionless face, immobile lips, and
grimaces inhibit speechreading proficiency (132). Careless, in-
distinct, exaggerated speech and an expressionless face
(versus a mobile face) are considered a hindrance to the

speechreader (297). In one study eighty-seven deaf subjects speechread two filmed speakers: one overemphasizing his facial expression and the other concentrating all expression in the area around his mouth and lower jaw (153). Overemphasized speech was understood the best. In another study speechreading exaggerated speech was not found to be significantly easier than speechreading non-exaggerated speech (386). Subjects were normal-hearing fourth grade students.

The possibility that increased vocal intensity levels might affect speechreading ease was investigated by Lynch and Bode (220). They employed the Modified Rhyme Test as a speechreading task and had a female speaker use "normal," "loud" (10 dB above normal), and "soft" (10 dB below normal) intensities. A full-face video recording of the speaker was seen by thirty-seven normal-hearing university students. Speechreading consonant scores increased within the 20 dB range employed: 51 percent for soft, 55 percent for normal, and 57 percent for loud speech. Most of the improvement in scores was in the identification of the initial consonant of test words. Although the results were based upon a single speaker, it appeared that the higher speech intensity levels may have produced a slight exaggeration in the articulatory movements which enhanced speechreading precision. An increased phonation time with the higher intensities may have also facilitated the speechreading task.

In a study involving black and white speakers, one of each with thick and one of each with thin lips, scores gradually and significantly deteriorated as lip thickness of the speaker increased (30). A secondary effort, also statistically significant, was the finding that black speechreaders were able to speechread black speakers best and white speechreaders could speechread white speakers best. It would appear that the speaker with thick lips is difficult to speechread because of reduced lip mobility and that a person can speechread a speaker of his own race better because of more practice in communication within the race.

RATE OF SPEECH. On a continuum of possible speech rates, "normal" is said to be faster than the "optimum" for speechreading purposes (266). Slower than average speech has been recommended during early speechreading training (102). However, Keith (184) criticized speechreading training where the teachers use slow, clearly enunciated speech. He recommended the use of normal speech rate and articulation by the teacher. In a rebuttal it was agreed that exaggerated or unduly slow speech was not good for practice, but the contention that this was typical of good speechreading teachers was disputed (289). On a questionnaire sent to hearing-impaired adults, a "slower than average" rate of speech was checked most frequently as the rate of speech easiest to speechread (25). Males and older respondents checked the "slower than average" rate in greater percentages than did females and younger respondents, and the few who checked "a little faster than average" as easiest were all younger respondents.

Rate of speech as compared to speechreading scores was investigated in a study with normal-hearing college students (252). It was found that a filmed test projected at sixteen frames per second was easier to speechread than was the same film when projected at the normal rate of twenty-four frames per second. In another study using deaf college students, projector speeds were increased from just over one-half of normal up to normal (120). The rate of twenty frames per second (about two-thirds of normal speed) produced the best speechreading scores, but differences were not significant.

In a similar study the rate of speech in comparison with speechreading scores among deaf students was investigated by using a filmed modification of the Utley sentence test (57). The subjects were divided into two groups, depending upon their speechreading proficiency. Films were projected at normal speed (120 words per minute) as well as at one-third, one-half, and two-thirds normal speed. No significant differences were found among viewing speeds between the two speechreading proficiency groups, either by correct scores or by word answer attempts made. Black et al. (35) also compared the multiple-choice speechreading test scores obtained when normal hearing university students were shown the same film twice, once projected at normal speed and once projected at a 15 percent reduction in speed. No significant differences were found in speechreading scores between the two rates.

The results of the various experiments with lip mobility and with speech rate suggest that the speechreader is not hampered by slower than average speech rates and their accompanying exaggerated or artificial lip movements. One might question, however, whether a child taught speechreading solely with a slow speech rate, which tends to be accompanied by exaggerated lip movements, would have difficulty understanding non-exaggerated lip movements and speech at normal rates. These matters were not investigated in the studies reported here. Nor do we know the effect of faster than average speech rates on speechreading scores. As a challenge for practice with advanced students, it has been suggested that the teacher speak fast, turn so the class sees a profile, drop the head so the speechreader is seeing mostly the lower lip, and walk around while speaking (133).

Cranwill (75) makes the statement that in normal speech the articulator movements average twelve per second but the eye can see only nine or ten. She is evidently quoting Nitchie (274), who reported the average time per movement in ordinary speech to be from 1/12 to 1/13 of a second. The source for the statement regarding the eye seeing only nine or ten movements is not given. Oyer (293) apparently contradicts this finding in his report of a study by Subar who used an experimental filmed test in which from 15 to 45 percent of the various test word parts were blacked out. No significant differences in speechreading performance under these conditions were found. Evidently the speechreader needs to see only a portion of a speech movement for adequate visual perception of it.

FAMILIARITY OF SPEAKER. Speechreaders often state that for best understanding of speech the speechreader need not know only the language and dialect of the speaker but also his other speech habits. Knowing the personality of a person is said to make it easier to understand him (300). Speechreaders typically report that relatives and close friends are easier to speechread than are persons more distantly known (25). Trask (376) suggested that speechreading proficiency could be judged on the basis of the person's success in speechreading persons ranging in relationship from a close relative to a casual acquaintance.

One indication of the value of knowing the speaker's speech habits is shown in the study by Day et al. (82). They presented sentences to the three most advanced classes in a number of schools for the deaf. Some sentences were given by the classroom teacher and others were spoken by the experimenter. The mean of all of the mean classroom speechreading scores for the forty-four classes was 54.5 percent for the teacher and 43.9 percent for the experimenter. In a further interpretation of this study, it was again pointed out that the students could understand their teacher better than they could the unfamiliar experimenter (303). Grouped scores were 51.7 percent and 40.0 percent, respectively. Using a filmed multiple-choice speechreading test, Black et al. found that normal hearing university students in brief practice periods improve in speechreading more with the same speaker than with a different speaker repeating the same material (35).

Speechreaders' attitudes toward the speaker have also been investigated as they relate to ease of speechreading (213). "Most preferred" group members were easier to speechread than "least preferred" group members. In a second experiment in role playing, it was found that speechreaders preferred to communicate with a "moderate" rather than an "aggressive" leader, but there was no significant difference in scores produced by speechreading either kind of speaker-leader. A congenial speaker did not seem to elicit a significantly better speechreading performance (93).

SEX OF THE SPEAKER. Petkovsek (300) was of the opinion that women are easier to speechread than men because the use of lipstick helps draw attention to their mouth and also because they use freer facial expression and more gesture. It is sometimes also mentioned that males with moustaches, beards, or pipes in their mouths are difficult to speechread. These seem to be more a matter of distractions than sex differences as such. There has been little research interest in possible differences caused by the sex of the speaker as they might relate to speechreadability. If such differences caused by the speaker's sex exist, they are probably hidden by the relatively insensitive speechreading tests employed and our inability to ferret out broader speaker differences.

Sahlstrom and Oyer (325) found that male and female speakers produce significant differences in the rate and intensity of movement occurring on the surface of the face during the production of selected homophenous words. That these differences, measured with a strain gauge made of silastic tubing attached to the speaker's face, are sufficient to influence speechreading scores by present tests from male and female speakers is doubtful.

Aylesworth (8) found no significant differences in speechreading scores produced by the sex of the speaker. In a questionnaire sent to hearing-impaired adults, male and female respondents were in general agreement about the ease of speechreading males, but the male respondents indicated that females were not easy to speechread more often than did female respondents (25).

VII
he environment

Just as certain environments can facilitate or detract from understanding the acoustic signal, so too we might expect some environmental factors to negatively or positively affect understanding by speechreading. Of major concern is the distance from speaker to the speechreader, the lighting on the speaker, and visual distractions.

Because the speechreader must function in an assortment of locations, not always predictable or easily altered, it follows that the environment can not usually be modified for optimum understanding by the speechreader. However, there are home and school environments that can be modified or otherwise manipulated so as to take advantage of those factors that might enhance the probable success with speechreading. On the other hand, environments that are detracting to speechreading success can be avoided by the speechreader. For these reasons environmental effects should be understood as to their effects on speechreading.

DISTANCE

It is obvious that as distance increases and vocal

intensity remains constant, the understanding of speech by audition will gradually diminish. In a similar manner we might expect that as distance increases, speechreading will become more and more difficult and at some point impossible. Just what critical distances are involved, however, is not yet completely clear. Nor do we know whether there is an ideal distance for speechreading practice and training.

Various distances have been used in studies of speechreading: a four-foot distance (344), a five-foot distance with a live test (364), a six-foot distance (74, 97, 149, 166, 235, 310), and an eight-foot distance (232, 282, 331). Other distances reported include five to eleven feet (361), six to ten and one-half feet (234), eight to ten feet (337), seven to ten feet (8), ten or eleven to fifteen feet with a filmed test (96, 212, 370, 395), nine feet to the television set (58), and seven to sixteen feet with a filmed test projected so as to be life size (117). It can be seen that an assortment of distances have been employed in these studies while in other reports distance or image size is not always mentioned. Suggested distances during training also vary. For instance, it has been recommended that speechreading therapy be done at a distance of no more than four feet (207, p.163), at a distance of two to four feet (222), at a six-foot distance (297), and ten feet has also been considered an optimum distance (329, p.285). It is difficult to argue with the suggestion that the distance used in training should be one that is comfortable to the speechreader (102).

The effect of distance has been examined in several studies. In one study no significant differences in scores were found for speechreading from zero to eighteen feet from the speaker (61). In another study no significant differences were found when distances of five, ten, fifteen, and twenty feet between subjects and the screen were used in a filmed test; but the best speechreading scores were found at ten feet (252). Speechreading at very close range was reported to be detrimental, but the distances involved are not clear (201).

Using normal-hearing subjects in noise, Neely (260) employed distances of three, six, and nine feet. He found no significant differences in speechreading scores at those three distances. No significant differences in speechreading scores with subjects between twelve and forty feet from the screen and no significant differences in scores as a result of two sizes of the projected image were found with normal-hearing adult subjects (366a). Using normal-hearing university students and older adults, another study examined the effect on speech-reading of distances of six, twelve, eighteen, and twenty-four feet (26). No significant differences in speechreading scores were found among these distances for either subject group, but it appeared that the twenty-four foot distance was beginning to affect the speechreading of the older adult group. It might be supposed that lessened visual acuity in the older population will begin to affect perception at about the twenty-four foot distance. In another study employing a limited number of young deaf subjects and special lighting on the face of the speaker, speechreading scores were found to deteriorate gradually as speaker and subjects were separated by five, ten, twenty, forty, seventy, and one hundred feet (96a).

From the evidence available it does not appear that distances of up to perhaps twenty or twenty-four feet have a significant effect on speechreading performance if the individuals have normal or corrected normal vision. On the other hand, there seems to be little value in regularly practicing speechreading at either extremely small or great distances. Training would, logically, be most meaningful if done at those distances most representative of typical daily conversational situations, that is, between five and ten feet.

LIGHTING ON THE SPEAKER

Often it is suggested that the deaf or hard-of-hearing child in the regular classroom be seated near the window side of the room so the natural light is on the teacher's face and not shining in the child's eyes. The suggestion is a good one. But we have little information as to the minimum or maximum amount of light that will permit speechreading or the optimum amount of light on the speaker's face. Distance, lighting, image size, and the speechreader's visual acuity are interrelated.

It is obvious that one cannot speechread in total darkness. That the lighting on the speaker can be far less than ideal and still not adversely affect the speechreader is suggested by the findings of one study (371). In this study it was found that individuals familiar with the message content produced slightly and non-significantly diminishing scores as the intensity of the room illumination decreased from thirty foot candles to one-half foot candle. However, in this experiment the subjects received the same test stimuli with decreasing amounts of light so it is possible that a practice or learning effect may have obscured significant differences in the reported small decrease in scores as the illumination became less. A light source low and in front of the speaker has been found to produce better speechreading scores than normal classroom lighting with relatively inexperienced speechreaders but not with more experienced speechreaders (170).

Based upon the limited research findings available, one can conclude that typical classroom lighting seems sufficient for optimum speechreading. It does not appear that special or increased amounts of light on the speaker serve a useful purpose in training, nor would this be typical of the usual lighting conditions encountered by the speechreader in daily life.

DISTRACTIONS

A distraction is a psychological factor, but if the distracting stimulus is at a high enough level, it may become masking, or a physical factor. It seems appropriate, therefore, to refer to visual masking just as audition is sometimes concerned with auditory masking. A number of experiments have inquired into the effects of visual and auditory distractions on speechreading performance.

We all know speakers who have distracting mannerisms, and we have all been in environments where there are distractions to the understanding of speech. For the speechreader visual rather than auditory distractions are probably the most critical, but since, as we saw in a previous chapter, auditory clues can play an important part in speechreading success, we should not discount the possibility that auditory distractions are detrimental to speechreading performance.

VISUAL DISTRACTIONS. One speechreading report states that it is distracting to speechread a person wearing dark glasses because part of the face is hidden (300). It might also be expected that speechreading a male sporting a beard or moustache or a female wearing long dangling earrings could be difficult because of the distractions. We have noticed that females who have long hair which tends to cover part of the face during head movements, even though the mouth area is not hidden, are distracting to speechread. Among the visual distractions reported by speechreaders were movements of the hands in the area of the face, exaggerated lip movements, and a speaker with a pipe or cigar in his mouth (25). The pipe or cigar in the mouth may be distracting, but they also may hinder speechreading performance by reducing lip mobility, as was discussed in the preceding chapter.

At present we know of no objective information as to the possible distractability to the speechreader if the speaker stutters,[1] has an articulatory defect, or speaks with a foreign accent. We have observed that foreign accents and geographic differences in vowel production are noticeable to the speechreader, but they don't seem to be so distracting to him as the same speech pattern is to the normal hearing population.

The effect on speechreading of the visual background behind the speaker was examined in one study (183). A neutral background and three differing pictorial backgrounds were used to determine their possible effect as distractors: (1) a colored slide of two females projected on each side of the speaker, (2) a colored background consisting of trees, a car, and a building behind the speaker, and (3) a black and white moving background of a busy street scene. No significant differences in speechreading scores were found among the four

---

[1]The abundant literature on deafness and on stuttering contains few references to the effects of their combination. Stuttering among the deaf is rare, but it does exist (9). A study of the stutterer's reaction to normal-hearing auditors and speechreaders was made by Shinn (339).

conditions with hearing-impaired or with normal-hearing speechreaders.

An assortment of moving visual distractors were examined in another study (234). No significant effect on speechreading scores was found to be caused by the presence of a flashing light or a red-on-white Archimedian spiral. A positive and significant relationship was found between a non-purposeful hand movement by the speaker and speechreading scores. It is difficult to understand how a non-purposeful hand movement could enhance speechreading performance, and this finding was surely spurious. In fact, in another experiment it was found that the speaker rubbing his chin, but being careful not to cover the mouth, caused the largest reduction in speech-reading scores of the four visual distractions investigated (29). However, none of the visual distractions caused a significant decrease in speechreading proficiency. The other visual dis-tractions employed were two females sitting very close to the male speaker and repeating unrelated speech material, flashing Christmas tree lights in an inverted U-shape behind the speaker, and two red-and-white bullseyes revolving at slow speed.

From the above it would appear that presumed visual distractions are not so detracting as might have been supposed. They did not achieve a masking level. Evidently the speechreader was able to select the meaningful sensations and filter out the unmeaningful ones. It may be that the subjects in these experiments quickly realized that the devised distractions offered no significant information and thereafter they were able to adapt to them and concentrate on the speaker's face. In daily life the visual distractions encountered are hardly so orderly or predictable and may have a greater negative effect on speechreading.

AUDITORY DISTRACTIONS. Inasmuch as hearing losses have such a large number of patterns and degrees, it would be difficult to ascertain the effect of auditory distractions on speechreading with hearing-impaired populations. However, the effects of auditory distractions on the speechreading of normal-hearing subjects need to be understood, since normal-hearing persons are used in much research. When normal-hearing subjects have been used, either placing the speaker behind a window in a sound-isolating room or using a masking sound have been the typical solutions to preclude hearing of the test speech stimuli.

Background masking noise has been employed in a number of experiments using normal-hearing subjects. A few studies have used a specified signal-to-noise ratio (96, 282, 364), but most have employed a constant sound pressure level. The following are some of the noise levels reported as being used: up to 100 dB of white noise (260), 90 dB (301), 84 to 86 dB noise (371), 85 dB (149), 80 dB of white noise (205, 234, 337, 343), 78 dB (235), and 70 dB noise (39, 363).

In one study continuous auditory distractions significantly and adversely influenced speechreading scores of trained subjects (205). Noises employed were white noise, speech, and background music, each at 80 dB SPL. The difference between scores while speechreading in quiet (55 dB background) and speechreading with each of the auditory distractions was significant beyond the .01 level, but the only significant difference among the three noise distractions was between white noise and music, and this difference may reflect a practice or learning effect.

The effects of cafeteria babble, traffic noise, and white noise were compared to quiet in another speechreading experiment (301). Each of the noises was at a 90 dB level, and the test consisted of monosyllabic words. In three of six comparisons the differences among mean scores for the conditions were statistically significant. Curiously, two of the non-significant comparisons were between quiet and traffic noise and between quiet and babble.

It might be speculated that intermittent noise would be more of a distraction than continuous noise, since the subjects would be expected to adjust to continuous noise more easily. In a study that investigated this hypothesis, it was found that intermittent white noise (one-half second on, one-half second off) did not significantly influence speechreading scores as compared to quiet or continuous noise conditions (28). However, the best scores were in the quiet condition and the worst scores in the intermittent noise. It may be that the regularly interrupted noise, like the predictable visual distractions, permits an adaptation by the speechreader so that proficiency is not significantly reduced.

One study that might appropriately be discussed in this section on auditory distractions was that done by Miller et al. (235). They tested the speechreading of normal-hearing adults and divided them into three groups. Group I then read essay materials for five minutes a day for five days, Group II read similar materials but with their own voice amplified back to them, and Group III read similar materials but with their own voice amplified back with .19-second delayed feedback. At the conclusion of five days an alternate form of the original speechreading test was given, and the group that had read with delayed feedback showed a significant increase in speechreading scores. The group with no amplification regressed significantly in speechreading, and the group with straight amplification did not change. The practical significance of these findings is not clear, and it is particularly difficult to reconcile the daily five-minute reading with no amplification to speechreading regression. Furthermore, even if delayed auditory feedback might in some way enhance speechreading proficiency, the very fact that the persons most in need of improvement have a significant hearing loss seems to rule out the usefulness of such a procedure.

VIII
ests of speechreading

Over the years a number of tests of speechreading have been developed. The earliest tests, and many of those presently used, are face-to-face or live tests. In the 1940's and 1950's several filmed tests were developed which presumably have better reliability than face-to-face tests, but their validity is still doubted (270).[1] The questionable validity may well relate to the matter of two- versus three-dimensional viewing of the speaker, among other things. At present no speechreading test can be said to be used nationally, nor has any test been adopted as a norm to which other speechreading tests can be compared. The Utley test (379, 380) probably came closer to a standard test than any other, but its use appears to be rapidly waning.

That speechreading proficiency can be evaluated by the experienced teacher or hearing clinician at least in gross

[1]Reliability refers to the stability or trustworthiness of a test, that is, the degree to which scores are consistent on repeated measures. Validity refers to the faithfulness with which a test measures what it purports to measure. For instance, a speechreading test that produces consistent test-retest scores is said to be reliable, and if its scores closely parallel the observed speechreading ability of the individuals tested, it is valid. Validity is usually more difficult to estimate than reliability, since we must agree upon the external criteria by which it is determined.

manner seems certain. But a reliable and valid test of speechreading, acceptable by a majority of the professionals in the field, is yet to be developed. The lack of a standardized measure for speechreading performance causes difficulties in the exchange of information from one class, school, or clinic to another and prevents speechreading research from making measurements with the desired precision. Just as importantly, speechreading progress cannot be accurately determined or the difference between two or more methods be meaningfully compared until such standardized tests become available.

An approach toward validating speechreading proficiency was suggested many years ago, but to our knowledge it has not been employed or pursued. Trask (376) suggested the following as levels of speechreading ability:

1. Good. The speechreader can understand most people with whom he comes into contact. He can sometimes follow a sermon or lecture.
2. Fair. The speechreader has little difficulty in understanding his family or his friends.
3. Poor. The speechreader can understand a few people readily and a few more a little.

Establishing the validity of speechreading measures as an index of performance in everyday life is a crucial problem. Demonstrated ability to identify isolated monosyllables does not necessarily mean that the respondent will also be able to speechread "real" conversation effectively or even better than the person who is poor at identifying monosyllables. Investigators have consistently made such assumptions. In an attempt to achieve reliability, investigators have controlled or eliminated from the test materials or test environment factors which may be of major importance in their effects on speechreading performance in everyday life. But a reliable test is of little value if it does not faithfully describe some crucial aspect of performance.

Materials for speechreading tests have been varied. They include syllables, isolated monosyllabic words, spondees, multiple-choice words, word pairs, phrases, isolated sentences, related sentences, and short stories. Scoring may be a function of the number or percentage of specific words correctly identified or may relate to the correct determination of the idea or thought expressed. The materials are typically spoken by one individual without other clues, although a few tests include sound and some of the stories involve several individuals in common everyday situations and in varying environments. The advantages and disadvantages of each of these types of speech materials and methods of scoring are not clearly evident, although the tests involving isolated words and syllables presumably have a lower face validity. Syllables also seem to be more difficult to speechread than sentences (102). One could assume that stories or a conversational situation would most nearly represent the speechreader's daily communication tasks, but quantifying such materials as a test has been difficult.

Careful examination of the effects of the types of speech stimuli used in tests is greatly needed, since we have an unclear understanding of their validity. Speechreading differences based upon the effect of the diversity of test materials used may be clouding many of the research report findings. For instance, experienced and inexperienced speechreaders were found to perform about alike with monosyllables, but experienced speechreaders scored higher on sentence materials than did inexperienced speechreaders (40). Curiously, in one study it was found that speechreading scores for PB words and spondees were similar (39).

Among deaf children, Heider and Heider (157) found a higher correlation between the ability to perceive vowels and speechreading achievement than between the perception of consonants and speechreading. Using normal-hearing adults as subjects, O'Neill (281) reported that vision contributed 57 percent to the recognition of consonants, 30 percent to vowel recognition, 39 percent to words, and 17 percent to phrases.

Nitchie (272) was of the opinion that the ability to repeat or understand stories was an ideal test of speechreading, and Utley (380) came to the same conclusion. While not stating that one type of speech material is better than another for speechreading testing, Frisina (119) reports high rank order correlations (.73 to .88) among assorted test stimuli.

FACE-TO-FACE TESTS

Although face-to-face tests were undoubtedly used many years earlier, the first published study employing such a test was that by Kitson in 1915 (194). Kitson ranked the speechreading ability of fifteen hearing-impaired adult students and correlated this ranking with other scores in an attempt to relate speechreading ability to synthetic reasoning ability. Day et al. (82) employed face-to-face tests in a survey with a large number of hearing-impaired students. Commenting on this survey, Simmons (341) stated that the "variability of speaking situations and among speakers contributed to low reliability." Simmons does not report how reliability was determined, nor did Day et al. A modification of the test employed by Day was used by Johnson (175, 176). Both Pintner (303) and Conklin (65) used a face-to-face test of speechreading with a large population of deaf children.

More recently, live speechreading tests have been employed in numerous studies (17, 18, 21, 26, 71, 93, 306, 363, 364). Quick (311) used a multiple-choice test and developed two lists of monosyllabic words for testing speechreading, hearing, and the two combined. Evans (97) employed words, phrases, and sentences that constitute his Progressive Discrimination Test, and Lott and Levy (213) used selected sentences from the test by Taaffe (366). The Utley sentence test materials have been employed in a live presentation (70, 135), and Craig (74) used a multiple-choice test. A test constructed by Kelly (185) consisted of alphabet letters, multiple-choice words, and sentences, all presented by live voice.

A face-to-face test for children by Butt and Chreist (55, 56) consists of seventy test items. Each item is a question or command of from three to five words. When a group of children between the ages of three and nine years was studied, the correlation between this test and teacher rankings of the subjects was .79. The split-half reliability of the test was .95.

Another face-to-face test was developed by Barley (172, 173). From the everyday American speech sentences developed at the Central Institute for the Deaf, designed for auditory discrimination testing, Barley constructed a speechreading test by using selected sentences. Two forms were made, A and B, with an intercorrelation of .87. When the Utley test forms (evidently the sentence portion only) were used for validation with the Barley Test, the correlations were .79 and .83.

An experimental speechreading test has been described by Cavaluchi (60). The test consists of simple unrelated sentences of the question-answer type. Most of the questions can be answered by a single word. A multiple-choice answer sheet is employed, and each of the twenty sentences on the two test forms revolves around a situational clue. The directions for administering the test call for the speaker to read the sentence, allowing the person being tested to use audition, but the voice of the speaker becomes inaudible during the key word in each sentence.

The primary criticism of live speechreading tests revolves mainly around the charge that the speaker may have considerable difficulty in repeating the same speech stimuli a second, third, or more times with the same rate and with the same degree of movement of the articulators. Although we have seen that rate may not be a critical factor, the movement of the articulators seems to have a substantial effect on the ease of speechreading. On the other hand, it can be argued that a live test is more natural than a filmed test and thus would be expected to have greater face validity. The speaker in a face-to-face test is more likely to have the same dialectal speech pattern as the speechreader than the speaker in a filmed test. Furthermore, and most importantly, no one to date has presented evidence that there is a superiority to either the live or the filmed test but only that the two tend not to correlate as highly as would be expected on the basis of the presumed similarity of the task.

An interesting procedure to insure a repeatable speech rate in speechreading testing in research was used by Schwartz and Black (337). They employed a live test, but the speaker listened to a pre-recorded tape of the speech stimuli and repeated it immediately.

FILMED TESTS

In an effort to overcome some of the problems of the live speechreading test, a number of filmed tests have been introduced. Presumably Nitchie (268) devised the first filmed speechreading test, but there is no evidence that it was actually used as a test. This was a 16mm film containing three proverbs. In 1934 Heider (159) reported a study of speechreading where a filmed test was employed, but she did not give details; evidently it was her own test or the one used later by Heider and Heider (157). The latter developed three test films. The first film consisted of phonetic units, names of animals, nouns, unrelated sentences, and related sentences. The second test film included names of animals, nouns, unrelated sentences, and two stories. The third film was much like the second.

The first motion picture films to receive considerable use, originally for training and then for testing, were those by Mason (225, 227, 228, 229). Mason's tests were designed for children, and later she added a filmed instruction sequence to show non-reading children how to respond to the test items. The first test film was in two equal forms, each having five simple test words spoken in isolation. The revision was similar except there were ten words that increased in difficulty in each form. The third version also had two equal forms that included the materials in the previous tests plus fifteen additional nouns. Test III was standardized on 187 children. The two parts correlated highly (r = .93 to .95) based upon scores from children below the age of twelve years. The films are in black and white and have a female speaker. Mason's work with a filmed approach began in 1932, and the last test version showed great promise as a test vehicle. Unfortunately, her efforts were not continued following her death.[2] Some of

---

[2]Marie K. Mason taught at the Ohio School for the Deaf and at St. Mary's School for the Deaf in Buffalo. In 1930 she was appointed Instructor in Phonetics at Ohio State University. She died December 8, 1949.

the answer sheets devised by Mason are presented by O'Neill and Oyer (286, p.143ff).

A series of ten filmed situations for adults, and a later series of five for children, was developed by Morkovin (249). The Morkovin films were designed for training purposes, but they have been used for testing and apparently serve that purpose where story materials are considered appropriate. The Morkovin films will be discussed further in the next chapter. In 1945 the staff at Deshon General Hospital in Butler, Pennsylvania, developed a speechreading test for use in military rehabilitation centers. The test consisted of twenty sentences filmed in black and white, using a female speaker. The test-retest correlation was reported to be .88 (381).

In 1946 Jean Utley (379, 380) published the results of her filmed test of speechreading, called "How Well Can You Read Lips?" The test consisted of two equivalent forms, A and B, each with three parts. The test was given as a trial to several hundred subjects, and on the basis of this preliminary work, it was reduced so that Part I was comprised of thirty-one unrelated phrases or sentences, Part II of thirty-six words in isolation, and Part III of six short story scenes, each involving several persons. A female speaker appeared in the first two parts, which were in black and white. Part III was in color. The final test version was standardized on 761 deaf and hard-of-hearing subjects with a minimum of a third grade reading ability. Intercorrelations between the two forms found by Utley were .87 for the sentences, .66 for the words, and .89 for the entire test. The stories were the same on both forms and thus cannot be intercorrelated.

In commenting on the Utley test, Heider (160) presented a number of criticisms. Among these were the distracting movements of the speaker, the difficulty in using the test with younger children, and the finding that roughly half of the Utley test items should be discarded as being non-functional. That is, since half of the test items were found to be too difficult for almost any speechreader to identify correctly, they did not contribute any information. A more devastating critique of the Utley test was given by DiCarlo and Kataja (86). In this comparison hearing-impaired and normal-hearing subjects were first shown the film "A Family Dinner" (249) and then asked twenty questions about it. From the results of this test the subjects were divided into proficiency groups and the groups compared with their performance on the Utley test. Although DiCarlo and Kataja found a fairly high correlation between the two tests, they presented the following criticisms of the Utley test: single words are given too much weight, sentences have no continuity, there is a lack of situational clues, all but two stories appear to be inadequate, and the novice speechreader obtains approximately the same score as the experienced speechreader. To our knowledge the criticisms of the Utley test by Heider and by DiCarlo and Kataja have not been answered, nor have recommended changes been made in the original Utley test films.

Within months of the publication of the Utley test, a similar filmed test was reported by Reid (316, 317). Reid's test was in color and had three forms, using two females and one male as speakers. The parts of each original form consisted of seventeen vowels and diphthongs, eleven consonants, ten unrelated sentences, a series of related sentences telling a story, and a short story that was followed by four questions. The speaker spoke the test item number just before each item, rather than holding up a numbered card as in the Utley test. Reid's test was standardized on ninety-nine deaf girls in two residential schools, and intercorrelations between forms ranged from .82 to .84. Since the first two test parts (vowels-diphthongs and consonants) were found to correlate poorly with the other parts (r = .38), they were dropped from the final test forms.

A filmed test employing fifteen colloquial sentences spoken by a young female, as well as another filmed test of 120 sentences spoken by three male and three female speakers, is reported by Keaster (182). At the John Tracy Clinic a filmed test of speechreading was developed by Taaffe (366). This test has two equal forms, each consisting of thirty unrelated sentences which, as just mentioned, were developed at the University of Iowa by Jacqueline Keaster. Split-half correlations from .89 to .91 were reported. Form C was added in black and white with a speaker different from the one used to film the first two forms. This form had a reported reliability of .93.

A filmed test of familiar monosyllabic words was constructed by Moser et al. in which four speakers were used (251). The Illinois Communications Scale consists of four 16mm color films and is described by Jackson (170). An 8mm color film showing two persons in a restaurant scene was used by Nielsen (264) to obtain normative data with a large number of hearing-impaired subjects. The test stimuli consist of nine related sentences. Another 8mm test film in two parts of sixteen sentences each was developed by Katt (180); a correlation of .94 is reported between the two parts.

Evans (98) also developed an 8mm filmed test in two parts. Part I consists of sentences and stories which are accompanied by fifteen questions answerable by either "Yes" or "No." Part II contains twenty-five multiple-choice items which can be responded to by the child's indicating the number of pictured alternatives. With prelingually deaf children the intercorrelation between the two test parts was .98, and the correlation with speechreading achievement scores was .89.

A "Diagnostic Test of Speechreading" was published by Myklebust and Neyhus (258). The test is on two 8mm film cartridges. Part one consists of words and part two of phrases and sentences. Vocabulary in the test is suitable for deaf children between the ages of four and nine years. It is said to be not only an educational achievement test but also a diagnostic tool in determining disorders of visual memory, speechreading aphasia, and, indirectly, reading disorders.

Intercorrelations within and among several of the available filmed tests of speechreading are presented in Figure 8-1. From this figure it may be seen that, with several exceptions (notably the Morkovin film versus Utley Parts I and III), the correlations are moderate to very high. This fact suggests that whatever one film tests, the others do also to a significant degree. Intercorrelation information with other filmed tests would be helpful.

	Utley I	Utley II	Utley III	Morkovin #101	Mason
Utley I	—	.68-.69[a] .69[e]	.69-.75[a] .61[c] .76[e]	.26[d] —	.75[b]
Utley II	—	—	.56-.67[a] .51[c] .58[e]	—	.78[b]
Utley III	—	—	—	.27[d]	.59[b]
Total Utley	.96-.96[a] .99[b]	.72-.78[a] .68[b]	.80[c] .77[b]	.77[b]	.80
Taaffe	.88[g]	—	—	.89[f]	—

[a]Utley (380)
[b]Simmons (341)
[c]Di Carlo and Kataja (86)
[d]O'Neill and Stephens (287)
[e]Strain (361)
[f]Taaffe (366)
[g]Frisina and Bernero (120)

FIGURE 8-1. Intercorrelations of Filmed Speechreading Tests

A method of selecting test items by means of scalogram analysis is described by Postove (*308*). She solicited test sentences from experienced speechreading teachers and from them constructed forty-nine declarative and fifty interrogative sentences. These were filmed in color with both a male and a female speaker. The test films were seen by hard-of-hearing adult males, and the rank-difference method between scores obtained with these films and the Deshon test of speechreading was .85. From these results sixteen test items were retained for a short test of speechreading divided into two forms. The final forms correlated .73 with the Deshon test, a correlation which, like that of her original test, was statistically significant.

A self-administered film program in speechreading was developed by Black et al. (35), containing multiple-choice words derived from an auditory test (34). Six males visible from the waist up read each of the lists. A somewhat different multiple-choice speechreading test was devised by Donnelly and Marshall (89). They tabulated the errors that were made in response to a filmed test (366) and from these errors constructed a test answer sheet showing the sentence that was spoken by the speaker as well as the two sentences most often incorrectly given as answers by the subjects. The completed test was divided into two equal forms. These forms included sound so subjects could be tested either with or without the assistance of audition. In a follow-up investigation using one hundred normal-hearing high school subjects, differences were found between these multiple-choice test forms and odd and even numbered questions (11). Multiple-choice words were also used in a test by Quick (311), and multiple-choice picture tests were employed by Mason (229), Craig (74), and Evans (98).

LIVE VERSUS FILMED TESTS

The question of relationships between filmed test scores and scores from face-to-face tests or teachers' judgments was raised at the beginning of this chapter. We need to consider also the consistency of one live test to another or the reliability of teachers' judgments of speechreading. Using the Utley sentence test in a live presentation for both test and retest, Coscarelli (70) obtained a significant correlation (r = .89). In an early comparison with children, scores from a live test consisting of consonants, words, and sentences produced a correlation of .79 with teachers' judgments (65).

Teachers' ratings of speechreading were compared by Costello (71) to the results of a face-to-face test. Although

Costello described the latter as objective, it seems to have been quite informal. Nevertheless, intercorrelations were high. The teachers' ratings and the live test score correlation for words was .74 for the deaf and .69 for the hard of hearing, and for sentences the correlations were .83 and .88, respectively. However, when the hard-of-hearing and deaf groups were combined, the correlations were only .58 for words and .66 for sentences. The lower correlations when the two levels of hearing were combined suggests that teachers rate students' speechreading ability within their own degree of hearing-loss group.

When scores from Form A of his test were compared to scores of tests using three face-to-face speakers, Taaffe (366) obtained correlations of .74, .46, and .36. Each of the three speakers produced significantly different scores from those produced by the filmed test, and in each instance the live-test scores were lower than were the scores from the film. It is not clear whether differences obtained reflect speaker variations or live-versus-film differences. On the other hand, Jackson (170) found no significant differences between a televised and a live presentation. Likewise, DiCarlo (84) did not find significant differences between a live and a filmed presentation, and like Jackson, he obtained higher scores in the live presentation for both experienced and inexperienced normal-hearing college-age speechreaders. Since the filming was done during the live presentation, this may have penalized the scores for the live condition by introducing distractions, thereby minimizing differences between the two types of presentation. Heider (160) and Goetzinger (136) also reported a live presentation as easier to speechread than a filmed one.

Some available comparisons between filmed and live speechreading tests are presented in Figure 8-2. Although few of these correlations are low, neither are they high. In comparison with correlations among filmed tests, as were shown in Figure 8-1, it may be noted that the highest correlations between filmed-live tests tend to be no better than the lowest correlations between two filmed tests. The correlations shown in Figure 8-2 result from the combined ratings of five judges by Simmons (341) and of three ratings by O'Neill and Stephens

(*287*). Reid (*317*) and Utley (*380*) used ratings of various teachers who knew their subjects. Although many of the correlations shown in Figure 8-2 are statistically significant, it must nevertheless be acknowledged that they are, generally, much lower than intercorrelations among filmed tests and have only modest predictive value.

	Simmons (341)	O'Neill & Stephens (287)	Utley (380)	Reid (317)
Filmed Tests:				
Utley I	.52	.60		
Utley II	.37			
Utley III	.61	.49		
Total Utley	.57		.43	
Mason	.61			
Morkovin		.63		
Reid A				.53
Reid B				.46
Reid C				.53

FIGURE 8-2. Intercorrelations Between Filmed and Live Speechreading Tests

Because of the relatively poor relationship between live and filmed speechreading tests, Simmons (*341*) concluded that filmed and live tests "do not measure exactly the same thing . . . but what they do measure involves a fair amount of ability that is common to the two kinds of tests." Explanations for the low live-film test correlations as compared with intercorrelations of filmed tests have been elusive. It might be argued that the teacher or interviewer allows more subjective values to enter into the speechreading rating than would a filmed test, such as subtle personality factors. Possibly, on the other hand, the films are primarily tests of *lipreading* and the live tests more nearly represent those of *speechreading*. Or perhaps the filmed test is not a valid tool to use because it employs a two-dimensional presentation of the speaker, whereas the speechreader typically operates in a three-dimensional situation. Generalizing results of a two-dimensional test to the speechreader's usual task of receiving speech via a three-dimensional process is hazardous (292, 366).

One approach to this question was made by Goetzinger (135), who used a live presentation with subjects who viewed the speaker with both eyes, with only the dominant eye, or with only the non-dominant eye. No significant differences in speechreading scores were found to be caused by any of the three conditions. It may be noted that in this approach the depth perception of the subjects was presumably altered. However, it can be questioned whether the image seen by the viewers was materially changed, and the results by Goetzinger seem either to confirm this conclusion or to suggest that the third dimension is not important. The difference between two- and three-dimensional viewing seems to be that the former minimizes or nullifies clues based upon shadow, movement, and depth (293). Since the viewer still retains learned shadow and distance clues with a monocular view of the speaker, the Goetzinger approach may not have answered the basic question.

A difference in the viewing dimensions is suggested by a questionnaire response indicating that speechreaders preferred two-dimensional films to three-dimensional films or television (62). Our own students seem to prefer televised to filmed presentation of speechreading materials.

Another approach to the question of differential effects between filmed and live presentation was made by Strain (361). In this study normal-hearing college students were tested with a filmed test of speechreading, and on the basis of the results placed into two proficiency categories. Matched groups then received speechreading instruction for fifteen minutes per day for ten days by either closed circuit television or by a live presentation. After the training program the subjects were again tested with a filmed test. Although both groups significantly improved their scores, no significant differences between their scores were found, thus seeming to indicate no different effects produced by the different methods of instruction. Again, differences between two- and three-dimensional viewing seem to be only indirectly examined in this study, and the use of film for pre- and post-testing may have penalized the group which received live instruction.

A more absolute two-dimensional view of the speaker was used in another investigation (363). In this study a regular profile and a silhouette profile were used in speechreading tests. Although the silhouette is an artificial speechreading situation, it does rule out distance as well as small shadow effects on the face and articulators of the speaker. A significant difference in favor of the regular profile (three-dimensions) over the silhouette profile (two-dimensions) was found. It might be speculated that there will be a gradual improvement in reception of speech visually from silhouette to filmed or televised two-dimensional viewing to three-dimensional viewing.

Another possibility in measuring speechreading proficiency is to ask the speechreader to make such a rating himself. This approach was used as a part of two studies with normal-hearing untrained subjects (22, 26). In the first study university students were asked to rate their speechreading performance on a five-point scale immediately after having completed a face-to-face speechreading test but before the scores were known. The second study followed the same procedure but with university students and older subjects. Although the correlations between speechreading scores and self-ratings in each instance were statistically significant (r = .32 and .41), neither is high enough for predictive purposes. Whether hearing-impaired persons can rate their speechreading proficiency more accurately or whether there is a difference in the ratings between experienced and inexperienced speechreaders remains to be determined.

That experience with speechreading enables one to rate more accurately his ability is suggested from the results of a study employing normal-hearing college students (208). The subjects were enrolled in a speechreading course for teachers. At the beginning of the course the subjects did not accurately predict their speechreading ability (r = .15) as measured with the Utley filmed test. After nine one-hour training periods the subjects improved significantly in speechreading performance. The mean pre-training score was 61.3, and the mean post-training score was 81.7. Following training, a new self-rating produced a higher correlation (r = .52) , but the subjects still underestimated their speechreading proficiency.

A broader assessment of communication function was investigated by Olsen et al. (280). Noting the difficulty in validating the available speechreading tests, they attempted to determine the real-life communication function of hearing-impaired adults. The result of this effort was the Denver Scale, which is intended as an assessment of communication function and of anxiety experienced by adults with hearing impairment. In Part I of the Denver Scale, an open set of questions allows the hearing-impaired adult to report communication problems encountered, so as to determine how accurately he assesses his communication ability as compared to others in his environment who are in a position to judge his communication function. Parts II and III of the scale are modifications of a semantic differential scale. The purpose of Part II is to sample the individual's anxiety as it relates to communication, and Part III serves to assess his feelings regarding certain aspects of communication function. When this battery was used with twenty-five hearing-impaired adults, it was found that after ten weeks of rehabilitative therapy there was an improvement in communication function accompanied by a reduction in anxiety. However, scores from a videotaped speechreading test consisting of twenty common expressions did not correlate highly with either the improved communication or the anxiety reduction.

In summary, a standard test of speechreading is not presently available and is greatly needed. A large number of filmed and face-to-face tests have been developed. Perhaps among these tests some will prove useful once they have had broader examination by various clinicians. Many of the existing speechreading tests have been shown to be reliable measures, but their validity is still in question, and validity is of utmost importance. Filmed and live tests of speechreading appear to test somewhat different aspects of receptive speech by vision, and the most suspect of the reasons for their differences is that of the absence of a third dimension in filmed tests.

IX
speechreading methods

The purpose of speechreading instruction is to help the student to gain maximum understanding of the visible aspects of speech, a partial compensation for hearing impairment. In previous chapters of this book an attempt was made to review and collate reports on the well-understood and the only partially-known elements involved in speechreading, with the aim of filtering myth from fact. Because of conflicting research reports, only discrepant findings could be given in some instances. In other cases some of the skills that might be presumed to be involved in speechreading have not been investigated. Nevertheless, it is trusted that this review has furnished a number of meaningful, even though not always clear-cut, ideas for the teacher or the clinician for some "do's" and "don't's." In this final chapter some methodological approaches and materials will be briefly summarized with the hope that this survey will point the reader toward resources and ideas that can be profitably used. This review of methods and materials will not be in detail, since in the final analysis the teacher or clinician will want to read and digest many of the publications in their original form.

In the first part of the twentieth century, there was a

phenomenal increase in reported use of speechreading in the United States along with a proliferation of speechreading "schools." Then two important events intervened. The first was the Depression, which forced many schools to close or to diminish their activities because students could not afford to pay for training. The second factor causing a drastic slowdown of the mushrooming speechreading "business" was the gradual improvement in hearing aids which permitted more and more hearing-impaired persons to benefit from amplification. The present status of methodology in speechreading is much like the situation described three decades ago:

> At present, the whole business of imparting lip-reading . . . is at the crossroads. The older methods are forty years old; the newer methods are not very radical departures, but are more or less a composite of the old. Can anything new be learned? (239).

We still seem to be at the crossroads in speechreading. That anything new can be learned seems highly probable, even though the approach to speechreading instruction today does not seem to be substantially different from that in the 1940's even though at that time it had not changed significantly since the turn of the century. Perhaps the teacher of the deaf and the hearing clinician need to be reminded again that speechreading is as much a science as an art, that they should continually re-evaluate and update their methods. Too often speechreading methods and materials have been learned in a rote manner by a prospective teacher from her teacher, who in turn learned the same methods and materials from her teacher, and . . . soon we are back to the beginning of the century and may have not improved on the methodologies in vogue at that time.

What appears to be needed today are more dedicated and better trained teachers and clinicians who are willing to apply those linguistic and learning-theory approaches that have been found to be valid in order to modify the receptive and expressive speech behavior of the hearing-impaired child or adult in the most efficient manner possible. The theoretical construct of Jeffers (171) and the description of approaches to speechreading research and training by O'Neill (284) offer possible models with which to begin a broad and organized effort to understand the speechreading process better. Only with such understanding can training programs to increase speechreading skills be improved. In most of this book pertinent literature as it relates to speechreading processes has been reviewed and discussed. Until these complicated processes are better understood, we can expect no major improvements in methodology or pedagogy.

Until the critical factors involved in speechreading come into clearer focus, the teacher of the deaf and the hearing clinician will find worthwhile the time spent and patience required to become familiar with the myriad methodological books and journal articles published on the subject of speechreading in the past few decades. From this search will come ideas for assorted speechreading needs that can be applied to various student interest and proficiency levels. This eclectic approach of updating the old, discarding the useless, trying the promising new, and modifying the borrowed should enhance individual or classroom speechreading lessons. At the present time no good shortcut is known. Although broad principles of speechreading apply to any teaching situation, individual differences of hearing-impaired students require that instruction be varied to meet different needs (297).

In his classes teaching speechreading to teachers in training, the author has found it appropriate to have each student conduct a brief class lesson, using one of several assigned methods. Most of these published methods proceed, lesson by lesson, through a series of speech sounds or visemes in an orderly fashion. In a second assignment the class members independently develop and then present a brief lesson combining materials and approaches from three or more published method books or articles. In this second assignment the student is required to teach a lesson in the subject matter of his choice, but with age range prescribed, by combining several speechreading methodological approaches. The philosophy behind this assignment is to show the teacher in training the usefulness of speechreading as a means toward an end and also the advisability of using an eclectic approach.

The advisability of an individualized approach to speechreading training is underscored by O'Neill and Oyer (286), who present case histories to illustrate personalized differences in communication needs which therefore require differences in speechreading methods and materials. An eclectic approach is also recommended by Sanders (329, p.10) with updating and modification to be made as new facts become known.

It should be recognized that the individualized approach to speechreading does require high sophistication of and great dedication from the teacher. The hearing-impaired population can no longer tolerate a teacher who is minimally prepared and poorly motivated. Indeed, such a teacher was always a hindrance to the profession. Our belief is that each teacher or clinician should use a personalized approach with individuals or classes. Attempting to employ typical published speechreading method books with every individual or group, unless extensively supplemented by other materials, will produce less than ideal progress from the students.

A particularly barren area of speechreading relates to research, methods, and materials concerned with the very young deaf child. For the young, beginning speechreader at the initial stages of training, some teachers recommend the use of sequential matching that leads to actual speechreading. In this procedure the child is taught to match identical objects, and once he is successful at that task, he is taught to match an object to similar objects. Next the child matches objects to pictures of the object, a picture to an identical picture, and then a picture to similar pictures. Finally the pictures are matched to words presented orally. This procedure is sometimes referred to as teaching speechreading in specific situations. For adults the specific situation might simply involve matching printed words to the same words presented orally.

Other teachers prefer to teach speechreading within a framework of general situations. In this procedure speechreading occurs incidentally to communication in general or to academic-subject teaching. The specific and general situation procedures reflect analytic and synthetic orientations in teaching that were discussed in a previous chapter. Some teachers prefer to begin speechreading instruction by using general situations, while other teachers begin with specific situations and gradually include general situations as the child or adult gains proficiency in speechreading. Vuillemey (387) feels that there are five levels of recognition difficulty in speechreading that can be used in planning lessons for the child or adult. These levels are (1) learning to recognize photographic or pictured articulatory positions, (2) transferring this learning to identifying live articulation of vowels and consonants, (3) identifying consonants and vowels as comprising syllables, (4) identifying syllables as combined into words, and (5) learning to recognize words as constituting sentences. It may be noted that Vuillemey is describing one way of developing speechreading skills by emphasizing analysis. Although many teachers of the deaf do not support the analytic rationale, there is little good evidence that this method is inferior to synthesis as a teaching procedure, nor is there evidence to refute the claim by some teachers that beginning the child or adult with lessons predominantly analytic and then gradually stressing synthesis is an efficient procedure.

A SURVEY OF SPEECHREADING METHODS

Lillie Eginton Warren was one of the first Americans to recognize the communication needs of the hearing-impaired child, and she was a pioneer teacher of speechreading to adults in this country. She also realized the importance of developing a method and of trying to improve it. Her ideas appeared in print in 1895, but the book was a general discussion rather than a description of her method as such (390). A feature of her method was to have the student associate numbers with the sixteen sounds that she believed could be revealed on the face of the speaker. For this reason her method was often referred to as the numerical-cipher method.

Another pioneering method in the United States was developed by Louise I. Morgenstern, who later became Mrs. Kurt Neuschutz. Many of her ideas appeared in the book *Lip-Reading for Class Instruction* (245), which contained sixty-five short lessons on sounds and sound combinations and thirty-five lessons on conversation and lecture materials. Miss Morgenstern, herself having impaired hearing, taught the first public school evening class in speechreading in New York City.

These were but several of many early speechreading methods published in the United States. Soon four methods in speechreading gained widespread popularity in America, and these are briefly described below. These are the methods published by Bruhn, Nitchie, the Kinzies, and Bunger. Although these were the leading methods and texts on speechreading methodology, their popularity has gradually dimished. Nor have any other methods or books replaced them in popularity. Perhaps the reason for no present-day "best seller" speechreading method book is that it is now realized that no one method or book is equally applicable to the various circumstances in which speechreading is taught. Certainly no one method or book could be expected to be of equal value for the deaf and the hard of hearing, the prelingually deaf and the deafened, the beginner and the more experienced speechreader, or the child and the older student. These and numerous other differences within the category of hearing impairment preclude the meaningful use of any single method or book for the diverse applications needed.

Mueller-Walle Method. Martha Emma Bruhn[1] was born in Boston and was educated to become a teacher. She was teaching French and German in the public schools of Massachusetts when her hearing began to deteriorate. When her hearing became increasingly worse, she decided to go to Germany, where she took a six-week course in speechreading from Julius Mueller-Walle. She was the first hard-of-hearing pupil that Mueller-Walle accepted. Watching her work with the other pupils, Mueller-Walle noted her natural ability and also recognized that she was proficient in several languages. He suggested that she carry his method to America.

After Miss Bruhn completed the course of study under Herr Mueller-Walle, she remained in Germany to teach in his

[1]Miss Bruhn was born in 1871 and died in 1960. Her most recent position had been with the Boston Guild for the Hard of Hearing.

school for several months. She then selected from the methodology and materials of his course what she wanted, translated the fundamental principles of the method into English, and returned to the United States to open her own school of speechreading in Boston in 1902.

Miss Bruhn gave the first public exposition of her teaching approach in 1912 at a meeting of the American Association to Promote the Teaching of Speech to the Deaf held in Providence (83). She showed that the Mueller-Walle method of instruction differed from typical articulation teaching which stressed detailed attention to the positions of speech sounds.[2] After seeing Miss Bruhn's students and hearing her remarks, Alexander Graham Bell stated, "I am bound to confess that there is a great deal in this lipreading of Miss Bruhn that is valuable to our work, but there is one point that has struck me—there is a radical difference between her method of looking at lipreading and ours. We look to positions of the vocal organs. She looks to movements. There is something very significant there."

The Mueller-Walle method stresses rapid syllable drill rather than drills on sounds, and this emphasis is one of its unique features. The use of rapid syllable drill is carefully graded in difficulty to accustom the students to recognize assorted visible movements of speech. Gradually the student receives more meaningful and interesting material, but syllable drill also continues. Although syllable drill has been criticized as being too artificial, it has been found that the more often a syllable is encountered, the smaller the fragment needed for identification of the total item (307).

In the Mueller-Walle method book (49) the twenty-four lessons might have been better if they had been divided into more than twice that number. Although today many teachers feel that the method book is out of date and probably too analytic in orientation, combining the materials and approach

---

[2]Articulation teaching, or the articulation method, was an early term referring to oralism. Speechreading was included and used as much for improving speech production as it was for receiving speech.

from this method with one or more other methods makes it a valuable reference and method book.

Nitchie Method. Edward B. Nitchie was born to an old Brooklyn family of German origin. He became deaf at the age of fourteen years. After graduation from Amherst College he enrolled in one of Lillie Warren's speechreading classes. Soon afterwards he began to write his first book, *Self-Instruction in Lip-Reading,* in which Warren claimed he plagiarized her ideas. In 1903 Nitchie opened his own school for hard-of-hearing children in New York. However, he had so many adult applicants that he soon devoted himself to developing his method for adults.

Nitchie's first book on speechreading, mentioned above, was an improvement over the Warren method in that he substituted symbols for her arbitrary system of numbering the sounds. However, it still resembled her method to a great extent, stressing positions of the mouth rather than movements or linguistic clues. Each position was given a name "descriptive of its cardinal point of individuality." Like Warren, Nitchie stressed the use of a mirror in practice. The student was to watch his articulator positions in a mirror and match his speech production with that of his teacher. His books show a modification of his views on speechreading as they were issued over the years. Each deals less with phonetic analysis of the speech signal and visual positions of the speech mechanism and more with synthetic grasp or the mental processes. In 1912 Nitchie published *Lip-Reading Principles and Practices* (266) with minor revisions made by his widow in 1919 and 1930.[3] Following the same general format of this book was *Advanced Lessons in Lip-Reading* by Mrs. Nitchie, Elizabeth Helm Nitchie, published in 1923 (273).

In 1940 Elizabeth Nitchie revised *Lip-Reading Principles and Practices* by Edward B. Nitchie, calling the new version *New Lessons in Lip Reading,* and minor changes were made in the editions of 1947 and 1950 (274). This book has been one of

---

[3]Edward Bartlett Nitchie was born in 1876 and died in 1917. Mrs. E.H. Nitchie was born in 1881 and died in 1961. She retired as principal of the Nitchie School of Lip Reading in 1946.

the most popular speechreading method books in the United States, particularly with those of junior high school age and older. It is of less value for the younger speechreader and for the prelingually deaf child. With a small amount of updating of the materials, this is a practical and easy-to-use collection of orderly materials for the speechreader.

Nitchie's major contribution to speechreading teaching was his stress on the psychological process of the technique, the idea that speechreading success depends upon the mind as well as the eye. In his method the teacher is to repeat the sentence materials as a whole and never speak in single words, much less employ syllables or isolated sounds. Nitchie was not a believer in syllable drill or in memorizing vocabularies (267). The student is motivated to grasp any part of the statement spoken and to make a judgment about the entire idea from the context of what was understood. Word lists are used, but only to give the speechreader clues. The lessons cover all of the sounds of speech in an orderly manner. Nitchie can also be credited with stressing the practice of homophenous words and the determination of their meaning from context. His homophenous-word drill is much like that in the Mueller-Walle method.

Kinzie Method. Cora Kinzie was training to become a medical missionary when she became deaf. After studying with Martha Bruhn and Edward B. Nitchie, she decided to become a speechreading teacher. In 1917 the Mueller-Walle School of Lip-Reading in Philadelphia, where Kinzie had been teaching, became known as the Kinzie School of Speech Reading. With her sister Rose, she developed the Kinzie speechreading method (191, 192). It is to be expected that the Kinzies would combine certain principles of the Mueller-Walle and the Nitchie methods in their own approach. From the Mueller-Walle method they took the classification of introductory sounds, and from the Nitchie method, the basic principles of psychology (synthesis, intuition, and attention) as applied to speechreading (189).

The Kinzie book of graded lessons in speechreading for adults was published in 1931 and their lessons for children in 1936. The contributions of the Kinzie sisters were that their lessons were thorough and graded and were designed to meet the requirements and progress of various pupil ages. They also stressed following a specific technique, a fact which helped to raise instruction in the subject to more of a science than it had previously been. The Kinzie method books can be considered to be among the first published efforts toward an eclectic approach in speechreading methodology.

Jena Method. In the city of Jena,[4] Germany, Karl Brauckmann (1862-1938), like his father before him, directed a school for teaching deaf children. Some adults received training there also, as did teachers who wished to learn how to instruct the deaf. Dissatisfied with the current methods of teaching speechreading, in 1900 Brauckmann began to experiment with new and different techniques. In 1925 he published two small books on speechreading for the deafened adult. In the first of these books he reviewed and criticized the twelve German books on speechreading that had been published between 1841 and 1925 (319). A major criticism was that they were, in reality, all alike. They all included a detailed analysis of visible speech positions and followed with practice of observing these positions in syllables, then words, and finally sentences. However, since only about half of the positions of speech sounds were considered to be visible, the student had in some way to supply the missing movements and combine them with the visible positions in order to obtain meaning from what was spoken.

Out of his searches and experiments Brauckmann came to treat speech as having five forms: audible, visible, tactual, kinesthetic, and mimetic. Obviously the speechreader should use hearing to the degree permitted by the hearing loss and also use vision to the greatest extent possible in determining what was spoken. The unique approach by Brauckmann was his stress on the mimetic and kinesthetic forms. This method utilizes drills during which the individual or class repeats an assortment of materials with the teacher, at the same time watching the teacher and paying attention to their own speech movements by means of kinesthesia. The Jena method is thus more closely allied with speech production than are most other

[4]Pronounced YAY-nuh. The city was heavily bombed during World War II because the Zeiss optical factory was located there.

speechreading methods. In the first chapter we saw that until the present century speechreading was primarily a technique used for obtaining better speech production rather than stressed as a receptive speech avenue. It is interesting that Brauckmann reversed priorities, and to him speech production provided kinesthetic clues for becoming a better speechreader. The clues by kinesthesia are patterned by imitating the teacher's speech and later by less overtly imitating the speech of any speaker encountered. In addition to the five forms of speech outlined by Brauckmann, his method places considerable emphasis on rhythm drills and the use of stress patterns in phrases commonly found in speech.

In Brauckmann's second book on speechreading he described conversational speech as automatic and subconscious. Jacob Reighard, a professor of zoology at the University of Michigan, translated Brauckmann's speechreading method into English in 1926, assisted by Bessie Whitaker. Whitaker introduced the method at Michigan Normal College that same year, but Anna Mae Bunger is credited with popularizing the method in the United States, and she also edited the published English version (53). Miss Bunger, who had a hearing loss, used and expanded the method while teaching at the University of Michigan.

The Jena method is not well suited to the non-reading child. But the method features a number of techniques that can be used not only in working with this method but also as a supplement to other methods, such as vowel and consonant charts as well as drill that evolves into syllables and words. There are also rhythm drills and serial drills. Not explicit in the book, but used by Bunger in the method, was the concept that the speechreader do many of the drills accompanied by rhythmic movements of the hands or body. The teacher using this book will need to develop ideas for making the lessons realistic and current to the appropriate age and interest group. The published Jena method is still one of the more popular speechreading books in the United States. A modification of the Jena method for use with children has been published (309).

OTHER SPEECHREADING METHODS

A number of other speechreading methods and books have been published in English. Few of these have yet gained the past popularity of the Mueller-Walle, Nitchie, Kinzie, or Jena methods, and most are modifications or combinations of them. The following are some other published speechreading method books.

Hearing With Our Eyes, by Ena G. Macnutt (221), is a method designed for children. It follows the speech-sound orientation. That is, each lesson covers one or more specific speech sounds. The twenty-eight lessons appear to be an application of the Nitchie approach for children. A workbook for use by the child accompanied the method when published, and in 1959 a second workbook appeared in print.

Introduction to Lipreading was published by the Sonotone Corporation (168). More than half of this small book is devoted to general information for and encouragement to the person beginning to speechread. The book was written primarily to help the deafened adult. The last portion of the book includes word and sentence drill materials. The publication of these materials by a commercial hearing aid firm as a public service is to be applauded. Unfortunately, much of the material contained in the book is now outdated, and some of the materials designed for home practice would not be very useful without the help of a trained teacher.

The Key to Lipreading, by Lilian J. Dawson-Abbott (81), is a method book in eighteen lessons. The lessons are based upon the syllable approach, but these are not a mere rewriting of the Mueller-Walle method. In this method vowels and consonants are introduced in an orderly manner, with much repetition suggested so the vowel-consonant and consonant-vowel combinations become visually familiar to the student. Drills consist of identifying syllable variations, such as "far," "fay," and "fee." Some attention is given to feeling the sounds and movements, and the student is encouraged to feel the sounds as he produces them while at the same time also observing them in a mirror. Later lessons build the syllables into sentences, wherein a rapid grasp of the spoken sentences is en-

couraged. In the early lessons a precise word-for-word identification is strongly recommended. Mrs. Dawson-Abbott was
director for many years of the Australian Association for
Better Hearing.

Lip Reading, by J. Hounslow Burchett (54), was written
originally for use in Australia. The first three chapters are
introductory. Chapters five and six contain a number of useful
drills based primarily on comparisons between sounds. The
appendix contains a brief but good discussion of the congenital
deaf and speech of the deaf and also an unscientific discussion
on breathing.

Lip-Reading, by Olive M. Wyatt (410), contains a number
of good self-teaching ideas. It also includes a curious autobiographical section. The materials on speechreading are not
clearly for adults or for children, and they include vocabulary
artificial to Americans and probably to contemporary Britons.
One excellent technique stressed in the book is to vary and
expand word and sentence drill, thereby assuring a considerable practice with a limited speech vocabulary while avoiding
the boredom of exact repetition.

Lipreading and Hearing Aids, by Irene Rosetta Ewing
(102) [5] is a small book that attempts to cover a broad range of
topics relating to the hearing impaired. In its brevity it does a
surprisingly good job. The second part of the book includes
twenty short lessons on speechreading that for the most part
follow an approach based upon speech sounds.

Lip Reading for the Deafened Child, by Agnes Stowell,
Estelle E. Samuelson, and Ann Lehman (360), is an adaptation
blending the Nitchie and Mueller-Walle methods for hard-of-
hearing children. The method starts with consonants and then
adds vowels in a systematic manner. As did Nitchie, the
method stresses mirror practice. The students are taught to
recognize associations and contrasts of lip positions. The
method is geared for the primary school-aged child.

[5]Mrs. Ewing died July 16, 1959. She and her husband, Alexander W.G. Ewing,
brought the Department of Education for the Deaf at Manchester University to world
reknown.

Lip Reading Lessons for Adult Beginners, by Harriet Montague (240),[6] contains thirty lessons patterned after the Mueller-Walle method. As the title indicates, the book is intended primarily for the older beginning speechreader, the deafened adult.

Lip Reading Study and Practice, by Minnie Faircloth (104), is a small book that follows the speech-sound approach. Although this book was designed for use with hearing-impaired Canadian servicemen, it is appropriate for deafened adults in general.

New Aids and Materials for Teaching Lip-Reading was written for the New York City Board of Education as an official project of the Works Projects Administration (262). It was published by the American Society for the Hard of Hearing. This method follows the speech-sound approach, and it makes one of the first formal efforts to rate these sounds as to relative difficulty in speechreading.

Pattern for the Listening Eye, by Dorothy G. Clegg (63), consists of thirty short lessons. The book is based primarily upon a speech-sound orientation. Many useful supplementary materials are included, but unfortunately the phonetic symbols used are confusing and the organization of the material is not clear. The author previously wrote The Listening Eye.

Simplified Lip Reading, by Ella Marguerite Braunlich (41), is a small book containing thirty lessons based on a speech-sound approach. The drill materials seem to be patterned after those of the Nitchie and Mueller-Walle methods. Although the book was designed for home study, its value appears to be mainly as a supplementary book for use by the teacher. To be regretted is the inference in the title that speechreading is a simple skill to learn.

Speech Reading for the Hard of Hearing Child, by Olive A. Whildin and M. Agatha Scally (394), contains forty lessons

---

[6]Miss Montague was born in 1884 and died in 1959. She was deaf and her first teacher was Mary True. She was director of the John Tracy Correspondence Course and regularly edited a column in The Volta Review.

based on the speech-sound approach. Since directions and instructions are minimal in this book, it would seem to be of primary use for the teacher, who will need to develop a continuity in presentation of the materials. The book is written for children in the upper elementary grades.

A Synthetic Approach to Lip Reading, by George S. Haspiel (154), contains materials designed for children in the elementary grades, but many of the lessons would be appropriate up through high school age. There are twenty lessons based upon common and useful subjects and experiences. There is almost no attention given to speechreading individual sounds. Rather, as suggested by the book title, the emphasis is on the phrase and sentence. The book appears to have its greatest value as a supplementary one or one which would follow a basic introduction to speechreading.

What People Say, by Kathryn Alling Ordman and Mary Pauline Ralli (288), was designed as an introductory book for the Nitchie method. It follows the Nitchie approach and is divided into thirty lessons stressing the various speech sounds in an orderly manner but nevertheless not using these sounds in isolation. The interest level seems to be at a junior high school age and higher.

SUPPLEMENTARY MATERIALS

In addition to the many published speechreading methods, many of which have been briefly discussed above, there are also a number of supplementary materials published in book or pamphlet form. A few of these are mentioned below.

Jane Walker's Book of Art Lectures (389) is a series of lessons on various well-known works of art. These lectures were prepared for speechreading practice by Jane Walker, and they were published as a memorial to her. Jane Walker also wrote *Jane Walker's Book of Lipreading Practice Material* (388).

A Lipreader Must Practice, by Medary Reike Copeland (67), was designed to provide supplementary materials for secondary school-age and adult students. There are six parts in the book, with heavy emphasis on using key words in sentences and stories. There is little stress on the sounds of speech, but rather the book consists primarily of games and humorous stories. Another and similar book by Copeland is entitled *A Lipreading Practice Manual for Teenagers* (66).

Look, Listen and Lipread, edited by Betty C. Wright (409), is a collection of supplementary materials covering a fairly wide assortment of subjects. These materials were contributed by thirty-seven teachers of speechreading.

Stories and Games for Easy Lipreading Practice, by Rose V. Feilbach (107), is a small book containing numerous short stories, anecdotes, and games. The materials are geared to an interest level from upper elementary-age children to adults.

A Treasure Chest of Games for Lip Reading Teachers, by Estelle E. Samuelson and Minnie B. Fabregas (327), is a pamphlet containing sixty games. The games are classified as to where they might fit within a lesson or unit of study.

Three speechreading books containing supplementary materials were developed by Mae T. Fisher. *Lip Reading Practice Materials for Children* (113) contains twenty lessons which appear to be on a level broad enough for most elementary-aged children. Additional visual and story materials are suggested. *Let's Practice Lipreading* (112) and *Improve Your Lipreading* (114) were designed for teenagers and adults. These collections contain sentence, story, and quiz materials.

A number of books and materials on speechreading have been designed and published for specific schools or programs. Often these materials do not become generally known to teachers of the deaf or to hearing clinicians. *Lipreading for the Deaf and Hard of Hearing* (209) is a publication which grew from a research project at Junior High School #47 in New York City. The book consists primarily of supplementary ideas and materials. Louargand (214) has published a lesson manual that is built around units of study found in the teacher's guides developed by the California Curriculum Commission. Included are thirty-three lessons in social studies, thirty-three lessons in science, and ten in arithmetic. The manual is geared to the first through the sixth-grade level.

TRAINING FILMS. A series of ten films for adults and five films for children, called *Life Situation Films*, were developed by Boris V. Morkovin (1882-1962). Other materials, as well as procedures suggested for use with the films, are described in several reports (242, 246, 249). The films are 16mm and available in either black and white or in color. Each is approximately five minutes long and portrays a typical life situation for the speechreader. Questions about the spoken materials and also the situational clues shown are then asked of the viewers. The idea is that speechreaders, individually or in groups, can view a film, discuss it with the teacher, and then watch it again for review. The films form part of what is called the A-V-K Method, meaning audio-visual-kinesthetic.

The life-situation film series for children consists of the following titles: Tommy's Table Manners, A Lesson in Magic, The Little Cowboy, Barbara's New Shoes, and Bow Belinda. As was noted in the preceding chapter, these films were not designed for testing speechreading, but they have been used for such. "A Family Dinner" from the adult series has been the most popular one for testing purposes. Other films in the series for adults include "At The Bank" and "At The Grocery Store."

Four color 8mm films of five minutes each are described by Neyhus (263). Vocabulary used in the films is geared to the four to ten-year ages. The speakers are a teacher and a child in a classroom setting. Sound is also on the film, thereby permitting training in combined vision-audition if desired. This series of films was modified for speechreading testing, as was mentioned in the preceding chapter (258). The use of 8mm motion pictures, opaque pictures and filmstrips is briefly described by Withrow (398). Stepp (352, 353) describes the use of 8mm film loops for speechreading training with deaf children. The films may be used by an individual or shown to a group of children and form one means whereby speechreading practice can be increased and classwork supplemented. Films and film loops also present flexibility in individualizing training, the importance of which has previously been discussed.

JOURNAL ARTICLES. In addition to speechreading method books, supplementary drill books, and filmed materials, the interested teacher or clinician will often find valuable ideas and drill material suggestions in journal articles. The various professional journals have over a period of years frequently printed reports by experienced teachers which offer helpful lesson plans, drill materials, and other ideas for speechreading practice. Many of the materials and ideas in these articles have become outmoded, but they can be modified and updated for the particular hearing-impaired children in training with minimal effort on the part of the teacher. Only a very few of these many, varied reports are mentioned below.

Preschool speechreading principles and procedures are discussed by Magner (222), who believes that the ideal time to begin speechreading is before the age of two years. Craig (74), Lassman (202), and Van Wyck (382) also discuss preschool instruction. Published accounts and suggestions for speechreading training with the preschool child are far from plentiful, and teachers of these children should be encouraged to contribute their ideas and experiences with the preschool child. Materials and ideas on speechreading for children may be found in a number of articles (45, 59, 140, 181, 239, 349, 350, 372, 374, 391, 411). Haspiel (155) also discusses speechreading for the child, and he points out the need to individualize the available published materials.

Similar writings for adults are included in a number of published journal articles (43, 73, 132, 133, 163, 297, 369). Teaching speechreading by programmed learning techniques is introduced in several articles (35, 42, 230).

TELEVISION. Television has been used as a medium with which to test speechreading, as we saw in the preceding chapter. In addition television can be, and in a few localities has been, successfully employed as a medium for teaching speechreading to individuals who might not otherwise get to a teacher or a clinician for help. The extremely hopeful reports on and promising use of television as a medium for teaching speechreading that appeared in the early days of commercial television have not, however, turned out to be so fruitful. Nor should inexperienced speechreaders be advised to watch commercial television programs for practice, since the novice is likely to become quickly discouraged because of the rapidly changing camera views. Most television programs, because of rapidly changing scenes and alternating distant and close views, are less than ideal for speechreading practice. The typical motion picture is just as poorly designed for the beginning speechreader. Later the student can be encouraged to practice with television, starting with news programs and then watching televised speeches.

One use to which television can be put in speechreading training is to have the individual or class watch a short program and then answer questions about situational, gestural, and facial clues. For instance, the teacher can ask about the sex and age of certain speakers, their general appearance and manner of dress, the contents of their environment, and the activity in which they were engaged (329, p.116).

Descriptions or discussions of televised speechreading programs are given by a number of authors (62, 76, 77, 79, 179, 197, 206, 243, 283, 292, 346, 359). From these reports the interested reader will find suggestions for televising speechreading lessons and some problems inherent in that medium. The use of closed-circuit television in monitoring speechreading therapy and in giving demonstration lessons would seem to offer great value to the teacher in training. However, this idea seems not to have been instituted or used to any great extent, at least if the lack of published reports is any criterion.

GENERAL GUIDELINES

From some of the research findings mentioned in previous chapters, from statements made in some of the method books briefly reviewed in this chapter, from speechreaders, and from observations made by experienced teachers of the hearing impaired, a number of general guidelines emerge. These guidelines are summarized below as they pertain to the speaker, the teacher, and the speechreader. Many of the speechreading method books also present similar guidelines. It should be reiterated that some of these guidelines are based upon the results of experimental research, some come from experienced teachers of the hearing impaired, and some are from successful speechreaders. With time and a better understanding of the speechreading processes, such a list of guidelines can be based more upon experimental research evidence and less on mere observation.

GUIDELINES FOR THE SPEAKER. In typical speaking-hearing situations the listener depends less upon speaker cooperation than does the speechreader. This fact is true primarily because speechreading can be accomplished only with a good view of the speaker's face, and speechreading is complicated by its inexactness as an avenue for the accurate reception of speech. Although the speechreader cannot count on complete speaker cooperation from strangers and casual acquaintances, the speechreader's close friends and his family can assist understanding by following some basic guidelines.

> Before engaging the speechreader in conversation, make certain that you have his visual attention.
> Be natural in posture, use of gestures, and manner of speech.
> Avoid sudden head or body movements. Do not continue talking if you turn from the speechreader.
> Speak distinctly, in a conversational tone, and with a conversational rate. If the speechreader is having difficulty in understanding, try slowing down the speech a little and experiment with a *slight* exaggeration of the speech movements.
> If a speechreader enters your conversational group, indicate the subject under discussion. If the speechreader becomes lost in the conversation, repeat key phrases for him, perhaps with a slight rephrasing.
> Unless you are also a speechreader, attempt to position yourself so your face is in good light and so that any glare from lighting is not in the speechreader's eyes.

When possible, attempt to retain a reasonable distance between you and the speechreader, perhaps between three and twelve feet.

In conversations, where possible, draw the speechreader's attention to objects or items being discussed.

Don't shout, even though the speechreader is having difficulty understanding. When the speechreader is wearing a hearing aid, shouting will probably distort the sound that he receives, and it also draws the attention of others around you, thereby embarrassing the speechreader.

GUIDELINES FOR THE TEACHER. Most of the guidelines for the speaker mentioned above are applicable to the teacher. Some of the guidelines for the teacher are also applicable to the speaker, particularly where the speaker has the opportunity and interest to participate in more than a casual conversation with the speechreader. The good teacher is less concerned with a specific method of teaching speechreading than she is with building lessons around the needs of the individual. For this reason the teacher needs to know the children, their homes, their parents, their strengths, and their weaknesses. If the student is not in a class for hearing-impaired children, the teacher also needs to determine the child's school progress and know the curriculum being covered.

Organize the speechreading period or lessons to provide for a variety of activity. The salient points of the previous lesson should be reviewed before introducing new movements or materials. Remember that your immediate goals are to help the student increase his speechreading skills and his knowledge in general.

Be familiar with the lesson material and goals before you begin. Have all materials ready before the lesson starts.

Alternate drills, homophenous word exercises, games, provision for the children to speechread each other, and intervals of rest from concentrated attention.

Motivate the children to do their best according to their age and maturity. Use materials that are at the child's maturity and interest level. As much as possible, correlate the speechreading material to the child's curriculum and out-of-school needs.

Encourage the child to progress, but design the materials used so that he finds success readily at the beginning of the lesson. Avoid materials and tasks far beyond the child's comprehension.

Laugh *with* the child when he makes mistakes in speechreading, and explain why certain mistakes in speechreading are more probable than others.

Write out proper nouns when they are introduced.

Make extensive use of visual aids such as the blackboard, charts, pictures, maps, and diagrams.

Position yourself as nearly at the child's eye level as possible, avoid extreme facial angles between you and the child, and keep at a minimum gross body movements from one angle or position to another.

Watch your own appearance and possible distracting clothing, jewelry, or hair style. Become aware of mannerisms in your speech or gesture that may unduly assist the child's comprehension or that may distract him.

Use short, complete, direct sentences as much as possible. Where responses from the speechreader are desired, avoid questions that can be answered by "yes" or "no" as much as possible, since the speechreader may be guessing and you may not realize it.

When developing key words, use highly visible sounds as much as possible, particularly at the early stages of training. Where appropriate, use familiar words of two or more syllables.

Pause occasionally in lecture-type presentations

to permit the class to make notes, and do not continue speaking until all class members are again looking up.

Make extensive use of written assignments and written information on test scheduling.

In all lessons use repetition of materials as needed, and constantly check to determine that each class member is understanding each step of the lesson.

GUIDELINES FOR THE SPEECHREADER. To date the components of how to become a successful speechreader are but partially understood. It appears that an average or higher intellect, consistent effort to understand, a desire to improve speechreading abilities, and a good knowledge of linguistic clues, as well as the observation of non-verbal cues, are a minimum required for speechreading success.

Acknowledge your hearing impairment. Do not attempt to hide it or be ashamed of it.

Study the general situation, the speaker or speakers, the roles of the discussants, and objects being talked about.

Use a hearing aid that is properly selected. Seek professional advice from a speech and hearing clinic periodically regarding your hearing aid so as to determine whether it is still functioning as expected and to learn of possible new developments in amplification.

Whenever possible, position yourself so the speaker's face is well lighted and so that you are not facing the light directly.

Cultivate a liking for people, and challenge yourself to speechread everyone you meet.

Attempt to be alert without being tense.

Maintain a sense of humor. When you make a mistake in speechreading, laugh at your error rather than attempting to bluff your way. Don't be ashamed to ask people to repeat when you don't understand, but don't interrupt during a sentence since the latter part of the message may enable you to tell the part you missed.

Watch the visible movements of the lips and other articulators of the speaker, but not with such concentration that you are analyzing every small position or movement.

Since some speech sounds do not have unique positions or movements, try to get meaning from whole phrases or sentences. Don't worry if you miss a word or two; hopefully you can fill in the missing portion from linguistic, situational, gestural, or facial clues.

Since conversation is a two-way activity, don't monopolize it in an attempt to avoid speechreading. Also, cultivate good speech habits—voice quality and articulation—so your speech is pleasant and intelligible.

Maintain a wide range of interests, and keep up with the news of your community and the world. Keep building your vocabulary, including colloquial expressions.

Make a pledge to yourself to master speechreading and be determined to do so. Don't be discouraged that you miss some speech or that you have some "blank" spells. The best speechreaders have bad days, and they don't understand everything by speechreading alone.

Educating friends and relatives about the communication problems of the hearing impaired is your responsibility. Put people at ease by mentioning the things they can do to assist you in understanding.

When your interpersonal relationships with normal-hearing individuals are not good, don't immediately blame them on your speechreading. Take stock of your personality, your dress, your behavior, and your attitude as possible culprits.

Practice speechreading daily. Practice speechreading in assorted environments. Practice speechreading with different people. Practice!

bibliography

1. Albright, M. A. Ear, eye, or both. *Volta Review* 46 (1944): 11-13.
2. Albright, P., and N. M. Hipskind. A comparison of visibility and speechreading performance between matched English sentences and Slurvian utterances. Paper presented at the American Speech and Hearing Association convention, 1971.
3. Alich, G. W. New investigations in speechreading. *20th Convention Assn. German Teachers Deaf*, 1961. Abstract in *dsh Abstracts* 5 (1965): 149.
4. Alich, G. W. Language communication by lipreading. *Proceedings International Conference Oral Education Deaf*, 1967, 465-482.
5. Amsler, R. The Jena method of teaching speech reading. *Volta Review* 29 (1927): 107-109.
6. Arakawa, K., and K. Furumaya. The changes of flicker value resulting from lipreading. *Bulletin Faculty Education* (Tokyo University) 8 (1962): 133-143. Cited by Quigley (*312*).
7. Arthur, R. H. The effect of contextual and non-contextual motion pictures on the speechreading proficiency of comparable adult males. Ph.D. dissertation, University of

Florida, 1962.

8. Aylesworth, D. L. The talker and lipreader as variables in face-to-face testing of lipreading ability. M.A. thesis, Michigan State University, 1964.

9. Backus, O. Incidence of stuttering among the deaf. *Annals Otology and Rhinology* 47 (1938): 632-635.

10. Barnes, S. K. Intelligence tests and lipreading ability. M.S. thesis, University of Southern California, 1962.

11. Bartfield, S. An evaluation of the multiple-choice form of the film test of lipreading. M.A. thesis, University of Cincinnati, 1968.

12. Bartlett, R. Attention in speech reading. *Hearing News* 17 (March 1949): 1-2.

13. Bechinger, W. J. Amtliche Forthildungstagung fur die Lehrkrafte der Gehorlosen-, Schwerhorigen- und Sprachheilschulen (Convention to further informing and educating teachers of schools for the deaf, the hard of hearing, and speech defectives). *Neue Bl. Taubst.*, 15, 1961, 168. Abstract in *dsh Abstracts* 2 (1962): 209-210, and cited by Quigley (312).

14. Bender, R. *The Conquest of Deafness*. Cleveland: Western Reserve University, 1960, 208pp.

15. Bennett, E. An investigation of the relationship of speechreading ability to visual perception and delayed visual retention. M.A. thesis, University of Kansas, 1960.

16. Bergendorff, M. A. Application of prompts in teaching speechreading to deaf preschoolers, M.S. thesis, University of Kansas, 1968.

17. Berger, K. W. Vowel confusions in speechreading. *Ohio J. Speech and Hearing* 5 (1970): 123-128.

18. Berger, K. W. Motivation in speechreading. *Teacher of the Deaf* 29 (1971): 30-32.

19. Berger, K. W. Lipreading error patterns. *Ohio J. Speech and Hearing* 6 (1971): 80-86.

20. Berger, K. W. Relationships between word length and word frequency in speechreading performance. Unpublished research, 1972.

21. Berger, K. W. Two experiments in speechreading. Unpublished research, 1972.

22. Berger, K. W. Consonant confusions in speechreading. *Ohio J. Speech and Hearing*, 1972, in press.

23. Berger, K. W. Three experiments in speechreading. *J. Communication Disorders* 5 (1972), in press.
24. Berger, K. W. Visemes and homophenous words. *Teacher of the Deaf,* 1972, in press.
25. Berger, K. W., and R. A. DePompei. Speechreaders report on speechreading. Unpublished research, 1972.
26. Berger, K. W., R. A. DePompei, and J. L. Droder. The effect of distance on speechreading. *Ohio J. Speech and Hearing* 5 (1970): 115-122.
27. Berger, K. W., M. Garner, and J. A. Sudman. The effect of degree of facial exposure and the vertical angle of vision on speechreading performance. *Teacher of the Deaf* 69 (1971): 322-326.
28. Berger, K. W., and M. A. Lewis. The effect of noise on lipreading performance. *Sound* 6 (1972): 7.
29. Berger, K. W., J. Martin, and R. Sakoff. The effect of visual distractions on speechreading performance. *Teacher of the Deaf* 68 (1970): 384-387.
30. Berger, K. W., G. W. Perry, J. Hoffman, and D. L. Smith. Lip-thickness of the speaker as a speechreading variable. Unpublished research, 1972.
31. Berger, K. W., and G. R. Popelka. Extra-facial gestures in relation to speechreading. *J. Communication Disorders* 3 (1971): 302-308.
32. Biller, M. E. Lip reading as a means of social and occupational adjustment. *Volta Review* 42 (1940): 614-619.
33. Birch, J. W., and E. R. Stuckless. The relationship between early manual communication and later achievement of the deaf. United States Department of Health, Education, and Welfare. Research Project #1769, 1964. Also see Stuckless and Birch.
34. Black, J. W. *Multiple-choice Intelligibility Test.* Danville, Illinois: Interstate Printers and Publishers, 1963, 48pp.
35. Black, J. W., P. P. O'Reilly, and L. Peck. Self-administered training in lipreading. *J. Speech Hearing Disorders* 28 (1963): 183-186.
36. Blakeley, R. W. Auditory abilities associated with lip reading. M.A. thesis, University of Oregon, 1953.
37. Block, M. G., and S. W. Kinde. Compound and simple stimuli in paired-associate learning as an investigation of the Rochester Method. Unpublished research, University of

South Florida, 1971.

38. Bode, D. L., G. P. Nerbonne, and L. J. Sahlstrom. Speech-reading and the synthesis of distorted printed sentences. *J. Speech Hearing Research* 13 (1970): 115-121.

39. Brannon, J. B., Jr. Speechreading of various speech materials. *J. Speech Hearing Disorders* 26 (1961): 348-352.

40. Brannon, J. B. Jr., and F. Kodman, Jr. The perceptual process in speechreading. *A.M.A. Archives Otolaryngology* 70 (1959): 114-119.

41. Braunlich, E. M. *Simplified Lip Reading*. New York: Supplementary School for Lip Reading, 1933, 80pp.

42. Brehman, G. E., Jr. Programmed discrimination learning for lipreaders. *American Annals Deaf* 110 (1965): 553-562.

43. Brintnall, D. Lipreading is fun. *Volta Review* 57 (1955): 115-116.

44. Bruce, L. M. Giving lipreading its fair share of time. *Volta Review* 40 (1938): 665-668.

45. Bruce, L. M. Speech reading in schools for the deaf. *Volta Review* 44 (1942): 614-617.

46. Bruce, W. Social integration and effectiveness of speech. *Volta Review* 62 (1960): 368-372.

47. Bruhn, M. E. *Elementary Lessons in Lipreading*. Lynn, Massachusetts: Nichols Press, 1927.

48. Bruhn, M. E. Methods of teaching lip reading: a symposium. Lip reading as living language. *Volta Review* 44 (1942): 636-638.

49. Bruhn, M. E. *Mueller-Walle Method of Lipreading*. 7th ed. Washington: The Volta Bureau, 1949, 114pp. Originally published in 1915 by the Nichols Press in Lynn, Massachusetts.

50. Bunger, A. M. Appraising progress in speech reading. *Volta Review* 26 (1924): 503-504.

51. Bunger, A. M. On being converted to the Jena method. *Volta Review* 29 (1929): 705-708.

52. Bunger, A. M. Methods of teaching lip reading to adults: a symposium. College classes in speech reading: their present services, their future possibilities. *Volta Review* 44 (1942): 640-641, 658.

53. Bunger, A. M. *Speech Reading — Jena Method*. 2nd rev. ed. Danville, Illinois: The Interstate Co., 1952, 109pp. Originally published in 1944 by the same publisher.

54. Burchett, J. H. *Lip-Reading.* London: National Institute for the Deaf, 1944 (1950), 180pp.
55. Butt, D. S. The development of a clinical speechreading test for hearing handicapped children of pre-reading level. M.A. thesis, University of New Mexico, 1958.
56. Butt, D. S., and F. M. Chreist. A speechreading test for young children. *Volta Review* 70 (1968): 225-239.
57. Byers, V. W., and L. Lieberman. Lipreading performance and the rate of the speaker. *J. Speech Hearing Research* 2 (1959): 271-276.
58. Cancel, C. A. A video-taped visual hearing test for Spanish speaking people. *International Audiology* 9 (1970): 184-187.
59. Carr, J. A limited or limitless vocabulary through speechreading. *Volta Review* 56 (1954): 109-113.
60. Cavaluchi, D. E. A new speechreading test. Paper presented at the American Speech and Hearing Association convention, 1971.
61. Cavender, B. J. The construction and investigation of a test of lip reading ability and a study of factors assumed to affect the results. M.A. thesis, Indiana University, 1949.
62. Cirulis, I. Speechreading and television. *Visual Aids Review* 3:2 (1961): 4-9, 26-31.
63. Clegg, D. G. *Pattern for the Listening Eye.* London: National Institute for the Deaf, n.d. (1953?), 124pp.
64. Coats, D. G. Characteristics of communication methods. *American Annals Deaf* 95 (1950): 485-490.
65. Conklin, E. S. A method for the determination of relative skill in lipreading. *Volta Review* 19 (1917): 216-219.
66. Copeland, M. R. *A Lipreading Practice Manual for Teenagers and Adults.* Washington: The Volta Bureau, n.d. (1969?), 74pp.
67. Copeland, M. R. *A Lipreader Must Practice.* Washington: The Volta Bureau, 1961, 66pp.
68. Cornett, O. R. Cued Speech. *American Annals Deaf* 112 (1967): 3-13.
69. Cornett, O. R. The method explained. *Hearing and Speech News* 35 (Sept. 1967): 7-9.
70. Coscarelli, J. E. The relationship of visual synthesis skill to lipreading. M.S. thesis, Vanderbilt University, 1968.
71. Costello, M. R. A study of speechreading as a developing

language process in deaf and in hard-of-hearing children. Ph.D. dissertation, Northwestern University, 1957.

72. Costello, M. R. Individual differences in speechreading. *Proceedings International Congress Education Deaf*, 1963, 317-321.

73. Coulomb, B. M. Don't abandon lipreading. *Hearing News* 32 (Jan. 1964): 22.

74. Craig, W. H. Effects of preschool training on the development of reading and lipreading skills of deaf children. *American Annals Deaf* 109 (1964): 280-296. Based on his Ph.D. dissertation, University of Pittsburgh, 1962.

75. Cranwill, S. A. Lipreading. *American Annals Deaf* 107 (1962): 495-498.

76. Crawley, E. F. Television and the hearing handicapped. *Hearing News* 26 (Jan. 1958): 3-4.

77. Cross, B. G. At work and play — TV in the lives of the deaf and hard of hearing. *Volta Review* 69 (1967): 203-207.

78. Cutting, J. The relationship of certain visual perceptual tasks to speech reading ability. M.A. thesis, University of Kansas, 1960.

79. Cypreansen, L. E., and J. G. McBride. Lipreading lessons on television. *Volta Review* 58 (1956): 346-348.

80. Davidson, J.A.L. An investigation of the relationship between the lip-reading ability of normal-hearing individuals and measure of concept formation, visual perception and level of aspiration. M.A. thesis, Ohio State University, 1954. Also see O'Neill and Davidson.

81. Dawson-Abbott, L. J. *The Key to Lipreading*. Melbourne: The Australian Association for Better Hearing, 1956, 86pp.

82. Day, H. E., I. S. Fusfeld, and R. Pintner. *A Survey of American Schools for the Deaf 1924-1925*. Washington: National Research Council, 1928.

83. Deland, F. *Story of Lip Reading: Its Genesis and Development*. Revised by Harriet Montague. Washington: The Volta Bureau, 1968, 232pp. Originally published in 1931 by the same publisher. Deland was the superintendent of The Volta Bureau from 1914 to 1922.

84. DiCarlo, L. M. A comparison of live and filmed presentation of a lipreading lesson to a group of experienced and inexperienced college students. *Proceedings International*

Congress Education Deaf, 1963, 364-368.
85. DiCarlo, L. M. Much ado about the obvious. Volta Review 68 (1966): 269-273.
86. DiCarlo, L. M., and R. Kataja. An analysis of the Utley lip reading test. J. Speech Hearing Disorders 16 (1951): 226-240. Based on R. Kataja's Ph.D. dissertation, Syracuse University, 1950.
87. Dodds, E., and E. Harford. Application of a lipreading test in a hearing aid evaluation. J. Speech Hearing Disorders 33 (1968): 167-173.
88. Doehring, D. G., and J. Rosenstein. Speed of visual perception in deaf children. J. Speech Hearing Research 12 (1969): 118-125.
89. Donnelly, K. G., and J. A. Marshall. Development of a multiple-choice test of lipreading. J. Speech Hearing Research 10 (1967): 565-568.
90. Duffy, J. K. Audio-visual speech audiometry and a new audio and audio-visual speech perception index. Maico Audiological Library Series, 5:9, 1967.
91. Dyer, R., and F. S. Berg. Ratings of factors contributing to the speech-readability of instructors. Paper presented at the Summer Meeting of the Alexander Graham Bell Association for the Deaf, 1968. Cited by Berg in "Educational Audiology." In The Hard of Hearing Child, edited by F. S. Berg and S. G. Fletcher. New York: Grune and Stratton, 1970, 275-318.
92. Eggermont, J.P.M. Taalverwerving bij een Groep Dove Kinderen. Een Experimenteel Onderzoek Naar de Betekenis van een Geluidmethode voor Spraakafzien (Acquisition of Language in a Group of Deaf Children. An Experiment on the Significance of a Method of Sound Perception to Lipreading). Groningen: J. B. Wolters, 1964, 159pp. Cited by Quigley (312).
93. Eisman, B., and L. Levy. Interpersonal factors related to lipreading performance: performance as a function of characteristics of known communicators. John Tracy Clinic Research Papers, VII, 1957.
94. Ellis, M. A. A preliminary investigation of a lipreading test for young deaf children. M.S. thesis, University of Tennessee, 1964.
95. Erber, N. P. Interaction on audition and vision in the

recognition of oral speech stimuli. *J. Speech Hearing Research* 12 (1969): 423-425.

96. Erber, N. P. Auditory and audiovisual reception of words in low-frequency noise by children with normal hearing and by children with impaired hearing. *J. Speech Hearing Research* 14 (1971): 496-512. Based on his Ph.D. dissertation, Washington University, 1970.

96a. Erber, N. P. Effects of distance on the visual reception of speech. *J. Speech Hearing Research* 14 (1972): 848-857.

97. Evans, L. Factors related to listening and lipreading. *Teacher of the Deaf* 58 (1960): 417-423.

98. Evans, L. Psychological factors related to lipreading. *Teacher of the Deaf* 63 (1965): 131-136. Based on his M.A. thesis, University of Liverpool, 1964.

99. Ewing, A., ed. *The Modern Educational Treatment of Deafness*. Washington: The Volta Bureau, 1960.

100. Ewing, A. Demonstration with inductance loops. In *The Modern Educational Treatment of Deafness*, edited by A. Ewing. Washington: The Volta Bureau, 1960.

101. Ewing, A. Research on the educational treatment of deafness. *Teacher of the Deaf* 60 (1962): 151-168. Reprinted from *Educational Research* 4, 1962.

102. Ewing, I. R. *Lipreading and Hearing Aids*. 3rd ed. Manchester: Manchester University Press, 1959, 73pp. Originally published in 1930 as *Lipreading*. Revised in 1967 as *Hearing Aids, Lipreading and Clear Speech*.

103. Ewing, I. R. Lip-Reading for adults. *Teacher of the Deaf* 39 (1941): 3-6.

104. Faircloth, M. *Lip Reading Study and Practice*. Toronto: The Ryerson Press, 1946, 64pp.

105. Falconer, G. A., and R. B. Mefferd, Jr. The effect of field dependency, extraversion and neuroticism on lipreading. Paper presented at the American Speech and Hearing Association convention, 1970.

106. Farrimond, T. Age differences in the ability to use visual cues in auditory communication. *Language and Speech* 2 (1959): 179-192.

107. Feilbach, R. V. *Stories and Games for Easy Lipreading Practice*. Washington: The Volta Bureau, 1952, 108pp.

108. Ferreri, G. Speech reading. *Volta Review* 12 (1910): 161-165.

109. Fiedler, M. Good and poor learners in an oral school for the deaf. *Exceptional Children* 23 (1957): 291-295.

110. Fisher, C. G. Confusions among visually perceived consonants. *J. Speech Hearing Research* 11 (1968): 796-804. Based on his Ph.D. dissertation, Ohio State University, 1963.

111. Fisher, C. G. The visibility of terminal pitch contour. *J. Speech Hearing Research* 12 (1969): 379-382.

112. Fisher, M. T. *Let's Practice Lipreading*. Washington: The Volta Bureau, 1945 (1957), 42pp.

113. Fisher, M. T. *Lip Reading Practice Material for Children*. New York: Comet Press Books, 1957, 27pp.

114. Fisher, M. T. *Improve Your Lipreading*. Washington: The Volta Bureau, 1965 (1968), 68pp.

115. Follwell, S. N. The use of speech in after-school life. *Teacher of the Deaf* 41 (1943): 97-102, 121-124; 42 (1944): 8-12, 117-120.

116. Franks, J. R. The influence on lipreading skill of tachistoscopic training in discriminating non-linguistic lip configurations. Paper presented at the American Speech and Hearing Association convention, 1971.

117. Franks, J. R., and H. J. Oyer. Factors influencing the identification of English sounds in lipreading. *J. Speech Hearing Research* 10 (1967): 757-764. Based on Franks' Ph.D. dissertation, Michigan State University, 1964.

118. Frisina, D. R. Comparison of the performance of day students and residential students in residential schools for the deaf. *Proceedings 40th Convention American Instructors Deaf*, 1961, 149-165.

119. Frisina, D. R. Speechreading. *Proceedings International Congress Education Deaf*, 1963, 191-207.

120. Frisina, D. R., and R. J. Bernero. A profile of the hearing and speech of Gallaudet College students. *Volta Review* 60 (1958): 316-321.

121. Fulton, R. M. Comparative assessment of visible differences between voiced and unvoiced words. M.A. thesis, Michigan State University, 1964.

122. Furth, H. G. Visual paired associates task with deaf and hearing children. *J. Speech Hearing Research* 4 (1961): 172-177.

123. Furth, H. G. *Thinking Without Language*. New York: The

Free Press, 1966, 236pp.

124. Fusfeld, I. S. Factors in lipreading as determined by the lipreader. *American Annals Deaf* 103 (1958): 228-242.

125. Gaeth, J. H. Verbal learning among children with reduced hearing acuity. United States Department of Health, Education, and Welfare. Project #289, 1960.

126. Gault, R. H. The interpretation of speech by tactual and visual impression. *Archives Otolaryngology* 4 (1926): 228-239.

127. Gault, R. H. "Hearing" through the sense organs of touch and vibration. *J. Franklin Institute* 204 (1927): 356-357.

128. Gault, R. H. On the identification of certain vowel and consonant elements in words by their tactual qualities and by their visual qualities as seen by lipreading. *J. Abnormal Psychology* 22 (1927): 33-39.

129. Gault, R. H., and L. D. Goodfellow. An empirical comparison of audition, vision and touch in the discrimination of temporal patterns and ability to reproduce them. *J. General Psychology* 18 (1938): 41-47.

130. Geldard, F. A. Adventures in tactile literacy. *American Psychology* 12 (1957): 115-124.

131. Getz, S. *Environment and the Deaf Child.* Springfield, Illinois: Charles C. Thomas, Publisher, 1953, 173pp.

132. Gilliat, M. E. If I were teaching children again. *Teacher of the Deaf* 59 (1961): 55-59.

133. Gilliat, M. E. Suggestions for lip-reading classes for deaf adults. *Teacher of the Deaf* 60 (1962): 36-45.

133a.Glaser, R. G. The relationship of speechreading performance to altered visual acuity. M.A. thesis, Kent State University, 1972.

134. Goda, S. Language skills of profoundly deaf children. *J. Speech Hearing Research* 2 (1959): 369-376.

135. Goetzinger, C. P. A study of monocular vs. binocular vision in speechreading. *Proceedings International Congress Education Deaf,* 1963, 326-333.

136. Goetzinger, R. B. A study of speechreading ability in relation to memory for motion and to visual perception with deaf subjects. M.S. thesis, University of Kansas, 1967.

137. Goldstein, M. A. *The Acoustic Method for Training of the Deaf and Hard of Hearing Child.* St. Louis: The Laryngoscope Press, 1939, 246pp.

138. Goodman, P. Untersuchengen uber das ablesen vom munde bei taubstummen und spatertauben. *Arch. Ges. Psychol.* 67 (1929): 441-504. Cited by Simmons (*341*).

139. Gopfert, H. Psychologische unter suchungen uber das ablesen vom munde bei ertraubten und horenden. *Kinderforsch.* 28 (1923): 315-367. Cited by Simmons (*341*).

140. Gordon, A. Lipreading in the primary department of the California School. *American Annals Deaf* 84 (1939): 350-362.

141. Graffydh-Williams, H. Education of the deaf in Russia before 1917. *Teacher of the Deaf* 57 (1959): 183-193.

142. Graffydh-Williams, H. Leaves in an eastern wind. *Teacher of the Deaf* 60 (1962): 169-175.

143. Graunke, W. I. Effect of visual-auditory presentation on memorization by children with hearing impairment. M.A. thesis, Northwestern University, 1959.

144. Green, P. Education? *Teacher of the Deaf* 59 (1961): 49-54.

145. Greenberg, H. J., and D. L. Bode. Visual discrimination of consonants. *J. Speech Hearing Research* 11 (1968): 869-874.

146. Grzebien, A. E. *Speechreading Through Sports (College Football)*. Washington: The Volta Bureau, 1967, 58pp.

147. Guthrie, V. S. A history of preschool education for the deaf. *Volta Review* 47 (1945): 5-9, 56-58, 72-76, 116-118, 142-146.

148. Handelman, N. S. The relationship between certain personality factors and speech-reading proficiency. Ph.D. dissertation, New York University, 1955.

149. Hannah, E. P. Nuclear stress variation as a factor in speechreading. Paper presented at the American Speech and Hearing Association convention, 1970.

150. Hannah, E. P. Speechreading: diagnosis and therapy on a linguistic base. Paper presented at the American Speech and Hearing Association convention, 1971.

151. Hardick, E. J., H. J. Oyer, and P. E. Irion. Lipreading performance as related to measurement of vision. *J. Speech Hearing Research* 13 (1969): 19-22.

152. Harrington, J. D. The preparation of a basic reference for teachers of lipreading and administrators of lipreading programs. Ed.D. dissertation, New York University, 1966.

153. Hartman, N. Cited by W. J. Bechinger (*13*).

154. Haspiel, G. S. *A Synthetic Approach to Lip Reading*. Magnolia, Massachusetts: The Expression Co., 1964, 175pp.
155. Haspiel, G. S. A rationale for lipreading therapy. *Volta Review* 67 (1965): 684-687.
156. Haycock, G. S. The education of the deaf in America. *Teacher of the Deaf* 21 (1923): 142-145, 156-164.
157. Heider, F., and G. M. Heider. An experimental investigation of lipreading. *Psychological Monographs* 52 (1940): 124-133.
158. Heider, F. Acoustic training helps lipreading. *Volta Review* 45 (1943): 135.
159. Heider, G. M. Psychological research in lip reading and language. *Volta Review* 36 (1934): 517-520.
160. Heider, G. M. The Utley lipreading test. *Volta Review* 49 (1947): 457-458.
161. Hester, M. S. Manual communication. *International Congress Education Deaf*, 1964, 615-618.
162. Hofsommer, A. J. Lip reading and the intelligence quotient of the hard-of-hearing child. *J. American Medical Association* 197 (1936): 648-650.
163. Howell, L. Lip-reading for the hard-of-hearing adult. *Volta Review* 19 (1917): 15-16.
164. Hubbard, G. G. *The Story of the Rise of the Oral Method in America*. Washington: The Volta Bureau, 1898, 49pp.
165. Hudgins, C. V. The development of communication skills among profoundly deaf children in an auditory training program. In *The Modern Educational Treatment of Deafness*, edited by A. Ewing. Washington: The Volta Bureau, 1960.
166. Hutton, C. Combining auditory and visual stimuli in aural rehabilitation. *Volta Review* 61 (1959): 316-319.
167. Hutton, C., E. T. Curry, and M. B. Armstrong. Semidiagnostic test materials for aural rehabilitation. *J. Speech Hearing Disorders* 24 (1959): 318-329.
168. *Introduction to Lipreading*. Elmsford, New York: Sonotone Corp., 1941, 63pp.
169. Jackson, D. Lipreading can help. *The Hearing Eye* 30 (March 1962): 6-9.
170. Jackson, W. D. Effects of lighting condition and mode of presentation on the speechreading accuracy of deaf children. Ed.D. dissertation, Indiana University, 1967.

171. Jeffers, J. The process of speechreading viewed with respect to a theoretical construct. *Proceedings International Conference Oral Education Deaf*, 1967, 1530-1561.

172. Jeffers, J., and M. Barley. The Barley Speechreading Test-C.I.D. "Everyday Speech" Sentences. *California J. Communicative Disorders* 1 (1971): 43-45.

173. Jeffers, J., and M. Barley. *Speech Reading*. Springfield, Illinois: Charles C. Thomas, Publisher, 1971, 392pp.

174. Johnson, D. R. A correlational study of lipreading, intelligence, and ability to synthesize. M.A. thesis, Texas Technological College, 1968.

175. Johnson, E. H. Testing results of acoustic training. *American Annals Deaf* 84 (1939): 223-233.

176. Johnson, E. H. The ability of pupils in a school for the deaf to understand various methods of communication. *American Annals Deaf* 93 (1948): 194-213, 258-314. Based on her M.A. thesis, MacMurray College, 1947.

177. Johnson, G. F. The effects of cutaneous stimulation by speech on lipreading performance. Ph.D. dissertation, Michigan State University, 1963.

178. Jones, J.W. One hundred years of history in the education of the deaf in America and its present status. *Proceedings 21st Convention American Instructors of the Deaf*, 1917, 181-199. Cited by P. J. Schmitt, *Volta Review* 68 (1966): 85-105.

179. Kaho, E. This is lipreading on TV. *Hearing News* 26 (May 1958): 7-8, 18.

180. Katt, T. L. Construction and evaluation of an eight millimeter filmed lipreading test. M.A. thesis, Michigan State University, 1967.

181. Keaster, J. Communication techniques for the hard-of-hearing. *Transactions American Academy of Ophthalmology Otolaryngology* 53 (1949): 581-583.

182. Keaster, J. An inquiry into current concepts of visual speech reception. *Laryngoscope* 65 (1955): 80-84.

183. Keil, J. M. The effects of peripheral visual stimuli on lipreading performance. Ph.D. dissertation, Michigan State University, 1968.

184. Keith, J. Has lipreading missed the bus? — Yes. *Volta Review* 45 (1943): 286-288.

185. Kelly, J. C. *Audio-Visual Speech Reading*. Urbana, Illinois:

University of Illinois, 1955,39pp. Cited by O'Neill and Oyer (286).

186. Kelsch, A. F. Give the lipreader a chance. *Hearing News* 20 (April 1952): 3-8.

187. Kennedy, M., and M. W. Whitehurst. Suggestions for friends and relatives of the hard of hearing. *Volta Review* 71 (1969): 81-88.

188. Kincade, J. M. Lipreading for the deaf and hard of hearing: its place in otologic therapy. *Laryngoscope* 58 (1948): 118-137.

189. Kinzie, C. E. The Kinzie method of speech reading for the deaf. *Volta Review* 20 (1918): 249-252.

190. Kinzie, C. E. Methods of teaching lipreading to adults: a symposium. The Kinzie method of graded instruction. *Volta Review* 44 (1942): 701-703.

191. Kinzie, C. E., and R. Kinzie. *Lip-reading for the Deafened Adult.* Philadelphia: John C. Winston Co., 1931, 363pp.

192. Kinzie, C. E., and R. Kinzie. *Lip-Reading for Children,* Parts 1, 2, and 3. Washington: The Volta Bureau, 1936.

193. Kitson, H. D. The role of association in lip reading. *Volta Review* 16 (1914): 619-620.

194. Kitson, H. D. Psychological tests of lip reading ability. *Volta Review* 17 (1915): 471-476.

195. Knudsen, V. O. Hearing with the sense of touch. *J. General Psychology* 1 (1915): 471-476.

196. Kohl, H. R. *Language and Education of the Deaf.* New York: Center for Urban Education, 1966, 34pp.

197. Kosh, Z. H. *Television Lessons in Lipreading.* Washington: Greater Washington Educational Television Association, 1964.

198. Krug, R. F. Effects and interactions of auditory and visual clues in oral communication. United States Department of Health, Education, and Welfare. Project #499, n.d. (1960?).

199. Lane, H. S. Influence of nursery school education on school achievement. *Volta Review* 44 (1942): 677-680.

200. Larr, A. L. Ability to distinguish between voiced and silent speech tested on closed circuit TV. *Hearing News* 27 (Jan. 1959): 16-17.

201. Larr, A. L. Speechreading through closed circuit television. *Volta Review* 61 (1959): 19-22.

202. Lassman, G. H. Lipreading in nursery school. *Volta*

Review 50 (1948): 445-459.

203. Lassman, G. H. *Language for the Preschool Deaf Child.* New York: Grune and Stratton, 1950, 263pp.

204. Lavos, G. The reliability of an educational achievement test administered to the deaf. *American Annals Deaf* 89 (1944): 226-232.

205. Leonard, R. The effects of continuous auditory distractions on lipreading performance. M.A. thesis, Michigan State University, 1962.

206. Letzler, A. P. Let's lipread television audience expanding in every direction. *Hearing News* 33 (May 1965): 9-11.

207. Levine, E. *Psychology and Deafness.* New York: Columbia University Press, 1960, 383pp.

208. Lieberth, A. K., and J. J. Egan. Self-rating of lipreading ability, *Ohio J. Speech Hearing* 5 (1970): 129-132.

209. *Lipreading for the Deaf and Hard of Hearing.* New York: Board of Education of the City of New York, n.d. (1960?), 103pp.

210. Lloyd, L. L. Sentence familiarity as a factor in visual speech reception. *J. Speech Hearing Disorders* 29 (1964): 409-413.

211. Lloyd, L. L., and J. G. Price. Sentence familiarity as a factor in visual speech reception (lipreading) of deaf college students. *J. Speech Hearing Research* 14 (1971): 291-294.

212. Logan, S. A. Lipreading and visual retention as a function of age in normal-hearing adults. M.S. thesis, Vanderbilt University, 1967.

213. Lott, B. E., and G. Levy. The influence of certain communicator characteristics on lip reading efficiency. *J. Social Psychology* 51 (1960): 419-425.

214. Louargand, E. M. *Curriculum Correlated Speechreading.* Sacramento: Published by the author, 1961, 187pp.

215. Love, E. B. Growing deaf and learning lip reading. *Volta Review* 45 (1943): 36-38.

216. Lovering, L. J., and E. J. Hardick. Lipreading performance as a function of visual acuity. Paper presented at the American Speech and Hearing Association convention, 1969.

217. Lowell, E. L. Research in speech reading: some relationships to language development and implications for the

classroom teacher. *Proceedings 39th Convention American Instructors Deaf,* 1959, 68-75.

218. Lowell, E. L. New insight into lipreading. *Rehabilitation Record* 2 (July-Aug. 1961): 3-5.

219. Lowell, E. L., G. Taaffe, and G. Rushford. The effectiveness of instructional film in lipreading. *Western Speech* 23, Summer 1959.

220. Lynch, M., and D. L. Bode. An experiment on the intensity variable in speechreading. Unpublished research, Purdue University, 1967.

221. Macnutt, E. G. *Hearing With Our Eyes.* Washington: The Volta Bureau, 1952, 147pp. An accompanying workbook, 1952, 28pp., and a second workbook, 1959, 30pp., are available.

222. Magner, M. E. Parents can help deaf children acquire ability in speech-reading. *American Annals Deaf* 105 (1960): 431-433.

223. Mahaffey, R. B. An investigation relating short-term tachistoscopic training to improvement in basic speechreading abilities. Abstract in *ASHA* 6 (1964): 388.

224. Manson, A. M. The work of the Protestant churches for the deaf in North America. *American Annals Deaf* 95 (1950): 265-279, 387-433, 461-485; 96 (1951): 363-381. Based on his M.A. thesis, Gallaudet College.

225. Mason, M. K. A laboratory method of measuring visual hearing ability. *Volta Review* 34 (1932): 510-513.

226. Mason, M. K. Individual deviations in the visual reproduction of the speech of two speakers. *American Annals Deaf* 84 (1939): 423-424.

227. Mason, M. K. A cinematographic technique for testing more objectively the visual speech comprehension of young deaf and hard-of-hearing children. Ph.D. dissertation, Ohio State University, 1942.

228. Mason, M. K. Teaching and testing visual hearing by the cinematographic method. *Volta Review* 44 (1942): 703-705.

229. Mason, M. K. A cinematographic technique for testing visual speech comprehension. *J. Speech Hearing Disorders* 8 [1943]: 271-278.

230. McDearmon, J. R. A method of teaching lipreading using programmed learning principles. *Volta Review* 69 (1967):

316-318.
231. McEachern, A. W., and G. Rushford. Lipreading performance as a function of unknown communicators. *John Tracy Clinic Research Papers*, VIII, Feb. 1958.
232. Metz, D. A. Auditory-visual discrimination skills using CID W-22 words. M.A. thesis, Western Reserve University, 1965.
233. Milesky, S. D. Testing lipreading potential. *Volta Review* 62 (1960): 373-375.
234. Miller, C. A. Lipreading performance as a function of continuous visual distractions. M.A. thesis, Michigan State University, 1965.
235. Miller, J., C. L. Rousey, and C. P. Goetzinger. An exploratory investigation of a method of improving speech reading. *American Annals Deaf* 103 (1958): 473-478.
236. Misra, S. K., and M. F. Palmer. A comparison of speechreading in Hindi and English in a school for the deaf. *Volta Review* 66 (1964): 615-617.
237. Mlott, S. R. A paired-associate technique for training people to lip read. Ph.D. dissertation, University of Mississippi, 1964.
238. Montague, H. This little girl began a revolution. *Volta Review* 42 (1940): 343-345, 384-385.
239. Montague, H. Lip Reading — a continuing necessity. *J. Speech Hearing Disorders* 8 (1943): 257-268.
240. Montague, H. *Lipreading Lessons for Adult Beginners.* Washington: The Volta Bureau, 1945, 114pp.
241. Montgomery, G.W.G. The relationship of oral skills to manual communication in profoundly deaf adolescents. *American Annals Deaf* 111 (1966): 557-565.
242. Moore, L. M. Life situation motion pictures for teaching. *Volta Review* 44 (1942): 705-707. Based on her M.A. thesis, University of Southern California, 1942.
243. Moore, L. M. Television as a medium for teaching speech reading and speech. *Volta Review* 57 (1955): 263-264.
244. Moores, D. F. Cued Speech: some practical and theoretical considerations. *American Annals Deaf* 114 (1969): 23-27. Also see rebuttal, pp. 27-33.
245. Morgenstern, L. I. *Lip-Reading for Class Instruction.* New York: Hinds, Hayden and Eldredge Publishers, 1916, 162pp.

246. Morkovin, B. V. Rehabilitation of the aurally-handicapped through the study of speech reading in life situations. *J. Speech Disorders* 12 (1947): 363-368.

247. Morkovin, B. V. Experiment in teaching deaf preschool children in the Soviet Union. *Volta Review* 62 (1960): 260-268.

248. Morkovin, B. V. Language in the general development of the preschool deaf child: a review of research in the Soviet Union. *ASHA* 10 (1968): 195-199.

249. Morkovin, B. V., and L. M. Moore. *Life-Situation Speech-Reading Through the Cooperation of Senses*. 2nd ed. Los Angeles: University of Southern California, 1948, 115pp. Originally published in 1944 by the same publisher.

250. Morris, D. M. A study of some of the factors involved in lip-reading. M.A. thesis, Smith College, 1944.

251. Moser, H.M., H. J. Oyer, J. J. O'Neill, and H. J. Gardner. Selection of items for testing skill in visual recognition of one-syllable words. Ohio State University Development Fund Project #5818, 1960. Cited by O'Neill and Oyer (*286*).

252. Mulligan, M. Variables in the reception of visual speech from motion pictures. M.A. thesis, Ohio State University, 1954.

253. Murphy, A. T., J. Dickstein, and E. Dripps. Acceptance, rejection and the hearing handicapped. *Volta Review* 62 (1960): 208-211.

254. Muyskens, J. H. The building and maintenance of clear speech for the deaf. *Volta Review* 40 (1938): 655-657.

255. Myklebust, H. R. The federal survey of the deaf and hard of hearing. Present earnings. *American Annals Deaf* 80 (1935): 200-219.

256. Myklebust, H. R. *Your Deaf Child*. Springfield, Illinois: Charles C. Thomas, Publisher, 1950, 133pp.

257. Myklebust, H. R. *The Psychology of Deafness*. New York: Grune and Stratton, Inc., 1960, 393pp.

258. Myklebust, H. R., and A. I. Neyhus. *Diagnostic Test of Speechreading*. New York: Grune and Stratton, Inc., 1971.

259. Nakano, Y. A study on the factors which influence lipreading of deaf children. *Bulletin Faculty Education* (Tokyo University) 6 (1960): 141-146; 7 (1961): 315-342. Cited by Quigley (*312*).

260. Neely, K. K. Effects of visual factors on intelligibility of

speech. *J. Acoustical Society America* 28 (1956): 1276-1277.

261. Nelson, M. Visual communication; lip reading. *EENT Monthly* 42 (June 1963): 66, 68, 80.

262. *New Aids and Materials for Teaching Lip-Reading*. Washington: American Society for the Hard of Hearing, 1943, 169pp.

263. Neyhus, A. I. Self teaching in the development of speechreading in deaf children. *American Annals Deaf* 110 (1965): 586-587.

264. Nielsen, B. K. Measurement of visual speech comprehension. *J. Speech Hearing Research* 13 (1970): 856-860.

265. Nielsen, K. M. The effect of redundancy on visual recognition of frequently employed spoken words. Ph.D. dissertation, Michigan State University, 1966.

266. Nitchie, E. B. *Lip-Reading: Principles and Practices*. Revised by E. H. Nitchie. New York: F. Stokes & Co., 1930, 372pp. Originally published in 1912 by the same publisher and revised in 1919 by E. H. Nitchie.

267. Nitchie, E. B. Lip-reading, an art. *Volta Review* 15 (1913): 276-278.

268. Nitchie, E. B. Moving pictures applied to lip reading. *Volta Review* 15 (1913): 117-125.

269. Nitchie, E. B. Synthesis and intuition in lipreading. *Volta Review* 15 (1913): 311.

270. Nitchie, E. B. Lip reading for the hearing. *Volta Review* 17 (1915): 435-436.

271. Nitchie, E. B. The use of homophenous words. *Volta Review* 18 (1916): 3.

272. Nitchie, E. B. Tests for determining skill in lip-reading. *Volta Review* 19 (1917): 222-223.

273. Nitchie, E. H. *Advanced Lessons in Lip-Reading*. New York: Frederick A. Stokes Co., 1923, 313pp.

274. Nitchie, E. H. *New Lessons in Lip Reading*. Philadelphia: J. B. Lippincott Co., 1940 (1950), 251pp.

275. Northern, J. L., D. Teter, and R. F. Krug. Characteristics of manually communicating deaf students. *J. Speech Hearing Disorders* 36 (1971): 71-76.

276. Numbers, M. E. An experiment in lip reading. *Volta Review* 41 (1939): 261-264.

277. Numbers, M. E., and C. V. Hudgins. Speech perception in present day education for deaf children. *Volta Review* 50

(1948): 449-456.

278. Ojima, S., and Y. Nakano. An experimental study of lipreading practice. *Bulletin Faculty Education* (Tokyo University) 7 (1961): 243-287; 8 (1962): 91-120. Cited by Quigley (*312*).

279. Ojima, S., and Y. Nakano. Visual communication. *Bulletin Faculty Education* (Tokyo University) 9 (1963): 163-167. Cited by Quigley (*312*).

280. Olsen, B. D., J. G. Alpiner, W. Chevrette, G. J. Glascoe, and M. J. Metz. The Denver Scale for assessment of communication function of hearing-impaired adults. Paper presented at the American Speech and Hearing Association convention, 1971.

281. O'Neill, J. J. An exploratory investigation of lipreading ability among normal-hearing students. *Speech Monographs* 18 (1951): 309-311.

282. O'Neill, J. J. Contributions of the visual components of oral symbols to speech comprehension. *J. Speech Hearing Disorders* 19 (1954): 429-439.

283. O'Neill, J. J. A televised lipreading series. *Central States Speech J.* 10 (Winter 1959): 35-37.

284. O'Neill, J. J. Frontiers of research in visual communication. *Proceedings International Conference Oral Education Deaf,* 1967, 1562-1571.

285. O'Neill, J. J., and J.A.L. Davidson. Relationship between lipreading ability and five psychological factors. *J. Speech Hearing Disorders* 21 (1956): 478-481. Based on Davidson's M.A. thesis.

286. O'Neill, J. J., and H. J. Oyer. *Visual Communication for the Hard of Hearing.* Englewood Cliffs: Prentice Hall, 1961, 163pp.

287. O'Neill, J. J., and M. C. Stephens. Relationships among three filmed lip-reading tests. *J. Speech Hearing Research* 2 (1959): 61-65. Based on Stephens' M.A. thesis.

288. Ordman, K. A., and M. P. Ralli. *What People Say.* 3rd ed. Washington: The Volta Bureau, 1955, 117pp. Originally published in 1949 by the same publisher.

289. Ordman, T. Has lip reading missed the bus? — No. *Volta Review* 45 (1943): 288-290, 316-318.

290. Overbeck, J. C. van. Response to speech and music. In *The Modern Educational Treatment of Deafness,* edited by A. Ewing. Washington: The Volta Bureau, 1960.

291. Owrid, H. L. Measuring spoken language in young deaf children. *Teacher of the Deaf* 58 (1960): 124-128.
292. Oyer, H. J. Teaching lipreading by television. *Volta Review* 63 (1961): 131-132, 141.
293. Oyer, H. J. An experimental approach to the study of lipreading. *Proceedings International Congress Education Deaf,* 1963, 322-326.
294. Oyer, H. J., and M. Doudna. Word familiarity as a factor in testing discrimination in hard-of-hearing subjects. *Archives Otolaryngology* 72 (1960): 351-371.
295. Paget, G. The Systematic Sign Language. *Hearing* 24 (1969): 75-76.
296. Parsons, M. M. *The Reading of Speech from the Lips.* Providence: Ackerman & Co., 1900, 77 pp.
297. Pauls, M. D. Speechreading. In *Hearing and Deafness,* edited by H. Davis and S. R. Silverman. Rev. ed. New York: Holt, Rinehart and Winston, 1960, 353-367.
298. Pelligrini, A. Speech audiometry and lip reading. Fifth International Congress Oto-Rhino-Laryngo-Broncho-Oesophalology, 1953. Abstract in *Excerpta Medica Sec. XI* 6 (1953): 189.
299. Pesonen, J. Phoneme communication of the deaf. *Annales Academiae Scientiarum Fennicae* (Helsinki) B151(2) (1968): 1-207. Abstract in *dsh Abstracts* 9 (1969): 151; and in *Teacher of the Deaf* 67 (1969): 130-131.
300. Petkovsek, M. The eyes have it. *Hearing News* 29 (March 1961): 5-9.
301. Pettit, B. C. The effect of acoustical environment on speechreading performance. M.A. thesis, Ohio State University, 1963.
302. Pickett, J. M. Tactual communication of speech sounds to the deaf: comparison with lip reading. *J. Speech Hearing Disorders* 28 (1963): 315-330.
303. Pintner, R. Speech and speech reading tests for the deaf. *J. Applied Psychology* 13 (1929): 220-225. Also, *American Annals Deaf* 74 (1929): 480-486.
304. Pollack, C. The effects of the oral and simultaneous methods of communication on test performance involving comprehension of concrete and abstract concepts among deaf high school students. Ph.D. dissertation, New York University, 1966.
305. Pollack, D. Acoupedics: a uni-sensory approach to auditory

training. *Volta Review* 66 (1964): 400-409.

306. Popelka, G. R., and K. W. Berger. Gestures and speech reception. *American Annals Deaf* 116 (1971): 434-436. Based on Popelka's M.A. thesis, Kent State University, 1970.

307. Postman, L., and M. R. Rosensweig. Practice and transfer in the visual and auditory recognition of verbal stimuli. *American J. Psychology* 61 (1958): 376-379.

308. Postove, M. J. Selection of items for a speechreading test by means of scalogram analysis. *J. Speech Hearing Disorders* 27 (1962): 71-75. Based on her M.A. thesis, University of Maryland, 1959.

309. Powrie, G. S. *Speechreading for Young Deaf Children.* Ypsilanti: Published by the author, 1954, 54pp. Based on her M.A. thesis, University of Michigan, 1953.

310. Prall, J. Lipreading and hearing aids combine for better comprehension. *Volta Review* 59 (1957): 64-65.

311. Quick, M. A test for measuring achievement in speech perception among young deaf children. *Volta Review* 55 (1953): 28-31.

312. Quigley, S. P. Language research in countries other than the United States. *Volta Review* 68 (1966): 68-83.

313. Ralli, M. P. Methods of teaching lip reading to adults: a symposium. *Volta Review* 44 (1942): 638-640.

314. Raymond, C. A preliminary investigation in the development of a test of lipreading ability for the students of a residential school for the deaf. M.A. thesis, State University of Iowa, 1948.

315. Reams, M. H. An experimental study comparing the visual accompaniments of word identification and the auditory experience of word intelligibility. M.A. thesis, Ohio State University, 1950.

316. Reid, G. A. Problems in testing. *Volta Review* 48 (1943): 660-661.

317. Reid, G. A. A preliminary investigation in the testing of lip reading achievement. *American Annals Deaf* 91 (1946): 403-413. Also, *J. Speech Hearing Disorders* 12 (1947): 77-82. Based on her M.A. thesis, University of Wisconsin, 1942.

318. Reighard, J. A. A Dutch view of the Jena method. *Volta Review* 37 (1935): 597-600.

319. Reighard, J. A. Karl Brauckmann. *Volta Review* 40 (1938): 407-408, 419-420.

320. Richardson, J. A review of four methods of lipreading. *Volta Review* 70 (1968): 39-41.
321. Roback, I. M. Homophenous words. M.A. thesis, Michigan State University, 1961.
322. Rosenbaum, S. B. An investigation of low intensity auditory stimulation in the measurement of results of training in speech reading. M.A. thesis, University of Maryland, 1957.
323. Rowe, F. B., and B. Watson. Communication through gestures. *American Annals Deaf* 105 (1960): 232-237.
324. Ruesch, J., and W. Kees. *Nonverbal Communication.* Los Angeles: University of California Press, 1956, 205pp.
325. Sahlstrom, L. J., and H. J. Oyer. Objective measurement of certain facial movements during the production of homophenous words. Paper presented at the American Speech and Hearing Association convention, 1967.
326. Saltzman, M. Factors in learning speechreading. *A.M.A. Archives Otolaryngology* 65 (1957): 425-427.
327. Samuelson, E. E., and M. B. Fabregas. *A Treasure Chest of Games for Lip Reading Teachers.* Washington: The Volta Bureau, 1951, 21pp.
328. Sanders, D. A. The relative contribution of the visual and auditory components of speech to speech intelligibility. *Proceedings International Conference Oral Education Deaf,* 1967, 865-873.
329. Sanders, D.A. *Aural Rehabilitation.* Englewood Cliffs: Prentice-Hall, Inc., 1971, 374pp.
330. Sanders, D. A. A follow-up study of fifty deaf children who received pre-school training. Ph.D. dissertation, Royal Victoria University, 1961.
331. Sanders, D. A., and S. J. Goodrich. The contribution of vision to speech intelligibility under three conditions of frequency distortion. *J. Speech Hearing Research* 14 (1971): 154-159. Based on Goodrich's M.A. thesis, State University of New York at Buffalo, 1967.
332. Sanders, D. A., and J. E. Coscarelli. The relationship of visual synthesis skill to lipreading. *American Annals Deaf* 115 (1970): 23-26.
333. Sarrail, S. Basic percentage of error in lip reading. *Otolaryngology* (Buenos Aires) 2 (1951): 271-277. Abstract in *Excerpta Medica Sec. XI* 5 (1952): 333.
334. Sato, S. Some experimental studies on receptive language in

hearing defectives. Part I. Lipreading. *Tohoku J. Educational Psychology* 1 (1963): 33-39. Abstract in *dsh Abstracts* 4 (1964): 57.

335. Schaffer, C. M. The kinesthetic method of speech development and speechreading. *American Annals Deaf* 87 (1942): 421-422.

336. Scherer, P. Visual learning processes in deaf children. *Proceedings International Conference Oral Education Deaf,* 1967, 1997-2008.

337. Schwartz, J. R., and J. W. Black. Some effects of sentence structures on speechreading. *Central States Speech J.* 18 (1967): 86-90.

338. Scouten, E. L. The Rochester Method, an oral multisensory approach for instructing prelingual deaf children. *American Annals Deaf* 112 (1967): 50-56.

339. Shinn, M. L. A study of the reaction of the stutterer to lip reading and normal-hearing auditors. M.A. thesis, University of Minnesota, 1942.

340. Siegenthaler, B. M., and V. Gruber. Combining vision and audition for speech reception. *J. Speech Hearing Disorders* 34 (1969): 58-60.

341. Simmons, A. A. Factors related to lipreading. *J. Speech Hearing Research* 2 (1959): 340-352.

342. Simmons, A. A. Language growth through lipreading. *Proceedings International Congress Education Deaf,* (1963): 333-338.

343. Smith, D. L. A comparison of shadowed and delayed response techniques in speechreading therapy. M.A. thesis, Ohio State University, 1966.

344. Smith, R. An investigation of the relationships between lipreading ability and the intelligence of the mentally retarded. M.A. thesis, Michigan State University, 1964.

345. Smith, R. C., and D. W. Kitchen. Lipreading performance and contextual clues. Unpublished research. Michigan State University, 1971.

346. Smith, R. D. Let's lipread—TV product criteria. *American Annals Deaf* 110 (1965): 571-578.

347. Soderberg, M. K. An investigation of the level-of-aspiration behavior of hard-of-hearing and normal-hearing lipreaders as measured by a lipreading task. M.A. thesis, Ohio State University, 1959.

348. Sortini, A. J. *Speechreading—A Guide for Laymen.* Washington: The Volta Bureau, 1958 (1965), 50pp.

349. Southard, P. Good stories for lipreading. *Volta Review* 48 (1946): 200, 252-254.

350. Steed, E.L. Speech reading and how it grew. *Volta Review* 48 (1946): 69-74.

351. Stephens, M. C. An experimental investigation of the relationships among three filmed lipreading tests and their relationship to teacher ratings. M.A. thesis, Ohio State University, 1956. Also see O'Neill and Stephens.

352. Stepp, R. E. Demonstration of learning laboratory established to facilitate lipreading practice. *American Annals Deaf* 110 (1965): 588-590.

353. Stepp, R. E. A speechreading laboratory for deaf children. *Volta Review* 68 (1966): 408-415.

354. Stewart, J. L., D. Pollack, and M. P. Downs. A unisensory program for the limited-hearing child. *ASHA* 6 (1964): 151-154.

355. Stobaschinski, R. L. Lip reading: its psychological aspects and its adaptation to the individual needs of the hard of hearing. *American Annals Deaf* 43 (1928): 234-242, 355-365.

356. Stone, L. Facial clues of context in lip reading. *John Tracy Clinic Research Papers,* V, Dec. 1957, 11pp.

357. Stone, M. E., and J. P. Youngs, Jr. Catholic education of the deaf in the United States 1837-1948. *American Annals Deaf* 93 (1948): 411-510.

358. Story, A. J. *Speech-Reading and Speech for the Deaf.* Stoke-on-Trent: Hill and Ainsworth, Ltd., 1915. Mr. Story (1864-1938) was editor of *Teacher of the Deaf.*

359. Stovall, J. D., J. V. Irwin, and C. S. Hayes. Teaching speechreading by television. *Rehabilitation Record* 3 (1962): 38-40.

360. Stowell, A., E. E. Samuelson, and A. Lehman. *Lip Reading for the Deafened Child.* New York: Macmillan, 1928, 186pp.

361. Strain, B. J. A comparative study of the effectiveness of lipreading instruction in a face-to-face situation and by closed-circuit television. M.A. thesis, Ohio State University, 1960.

362. Stuckless, E. R., and J. W. Birch. The influence of early manual communication on the linguistic development of deaf children. *American Annals Deaf* 111 (1966): 452-460, 499-504. Also see Birch and Stuckless.

363. Sudman, J. A., and K. W. Berger. Two-dimension versus

three-dimension viewing in speechreading. *J. Communication Disorders* 4 (1971): 195-198. Based on Sudman's M.A. thesis, Kent State University, 1970.

364. Sumby, W. H., and I. Pollack. Visual contributions to speech intelligibility in noise. *J. Acoustical Society America* 26 (1954): 212-215.

365. *Summary of Selected Characteristics of Hearing Impaired Students.* Washington: Gallaudet College, 1971, 37pp.

366. Taaffe, G. A film test of lipreading. *John Tracy Clinic Research Papers*, II, Nov. 1957, 11pp.

366a. Taaffe, G. The effects of image size and visual angle on lip reading. Technical Memo #1, Special Project #17, John Tracy Clinic, 1958. Cited by Erber (96a).

367. Taaffe, G. The cognitive structures of lipreading. Ed.D. dissertation, Wayne State University, 1968.

368. Taaffe, G., and W. Wong. Studies of variables in lip reading stimulus materials. *John Tracy Clinic Research Papers*, III, Dec. 1957, 21pp.

369. Taber, F. A. Adult lip reading classes in New York City. *Volta Review* 41 (1939): 355-358, 373.

370. Tatoul, C. M., and G. D. Davidson. Lipreading and letter prediction. *J. Speech Hearing Research* 4 (1961): 178-181.

371. Thomas, S. L. Lipreading performance as a function of light levels. M.A. thesis, Michigan State University, 1962.

372. Thomasia, M. Teaching lipreading in a school in South Africa. *Volta Review* 69 (1967): 45-49.

373. Thorndike, E. L., and I. Lorge. *The Teacher's Word Book of 30,000 Words.* New York: Teachers College, Columbia University, 1944.

374. Thornton, J. Pictures make words. *Volta Review* 61 (1959): 18, 43.

375. Tiffany, R., and S. L. Kates. Concept attainment and lipreading ability among deaf adolescents. *J. Speech Hearing Disorders* 27 (1962): 265-274.

376. Trask, A. N. More about lip-reading, and then some. *Volta Review* 19 (1917): 567-569.

377. Uden, A. van. Observations on the education of deaf in the Netherlands and the U.S.A. *Volta Review* 62 (1960): 10-14.

378. Upton, H. Wearable eyeglass speechreading aid. *American Annals Deaf* 113 (1968): 222-229.

379. Utley, J. Factors involved in the teaching and testing of lip-

reading ability through the use of motion pictures. *Volta Review* 38 (1946): 657-659.

380. Utley, J. A test of lipreading ability. *J. Speech Hearing Disorders* 11 (1946): 109-116. Based on her Ph.D. dissertation, Northwestern University, 1946.

381. VanBebber, M. L. A study of factors influencing improvement in speech reading ability. M.A. thesis, University of Maryland, 1954.

382. VanWyk, M. K. Beginning speechreading. *Volta Review* 59 (1957): 165-168.

383. Vaughan, V. D. A study of the value of certain tests in predicting success in speech reading. M.A. thesis, University of Oklahoma, 1954.

384. Vernon, M., and E. D. Mindel. Psychological and psychiatric aspects of profound hearing loss. In *Audiological Assessment*, edited by D. E. Rose. Englewood Cliffs: Prentice-Hall, 1971.

385. Vivian, R. M. The Tadoma Method: a tactual approach to speech and speechreading. *Volta Review* 68 (1966): 733-737.

386. Vos, L. J. The effects of exaggerated and nonexaggerated stimuli on lipreading ability. M.A. thesis, Michigan State University, 1965.

387. Vuillemey, P. P. From objective audiometry to lipreading. *Annuals Oto-Laryngology* (Paris) 62 (1952): 321-325.

388. Walker, J. B. *Jane Walker's Book of Lipreading Practice Material*. Washington: The Volta Bureau, 1945.

389. Walker, J. B. *Jane Walker's Book of Art Lectures for Lip Reading Practice*. Washington: The Volta Bureau, 1951, 61pp.

390. Warren, L. E. *Defective Speech and Deafness*. New York: Edgar S. Werner, 1895, 116pp.

391. Watson, C. Lipreading becomes competitive. *Volta Review* 50 (1948): 106, 138.

392. Watson, L. A. *How to Get the Most of Your Remaining Hearing*. Minneapolis: Maico Foundation, 1956, 118pp.

393. Wedenberg, E. Auditory training of deaf and hard-of-hearing children. *Acta Otolaryngologica*, Supplement 94, 1951.

394. Whildin, O. A., and M. A. Scally. *Speech Reading for the Hard of Hearing*. Westminster, Maryland: John William Eckenrode, 1939, 148pp.

395. Whitcomb, O. A. An attempt to determine the relationship of visual perception—visual memory span and proficiency in lipreading. M.A. thesis, Northern Illinois University, 1965.

396. Whitehurst, M. W. Integration of auditory training and lip reading. *Volta Review* 66 (1964): 730-733.

397. Whitehurst, M. W. *Integrated Lessons in Lipreading and Auditory Training.* Published by the author, 1964, 83pp.

398. Withrow, F. B. The use of audiovisual techniques to expand lipreading and auditory experiences of young deaf children. *American Annals Deaf* 110 (1965): 523-527.

399. Wong, W., and G. Taaffe. Relationships between selected aptitude and personality tests of lipreading ability. *John Tracy Clinic Research Papers*, VII, Feb. 1958, 8pp.

400. Wong, W., S. L. Dickens, and G. Taaffe. A bibliography of psychological characteristics of the aurally handicapped and of analytical studies in communication. *John Tracy Clinic Research Papers*, I, Oct. 1957, 49pp.

401. Wood, K. S., and R. W. Blakely. The association of lipreading and the ability to understand distorted speech. *Western Speech* 17 (1953): 259-261.

402. Woodward, M. F. Linguistic methodology in lipreading. *John Tracy Clinic Research Papers*, IV, 1957, 32pp.

403. Woodward, M. F. Linguistic methodology in lipreading research: an experiment in applied psycholinguistics. Ph.D. dissertation, University of California, Los Angeles, 1958.

404. Woodward, M. F. Linguistic criteria for classifying lipreading vocabulary. *Proceedings International Congress Education Deaf,* June 1963, 971-976.

405. Woodward, M. F., and C. G. Barber. Phoneme perception in lipreading. *J. Speech Hearing Research* 3 (1960): 212-222.

406. Woodward, M. F., and E. E. Lowell. A linguistic approach to the education of aurally-handicapped children. United States Department of Health, Education, and Welfare. Project #907, 1964.

407. Wooley, F. T. How we use the tachistoscope. *Hearing News* 17 (Oct. 1949): 3-4.

408. Worthington, A.M.L. An investigation of the relationship between lipreading ability of congenitally deaf high school students and certain personality factors. M.A. thesis, Ohio State University, 1956.

409. Wright, B. C. *Look, Listen and Lipread.* Washington: The

Volta Bureau, 1957, 110pp.

410. Wyatt, O.M. *Lip-Reading.* London: The English Universities Press, Ltd., 1960; and Springfield, Illinois: Charles C. Thomas, 1969, 159pp.

411. Yenrick, D. E. Speechreading materials for the primary public school grades. *Volta Review* 53 (1951): 249-251. Based on his M.A. thesis, Ohio State University, 1950.

412. Zerling, S. The art of lipreading. *New York State J. Medicine* 40 (1940): 1164-1167.

index